Oliver Wendell Holmes
Physician and Man of Letters

Daguerrotype of Holmes, circa 1855. From the collection of the Boston Medical Library in the Francis A. Countway Library of Medicine.

Oliver Wendell Holmes

Physician and Man of Letters

Scott H. Podolsky
Charles S. Bryan

Editors

Published for the
Boston Medical Library
by
Science History Publications/USA
a division of
Watson Publishing International LLC
Sagamore Beach
2009

First published in the United States of America
by Science History Publications/USA
a division of
Watson Publishing International LLC
Post Office Box 1240, Sagamore Beach, MA 02562-1240, USA

www.shpusa.com

ISBN 978-0-88135-381-5, paperback
ISBN 978-0-88135-379-2, hard cover

Library of Congress Cataloguing-in-Publication Data

Oliver Wendell Holmes : physician and man of letters / Scott H. Podolsky, Charles
S. Bryan, editors.
     p. ; cm.
  Includes bibliographical references and index.
  ISBN-13: 978-0-88135-379-2 (alk. paper)
  ISBN-10: 0-88135-379-5 (alk. paper)
  1. Holmes, Oliver Wendell, 1809–1894. 2. Physicians—United States—
Biography. 3. Holmes, Oliver Wendell, 1809–1894—Correspondence.
4. Physicians—United States—Correspondence. I. Podolsky, Scott H.
II. Bryan, Charles S. III. Holmes, Oliver Wendell, 1809–1894. IV. Boston
Medical Library.
  [DNLM: 1. Holmes, Oliver Wendell, 1809–1894. 2. Medicine—United
States—Biography. 3. Medicine—United States—Essays. 4. Homeopathy—
United States—Biography. 5. Homeopathy—United States—Essays.
6. Psychology—United States—Biography. 7. Psychology—United States—
Essays. WZ 100 H752o 2009]
  R154.H636O55 2009
  610.92—dc22
  [B]
                                   2009031959

Designed and manufactured in the USA.

For Ellen and Steve Podolsky
and in memory of Mark Silverman

Contents

Acknowledgments

E arly in the *Autocrat of the Breakfast Table*, Holmes declares that "all generous companies of artists, authors, philanthropists, [and] men of science, are, or ought to be Societies of Mutual Admiration." And indeed, the editors have had almost too good a time working together closely this past year. However, we could not have completed the volume without the valuable input and efforts of a number of colleagues.

At the Center for the History of Medicine at the Francis A. Countway Library of Medicine, Kathryn Hammond Baker has been supportive of and thoughtful regarding the volume from its inception; and Jack Eckert, as he does for all researchers, not only provided answers to particular (and numerous) queries but pointed us in fruitful directions we hadn't even considered. Lucretia McClure has long championed the relevance of Holmes to contemporary medicine and society and proved a skillful miner of the Holmes literary corpus; while Dominic Hall provided valuable information concerning the Warren Anatomical Museum, to which Holmes had been an important and frequent contributor. Our thanks also go to Elizabeth Cousins, Michael Dello Iacono, Suzanne Denison, Emily Gustainis, Giordana Mecagni, Jessica Murphy, Cheryl Ostrowski, Cathy Pate, Jessica Sedgwick, Bryan Sutherland, Joan Thomas, and Darla White. We have also been bolstered by the ongoing support of the Countway's leadership, provided by Isaac Kohane and Alexa McCray, as well as by the medical school's leadership, provided by Dean Jeffrey Flier.

We are grateful for the enthusiastic support provided by the Boston Medical Library. S. Jay Jayasankar, its president, has advocated the project from the beginning, and Roz Vogel has been a key supporter of Center activities. Such members as Ilan Mizrahi have played important roles in mining for quotes as well. We're fortunate to have had the input and support of such Center subcommittee members as Allan Brandt, Jeremy Greene, David Jones, Charles Rosenberg, Eleanor Shore, and Peter Tishler, as well as to have had the support of the library's Joint Library Committee and its president, Mitch Rabkin. Beyond the medical school, Rob Velella, Bree Harvey, Gavin Kleespies, Dawnielle Peck, and Wendell

Refior have proved models regarding how to bring nineteenth-century luminaries to twenty-first century audiences, while Steve Levisohn and colleagues at the Massachusetts General Medical Group have continued to embody the best of contemporary therapeutic skepticism.

Regarding the previously unpublished 1879 introductory lecture to the incoming Harvard Medical School class, we are grateful to Houghton Library at Harvard University for their valuable assistance and permission to bring this lecture to a wider audience. It's also a privilege to thank a true prince, Mark Saadeh, for his efforts in leading the transcription process.

We have learned a tremendous amount from the volume's essay contributors, and hope that the Holmesian notion that "every now and then a man's mind is stretched by a new idea or sensation, and never shrinks back to its former dimensions" has held true for the editors in this case. And Neale Watson and Mark Bergeron have insisted from the beginning on their commitment to the quality of the volume; they have proved more than true to their word!

We thank our families, as always. Amy Podolsky helped to catalyze the initial thoughts concerning the volume, while she, Josh, and Danny have tolerated a year's descent into Holmesiana with their usual good humor. Donna Bryan, compensated only by several memorable trips to Boston, graciously tolerated the omnipresence of Holmes in her household. Finally, we are grateful to "the amiable autocrat" himself for challenging us by leaving to posterity such bold insights into the human condition. May readers feel the same way!

Preface

SCOTT H. PODOLSKY

THIS VOLUME'S ORIGIN DATES TO MAY 5, 2008, when the American Osler Society held a special session in the Ether Dome of the Massachusetts General Hospital. Charles S. Bryan, co-editor of *The Quotable Osler*, spoke on "'The Greatest Brahmin Among Them'—Osler's Perspective on Oliver Wendell Holmes." Perhaps with tongue in cheek, Bryan compared the revered William Osler with the comparatively forgotten Holmes on their respective medical, literary, and philosophical merits—and found in favor of Holmes on all accounts. In this telling, Holmes—from his roles as investigator of the contagiousness of puerperal fever and proponent of therapeutic rationalism, to those as savior of Old Ironsides, best-selling author on both sides of the Atlantic, and forerunner of depth psychology—remained, in Osler's words, "the most successful combination which the world has ever seen, of the physician and man of letters." Afterwards, Charles suggested to me that there ought to be a *Quotable Holmes*.

Mind swimming with Holmesian fish-related epigrams, I took the bait. Imparting a sense of urgency was the observation that the year 2009 marks the bicentennial of the births not only of Darwin and Lincoln but also of Holmes. Given Holmes's roles as founding president of the Boston Medical Library and dean of Harvard Medical School (from 1847 to 1853), the Center for the History of Medicine at the Countway Library of Medicine (which represents the union of the Boston Medical Library and Harvard Medical Library) seemed the proper venue for drawing attention to, and further catalyzing, Holmes-related scholarship.

I write "drawing attention to," for scholarship on Holmes as both medical and literary figure already enjoys something of a renaissance. John Harley Warner, in *Against the Spirit of System: The French Impulse in*

Nineteenth-Century American Medicine, places the entire nineteenth-century American turn to therapeutic skepticism—of which Holmes would be perhaps the most articulate, if not original, spokesman—in historical and conceptual perspective, depicting a generation of American physicians and their formative experiences in "system"-exploding Paris. William Dowling, in *Oliver Wendell Holmes in Paris: Medicine, Theology, and the Autocrat of the Breakfast-Table*, focuses attention upon Holmes specifically, tying Holmes's therapeutic skepticism and belief in the healing power of nature (the *vis medicatrix naturae*) to a deeper *religio medici*, a belief in God's immanence in nature, which would further characterize Holmes's reception and articulation of Darwinism itself. Yet Holmes would perceive himself as an iconoclast—and indeed, society's own productive evolution as critically dependent upon such iconoclasm—and Peter Gibian, in *Oliver Wendell Holmes and the Culture of Conversation*, generalizes Holmes's skep-

Group photograph of members of the Boston Society for Medical Improvement (undated, but likely taken between 1846 and 1854). Holmes, seated second from the left, had delivered his lecture on "The Contagiousness of Puerperal Fever" before the BSMI in 1843. From the collection of the Boston Medical Library in the Francis A. Countway Library of Medicine.

ticism to his literary and cultural work, as evidenced most clearly in the Breakfast-Table series, which brought Holmes a massive readership on both sides of the Atlantic. And finally, Michael Weinstein, in *The Imaginative Prose of Oliver Wendell Holmes*, examines Holmes as a proto-psychologist and philosopher who wrestled with the medical and moral consequences of individual freedom and responsibility.

It's thus our overarching goal to offer a balanced perspective on Holmes the physician and Holmes the man of letters. After Charles Bryan's biographical sketch, John Haller, Amalie Kass, and Charles Rosenberg dissect Holmes's three most influential medical essays: "Homœopathy and its Kindred Delusions," "The Contagiousness of Puerperal Fever," and "Currents and Counter-Currents in Medical Science," the latter being the apotheosis of Holmes's therapeutic skepticism in which he famously declared that "if the whole materia medica, *as now used*, could be sunk to the bottom of the sea, it would be all the better for mankind, and all the worse for the fishes." Then, Peter Gibian and Michael Weinstein examine what seem at first the "non-medical" aspects of Holmes, namely, his role as literary figure, philosopher, and forerunner in the development of depth psychology.

We follow these essays with Charles Bryan's original suggestion: a *Quotable Holmes*, broken up into approximately 250 medical quotes and 250 non-medical quotes. Drawn from nearly all of Holmes's published prose and poetry, and some of his unpublished material, the quotes have been selected and organized to provide an overview of Holmes's work *in toto*, yet to reflect on their individual topics of concern and their frequent relevance to today's concerns, medical and otherwise. Holmes wrote that "it takes a generation or two to find out what are the passages in a great writer which are to become commonplaces in literature and conversation," and it is doubtful he foresaw that such terms coined by him as "anesthesia," "white plague," "Hub of the solar system," and Boston "Brahmin" would join the daily lexicons of later generations. Yet Holmes would also caution his readership, as he did in "The Contagiousness of Puerperal of Fever," that "this is a proper place to warn the student against skimming the prefaces and introductions of works for mottoes and embellishments to his thesis. He cannot learn anatomy by thrusting an exploring needle into his body. He will be very liable to misquote his author's meaning while he is picking off his outside sentences." And Peter Gibian has pointed out the very intention of Holmes to provoke and to stimulate; excerpts from the Breakfast-Table series, for example, must be read with the understanding that Holmes often uses his characters as devil's advocates rather than stand-ins for his own convictions. Thus, one reads many of these quotes in isolation at one's own risk, even if nodding, laughing, or scowling in the process. And certain quotes have been purposely excluded, on account of insufficient context or irony-proofing. We follow the quotes with the unedited (though annotated) transcript of Holmes's previously unpublished 1879 lecture to the incoming first-year class at Harvard Medical School, a lecture that epitomizes Holmes's style and overall emphasis upon therapeutic skepticism.

We came to realize, and perhaps should have anticipated, that one really can't separate Holmes the physician from Holmes the man of letters. Holmes's importance as a medical writer stems from the literary, rhetorical quality of his writings and talks (as will be seen in Amalie Kass's essay, woe to the Philadelphia physician who characterized Holmes's account of puerperal fever as "the jejune and fizenless dreamings of sophomore writers"!), while he introduced his medical concerns into each of his Breakfast-Table books and "medicated" novels. And as recent scholarship has shown, Holmes infused his works with interrelated concerns about the healing power of nature and divine immanence, the validity of received dogma and the reliability of the marketplace, and predestination as manifested in hereditary tendencies on this earth rather than in the afterlife.

In sum, we've predicated this volume on the belief that there is a great deal to be gained, in the twenty-first century, from a close investigation of Holmes's contributions in the nineteenth century. Much remains to be said and written about Holmes—for example, about his positions on race, gender, hereditary predispositions, or comparative anatomy and evolution. One of our hoped-for outcomes of this volume is to stimulate such research on this multifaceted personality. Indeed, during his presentation in the Ether Dome, Charles Bryan asked the audience rhetorically: "Why are we meeting as the Osler Society rather than as the Holmes Society"? We view this volume as a potential entry point for such exploration.

Part I
Essays

Spy

Vincent Brooks Day & Son Lith.

"the Autocrat of the Breakfast Table."

"Spy" (Sir Leslie Matthew Ward) portrait of Holmes for Vanity Fair, *June 19, 1886*

"The Greatest Brahmin"

Overview of a Life

CHARLES S. BRYAN

I T WAS WITH GOOD REASON that Sir William Osler (1849–1919), the
most famous physician in the English-speaking world at the turn of the
twentieth century, called Oliver Wendell Holmes "the most successful
combination which the world has ever seen, of the physician and man of
letters."[1] Holmes the physician seemingly had a hand in every breakthrough
of the nineteenth century. He anticipated the germ theory, opposed
"heroic" measures such as bloodletting, held up to critique such alternative
therapies as homeopathy, gave "anesthesia" and "anesthetic agents" their
names, and explored the possibilities of what would become the new depth
psychology and analytic psychiatry. Holmes the man of letters was for a
time the most widely-read American author on both sides of the Atlantic.
He co-founded *The Atlantic Monthly* and assured its success, achieved notoriety as a poet, pioneered the psychological novel, thrived among such literary companions as Ralph Waldo Emerson, Nathaniel Hawthorne, Henry
Wadsworth Longfellow, James Russell Lowell, and Herman Melville, and
found in England such admirers as William Makepeace Thackeray,
Anthony Trollope, and Oscar Wilde. For originality in both medicine and
literature Holmes remains unsurpassed.

Osler likewise saw a clear connection between Holmes the physician
and Holmes the belletrist. Osler included Holmes on his bedside reading
list for medical students on the grounds that "from the Breakfast Table

---

[1] William Osler, "Oliver Wendell Holmes," in *An Alabama Student and Other Biographical Essays* (London: Oxford University Press, 1908), 55–67.

Series of Oliver Wendell Holmes you can glean a philosophy of life peculiarly suited to the needs of a physician." He told members of the British Medical Association that Holmes exemplified those who had "influenced the profession less by their special work than by exemplifying those graces of life and refinements of heart which make up character," and that Holmes was indeed "the greatest Brahmin among them," an avatar of "the leaven which has raised our profession above the dead level of a business." He told members of the Association of Medical Librarians that "a complete set of the writings of Oliver Wendell Holmes should be in every medical library," and that if they could "find the original pamphlet on the *Contagiousness of Puerperal Fever*, a reprint from the *New England Journal of Medicine and Surgery*, 1843, have it bound in crushed levant [Levant, the most expensive morocco]—'tis worth of it." In 1889, Osler expressed his admiration for Holmes as the "most conscious modern example" of success in both medicine and literature, asking rhetorically:

> Would he [Holmes] rather go down to posterity as the man who, in this country at least, first roused the profession to a sense of the perils of puerperal fever as an infectious disease . . . or would he choose to be remembered as the author of "The [Chambered] . . . Nautilus" or "The Last Leaf?"

And when Osler, on a 1908 trip to Paris, led an expedition to the tomb of the great French clinician Pierre-Charles-Alexandre Louis, he laid a wreath "for the sake of James Jackson Jr., [Henry Ingersoll] Bowditch, & Holmes." Osler, in sum, viewed Holmes with awe bordering on reverence.[2]

It would no doubt surprise Osler that he, not Holmes, emerged from that era as the best-known reconciler of the old humanities with the new medical science. It would also surprise Osler that for most Americans—including physicians—the name "Oliver Wendell Holmes" conjures up the jurist, who displaced his father from the public eye to the extent that the appellation "Junior" became unnecessary. Moreover, Holmes's presence on Osler's recommended bedside reading list for medical students now seems as incongruous as Theodore Roosevelt's presence on Mount Rushmore and for the same reason: the erosion of a once-formidable reputation by Tincture of Time. Still, were Osler alive today, he would celebrate many of the things for which Holmes stood: the generalist in an

[2]William Osler, "The Master-Word in Medicine," in *Aequanimitas, With other Addresses to Medical Students, Nurses and Practitioners of Medicine*, third edition (Philadelphia: P. Blakiston's Son & Co., Inc., 1932), 347–71; Osler, "British Medicine in Greater Britain," in ibid., 161–88; Osler, "Some Aspects of American Medical Bibliography," in ibid., 291–309; Harvey Cushing, *The Life of Sir William Osler*, (Oxford: The Clarendon Press, 1925), 1: 301–2; and ibid., 2: 144.

age of spiraling specialization, the bedside teacher in an age of escalating technology, the poet's insights in an age where few allow quiet time for reflection, religious tolerance in a world endangered by divisive fundamentalism, and, perhaps above all, the joy of celebrating the human condition from as many perspectives as possible. Let us briefly review the life of this remarkable polymath.

Oliver Wendell Holmes (1809–1894)

Oliver Wendell Holmes was born in Cambridge, Massachusetts, on August 29, 1809, the son of the Reverend Abiel and Sarah Wendell Holmes, both from old New England families. Abiel Holmes was an introverted, serious man, against whose *gravitas* and rigorous Calvinism young Oliver would rebel. Sarah Wendell Holmes was her husband's antithesis: extroverted, playful, and light-hearted. Oliver would resemble both—he would be almost pathologically talkative, lively, and witty, yet capable of the bookishness and focus requisite to scholarly achievement. Indeed, he would develop an uncommon ability to hold in tension such polarities as solitude and sociability, gravity and levity, conservatism and progressivism, and what we now understand as the complementary voices and worldviews of the left and right cerebral hemispheres. Oliver Wendell Holmes would become one of the English-speaking world's last great generalists.

His boyhood did not foreshadow such brilliance. When he was not talking he was likely to be whistling, singing, playing his homemade flute, or getting into mischief. Whatever academic prowess he may have shown at Port School in nearby Cambridgeport was no match for that of classmate Margaret Fuller (1810–1850), the future transcendentalist and women's rights activist. And Oliver was easily distracted. He started many of the books in his father's library of some 2000 volumes, but finished few. His carved ball-in-cage lacked the meticulous workmanship of those carved by his friends. To his father's consternation he sought companionship, crowds, and entertainment wherever he could find them, as if heeding the advice of the physician-poet John Armstrong: "Go seek the cheerful haunts of men, and mingle with the bustling crowd." Taking his cue from his mother he would become, as Peter Gibian puts it, "the nation's symbol of Sociability."[3]

---

[3]Peter Gibian, *Oliver Wendell Holmes and the Culture of Conversation* (Cambridge: Cambridge University Press, 2001), 104.

Abiel Holmes's seriousness and bookishness showed nonetheless, for it was he who encouraged 12-year-old Oliver to write a poem on the theme of *Perdidi diem* (a lost day), the moral being to live every day to the fullest. Abiel Holmes sent him for a year to Phillips Andover Academy, the seat of Calvinist orthodoxy, and then to Harvard College. Oliver did well in the sciences, notably in chemistry and mineralogy, but his major reputation was that of a lively talker and, as the eventual class poet, the author of racy verse for the Hasty Pudding Club's festivities. While young Holmes studied at Harvard, his father's congregation splintered as members of the First Church in Cambridge sought other points of view. Abiel Holmes lost his pulpit, to his son's embarrassment. Young Holmes rejected the ministry, if indeed he had ever considered it, and toyed between medicine and the law before choosing the latter.

Courses at Harvard Law School were barely underway when, on September 14, 1830, the *Boston Daily Advertiser* carried a notice that the Secretary of the Navy advised scrapping the Boston-built frigate *Constitution*, veteran of engagements against the British, the French, and the Barbary pirates. Holmes dashed off a three-verse, 24-line poem, "Old Ironsides," railing against "the harpies of the shore" who would pluck "the eagle of the sea" and pleading:

O better that her shattered hulk
Should sink beneath the wave!
Her thunders shook the mighty deep,
And there should be her grave:
Nail to the mast her holy flag,
Set every threadbare sail,
And give her to the god of storms,
The lightning and the gale!

Published by the *Daily Advertiser* and picked up by other newspapers throughout the country, "Old Ironsides" evoked an outcry that rendered any plans to destroy the frigate—and whether there were indeed such plans remains arguable—a political impossibility, assuring the *Constitution* its destiny as the pride of Boston Harbor and the world's oldest commissioned vessel still afloat. The young poet became famous overnight if only by the signature "*H.*"

Holmes finished out the year but left the law for medicine. His enrollment at Boston Medical College rather than Harvard Medical School requires brief explanation. The medical schools in Boston including Harvard, as elsewhere in the United States with the possible exception of the

University of Pennsylvania, were essentially arrangements whereby local private physicians offered lectures and demonstrations for fees. The faculty at Boston Medical College included such then-famous physicians as James Jackson, John Ware, Walter Otis, and Winslow Lewis. Jackson's exceptionally promising son, James Jackson, Jr., became a close friend and the elder Jackson became for Holmes a surrogate father. At the end of Holmes's first year at medical school, the younger Jackson and two other friends sailed for Paris to further their medical educations. When Holmes followed in March 1833, the elder Jackson commended him to his son in Paris with the warning, "Do not mind his apparent frivolity."[4]

Although the "Paris school," a loose nexus of hospitals and private practices comprising the Mecca of medical education between roughly 1810 and 1860, is well-known to medical historians, a brief explanation may benefit the general reader.[5] When William Osler observed that "Minerva medicine has never had her chief temples in any one country for more than a generation or two,"[6] he had in mind the following broad if over-simplified sequence: Classical Greece → Rome → the Eastern and Western Caliphates of the Islamic Empire → Bologna and Montpellier → Padua → Leyden → Edinburgh → Paris (and subsequently Germany → the United States → the present era's globalization). To the obvious conclusion that academic medicine thrives in parallel with other aspects of culture, cynics suggest another reason students flocked to post-revolutionary Paris: an abundance of corpses for dissection. Be that as it may, Paris was famous for its great teachers and, when in 1882 Holmes entitled his farewell lecture to Harvard Medical Students "Some of My Early Teachers," he mentioned a string of them: Barons Boyer, Larrey, and Dupuytren, all famous in the history of surgery; Armand Velpeau, François Broussais, François Chomel, Gabriel Andral; and, last but not least, Pierre-Charles-Alexandre Louis (1787–1872). Although Holmes was not Louis's favorite pupil—that distinction went to the younger James Jackson, who described familial emphysema and whose death at age 24 from complications of typhus and dysentery deprived Boston medicine of its rising star—it was nonetheless Louis with whom he spent the most time. Holmes reminisced:

---

[4]James Jackson, *A Memoir of James Jackson, Jr., M.D.* (Boston: Houghton, Mifflin, and Company, 1905), 346; quoted in Eleanor M. Tilton, *Amiable Autocrat: A Biography of Oliver Wendell Holmes* (New York: Henry Schuman, 1947), 80.
[5]See John Harley Warner, *Against the Spirit of System: The French Impulse in Nineteenth-Century American Medicine* (Princeton: Princeton University Press, 1998).
[6]William Osler, "Vienna after Thirty-Four Years," *Journal of the American Medical Association* 50 (1908): 1523–5.

"Modest in the presence of nature, fearless in the face of authority, unwearying in the pursuit of truth, he was a man whom any student might be happy and proud to claim as his teacher and his friend."[7]

Louis, like most good mentors, directed Holmes toward independent study. Not being proficient in English, Louis asked Holmes to translate and report on recent work by the English physician and physiologist, Marshall Hall. In 1830, Hall had published *Observations on Blood-letting, founded on researches on the morbid and curative effects of loss of blood*. Hall's demonstration of the harmful physiological effects of bloodletting gave scientific rationale for what Louis, as the putative founder of medical statistics, would demonstrate with his "Numerical Method": the dubious benefits and possible harm of bloodletting for pneumonia. Hall's therapeutic conservatism, amplified by Louis and other Parisians as the *méthode expectante* of allowing nature to take her course, became the dominant theme of Holmes's medical writings, famously expressed in his opinion that if with a few exceptions "the whole materia medica, *as now used*, could be sunk to the bottom of the sea, it would be all the better for mankind, and all the worse for the fishes."[8] Also, in 1832 Hall had published a paper, "On the Reflex function of the Medulla Oblongata and Medulla Spinalis," in which he recorded how such animals as frogs, snakes, turtles, and hedgehogs respond to stimuli after ablation of portions of their nervous systems. Hall thereby discovered the reflex arc. Holmes, stimulated by this insight, would spend a lifetime considering the limits to free will imposed by inherited tendencies and previous life events, as evidenced in his three "medicated novels" (as he called them): *Elsie Venner* (1861), *The Guardian Angel* (1867), and *A Mortal Antipathy* (1885).[9] Holmes wrote in *Elsie Venner*: "Until somebody shall study this [behavior] as Marshall Hall has studied reflex nervous

---

[7]Oliver Wendell Holmes, "Some of My Early Teachers," in *Medical Essays, 1842–1882* [The Works of Oliver Wendell Holmes, Standard Library Edition, Volume IX] (Boston: Houghton, Mifflin and Company, 1892), 433.

[8]Oliver Wendell Holmes, "Currents and Counter-Currents in Medical Science," in *Medical Essays, 1842–1882*, 203.

[9]See Charles Boewe, "Reflex Action in the Novels of Oliver Wendell Holmes," *American Literature* 26 (1954): 303–19; Michael A. Weinstein, *The Imaginative Prose of Oliver Wendell Holmes* (Columbia, Missouri: University of Missouri Press, 2006). The extent to which Hall's discovery of the reflex arc prompted Holmes's explorations of psychology remains uncertain. Boewe's claim to that effect, and also the claim by Clarence P. Oberndorf (*The Psychiatric Novels of Oliver Wendell Holmes* [New York: Columbia University Press, 1943]) that Holmes anticipated much of Freudian psychiatry, may have been overstated. However, and as evinced by the quoted passage from *Elsie Venner*, the possibility that phenomena similar to the reflex arc govern much of our behavior clearly intrigued Holmes.

action in the bodily system, I would not give much for men's judgments of each other's characters."[10] Thus, Louis's request that Holmes study the work of Marshall Hall pointed the young student toward two lifelong paths of study. Louis also influenced Holmes by his scientific approach to clinical problems and by his personal traits, notably humility. Holmes later wrote Emerson that the "master key to all the success he [Louis] ever had . . . was honesty."[11] For Holmes, as for hundreds of American medical students and physicians during that era, Paris provided new insights into medicine and indeed into the broader themes of Western culture.

Returning to the United States, Holmes eventually received his M.D. degree from Harvard in 1836 by writing a dissertation on acute pericarditis and passing an examination. Although this may seem anomalous inasmuch as Holmes had never taken a course at Harvard Medical School, it was not unusual at the time. He hung out his shingle at 2 Central Court in Boston, declaring: "Small fevers gratefully received."[12] Although it would take him at least a decade to develop a self-supporting practice, as was again the norm, he steadily achieved prominence as a physician and citizen. In 1836 he won the first of his three Boylston Prizes offered by Harvard Medical School, recited a noteworthy poem at the Harvard commencement to celebrate the college's bicentennial, and had a collection of verse published. Holmes's growing popularity as a poet probably detracted from his medical practice, for he would later advise young doctors to avoid seeking reputations in other fields. Holmes also became a force in the Boston Society for Medical Improvement, comprised mainly of young doctors who like himself had studied in Paris. After his appointment to the Boston Dispensary under a system to care for the poor, Holmes began to advocate for reform in health care delivery. In 1837 he acquired still another source of income when Emerson sponsored him to become a public lecturer on the Boston Lyceum circuit. And he received stipends from teaching at the Tremont Medical School in Boston, where he introduced microscopy and histology for the first time to North American medical students, and at Dartmouth Medical School, where he taught anatomy for

---

[10]Oliver Wendell Holmes, *Elsie Venner* [The Works of Oliver Wendell Holmes, Standard Library Edition, Volume V] (Boston: Houghton, Mifflin and Company, 1892 [1861]), 227.
[11]Oliver Wendell Holmes to Ralph Waldo Emerson, 4 April 1856, quoted in William C. Dowling, *Oliver Wendell Holmes in Paris: Medicine, Theology, and The Autocrat of the Breakfast Table* (Durham, New Hampshire: University of New Hampshire Press, 2006), 82.
[12]Edwin P. Hoyt, *The Improper Bostonian: Dr. Oliver Wendell Holmes* (New York: William Morrow and Company, Inc., 1979), 72.

14 weeks during two successive years. Thus, within a few years of arriving back in the United States, Holmes had acquired status not only as a practicing physician but also as an educator, a rising young Turk in the medical profession, and a public speaker—not to mention a growing reputation as a wit and congenial companion.

In June 1840 Holmes married Amelia Lee Jackson, whose prosperous father gave the couple a furnished home. As Holmes's lectures became increasingly popular he began to hold forth at the prestigious Society for the Diffusion of Useful Knowledge, especially on the premise that American physicians dosed too much and observed too little. He spoke out against homeopathy, objecting not only to the dubious efficacy of diminutive drug doses but also to the effect homeopaths were having on American public health. Then in 1842, puerperal fever became increasingly prevalent in New England, especially among the Irish. Previously healthy women died after childbirth from what we now know to have been overwhelming sepsis caused by the group A streptococcus (*Streptococcus pyogenes*). The frequent association of one or another physician with a cluster of maternal deaths convinced Holmes of its contagiousness. Holmes assembled and published in 1843 a long series of anecdotes to the effect that puerperal fever was contagious. He argued that no physician preparing to deliver a child should participate in a postmortem examination. The medical profession, even in Boston, largely dismissed his paper, at least initially and in public. Never mind, the argument went, that several of Dr. Blank's patients developed puerperal fever; you must also consider that other women whom Dr. Blank delivered did just fine. Although Holmes's paper on the contagiousness of puerperal fever preceded that of the ill-fated Hungarian physician Ignaz Semmelweis, the latter now receives the lion's share of the credit mainly because he had better data. Still, Holmes deserves major credit for his eloquent and passionate communication to the medical profession, and many physicians likely changed their practice habits without openly admitting the possibility that they had been transmitting a deadly disease.

In 1846, Edward Everett, Harvard's president now remembered for the tedious two-hour speech that preceded Abraham Lincoln's two-minute Gettysburg Address, established new professorships of pathology and of anatomy and physiology. The latter was endowed by Dr. George Parkman, on whose land Harvard had built a new medical school that opened the same year. Holmes was appointed the first Parkman Professor of Anatomy and Physiology and also dean of the medical school. His blend of knowledge, enthusiasm, and flair for the English language made him immensely popular with the students. Humorously mocking excessively technical jargon, he would, for example, liken the brain exposed in the calvarium to an English walnut in its shell, the intestinal mesentery to the ruffles in a man's shirt, the fimbriated end of the Fallopian tubes to "the fringe of a poor woman's shawl," and the microscopic appearance of the coiled sweat glands to a fairy's intestines. The other professors insisted that Holmes give the last of the five morning lectures, as only he could keep students awake by that hour. In 1848 Holmes gave up his private practice as he now had a small salary at Harvard supplemented by outside activities.

However, as a medical school dean, he found himself embroiled in controversy almost from the start. On November 23, 1849, Dr. George Parkman, Holmes's and Harvard's benefactor, disappeared. He had been last seen entering the medical school from North Grove Street. Dr. John White Webster, the professor of chemistry, became the prime suspect when a man's pelvis and two pieces of a leg were discovered in a sewage holding tank connected to Webster's private lavatory. Webster, it turned out, had been living beyond his means and had used the same collateral for separate loans from Parkman and another wealthy Bostonian. What is now known as the Parkman-Webster murder trial began on March 17, 1850, lasted 12 days, and for public excitement became the nineteenth century's equivalent to the O.J. Simpson murder trial of the twentieth. An estimated 60,000 of Boston's 130,000 people flocked to the courthouse. Journalists came from as far away as London, Paris and Berlin. Attorneys for the two sides represented a who's who of legal circles. Holmes testified that whoever had dismembered the body knew something about anatomy and that the build was "not dissimilar" from Parkman's. Holmes also pointed out that Dr. Parkman had sported a new set of shiny teeth and suggested that the dentures recovered from Webster's furnace be examined with this in mind. The new dentures fit into a mold made by Parkman's dentist (although the defense showed that they fit molds from other mouths as well).

All of the evidence was circumstantial. The presiding judge, Chief Justice Lemuel Shaw of the Massachusetts Supreme Judicial Court, made a historic statement replete with bias against the defendant: The jury needed only to find *beyond a reasonable doubt* that the corpse was Parkman's (the previous standard had been "to an absolute certainty"). After less than three hours of deliberation the jury returned a verdict that the remains were indeed Parkman's, that Webster had killed him, and had done so deliberately. Only after appeals were exhausted did Webster confess to the crime. Webster had struck his creditor on the head with a walking stick, dismembered the body in a sink, burned some parts and hidden others in a chest and lavatory vault to decompose, and flushed the blood into the Charles River basin, which was directly beneath his laboratory.

Webster's public hanging on August 30, 1850, in Boston's Leverett Square did little for the reputation of Harvard Medical School, which like the mid-nineteenth-century medical profession as a whole struggled for public legitimacy. Holmes as dean was in the embarrassing position of having testified for both the prosecution and also for the defense as a character witness for Webster.

Holmes's life as dean was further complicated in 1850 when Harriot Kezia Hunt, whose 1847 application to be the first female medical student at Harvard had been rejected by the powers-that-be, reapplied and was joined by three black students: Daniel Laing, Jr., Isaac Humphrey Snowden, and Martin Robison Delany. Although Holmes's Victorian-era attitudes toward women and blacks (and also toward Native Americans) were complex, he endorsed all four with the reservation that he would privately instruct Miss Hunt in anatomy to spare her the embarrassment of examining genitalia in the presence of male students. When the students, all 113 of whom were white males, learned of the admission of the three black students to be followed by a woman, they sprang into action. They voted overwhelmingly to reject Miss Hunt. Nobody came to her defense. The case of the black students was more nuanced. Students argued that their presence would discourage white students from choosing Harvard Medical School and would cheapen their own diplomas. Although 23 percent of the students approved admitting the black students, a vocal majority prevailed with the following resolution: "*Resolved* That we have no objection to the education and elevation of blacks but do decidedly remonstrate against their presence in College with us." The black students, who by then were attending classes, were ostracized by their fellow students. They kept to themselves, as hardly anyone would speak to them.

Holmes had a crisis. He called a special meeting of the faculty. He suggested that perhaps Miss Hunt could be persuaded to withdraw her application, which she did. Holmes lacked faculty support for the black students and therefore bowed to the students' demands. Snowden and Laing were admitted to Dartmouth's medical school through Holmes's influence. Delany wouldn't budge, hoping that such abolitionists as William Lloyd Garrison, Charles Sumner, Henry Ward Beecher, and Wendell Phillips would come to his rescue. They did not. We should note in passing that

both Miss Hunt and Martin Delany went on to worldly success and posthumous notoriety despite denial of a Harvard medical degree. Hunt has been
called "the mother of the American woman physician" and Delany was
recently listed among the 100 greatest African Americans.[13]

If Holmes was not enjoying his deanship, he found sublimation
through outside interests and especially through his friendships among the
literati. He was, perhaps subconsciously, laying the groundwork for a second career as writer and public figure. The best-known story to that effect
concerns the "writer's picnic" of August 5, 1850, when Holmes, carrying
his black doctor's bag, led a small party of leading publishers and authors—
including Hawthorne and Melville—up the slopes of Monument Moun-
tain in the Berkshires of western Massachusetts. Reaching the summit,
Holmes opened the bag and pulled out bottles of fine champagne. Not
present on that joyful occasion was the writer who would give Holmes his
big break: the poet James Russell Lowell. Lowell had been invited to edit
a new literary magazine. Perhaps more than anyone, Lowell took Holmes
seriously as a writer and foresaw the popular appeal of Holmes's ability to
combine a breadth of knowledge with gentle humor, irony, and an interesting conversational style. Lowell specifically recalled two humorous
essays Holmes had written under the title "The Autocrat of the Breakfast
Table." In 1856, Holmes accepted Lowell's invitation to write a serial for
the new magazine for which Holmes then proposed a name: *The Atlantic
Monthly*. Although the *Atlantic* may have had more famous founding
members, notably Emerson and Longfellow, it was Holmes who scored

---

[13]See Ruth J. Abram, "Will There be a Monument? Six Pioneer Women Doctors Tell Their
Own Stories," in Abram, ed., *"Send us a Lady Physician": Women Doctors in America,
1835–1920* (New York: Norton, 1984), 71–106; Molefi Kete Asante, *100 Greatest African
Americans: A Biographical Encyclopedia* (Amherst, New York: Prometheus Books, 2002), 103–5.
Hunt and Delany were older applicants to Harvard Medical School, both having taken up the
practical study of medicine in the year 1833. Hunt, who later received an honorary medical
degree from the Woman's Medical College of Pennsylvania, practiced medicine and advocated for women's rights until her death in 1875. Delany wrote a novel, became as a major
the first black field line officer of the United States army, and, after the Civil War, explored
the possibility of a black nation in Liberia and practiced medicine in Charleston, South Carolina, until his death in 1885. He is today known as arguably the first proponent of American Black Nationalism. For further discussion of Delany's case, see Philip Cash, "Pride,
Prejudice, and Politics," in Werner Sollors, Caldwell Titcomb, and Thomas A. Underwood,
eds., *Blacks at Harvard: A Documentary History of African-American Experience at Harvard and
Radcliffe* (New York: NYU Press, 1993), 22–31. Harvard Medical School graduated its first
black student in 1869, but it was not until 1945 that women were admitted.

the biggest hit with the reading public. Indeed, Holmes literally made the *Atlantic*—and the *Atlantic* in turn made Holmes. Readers reveled in the conversational free-for-all among such characters as the bluntly-opinionated Autocrat, The Professor, The Divinity Student, The Lady in Black, Little Boston, The Astronomer, the Old Gentleman Opposite, That Boy ("a sort of expletive at the table") and the Landlady. There had been nothing like it in English since Laurence Sterne's *Tristram Shandy*, and there is perhaps nothing like it today except Garry Trudeau's *Doonesbury* comic strip—a playful yet ultimately serious running dialogue among stereotypical representatives of the larger society. By the late 1850s, *The Atlantic Monthly* had a circulation of 400,000 copies in a nation of 31 million people. Soon after *The Autocrat of the Breakfast-Table* appeared in book form in 1858, Holmes found himself famous.

Lowell did Holmes a second favor in 1856 by sponsoring his membership in the newly-minted Saturday Club. Although intellectual dinner clubs have since been formed in most if not all large cities in the United States, few if any have rivaled the Saturday Club for the prominence of its members. Here is Holmes's account of its early years:

> At one end of the table sat Longfellow, florid, quiet, benignant, soft-voiced, a most agreeable rather than a brilliant talker, but a man upon whom it was always pleasant to look,—whose silence was better than many another man's conversation. At the other end of the table sat Agassiz, robust, sanguine, animated, full of talk, boy-like in his laughter. The stranger who should have asked who were the men ranged along the sides of the table would have heard in answer the names of Hawthorne, Motley, Dana, Lowell, Whipple, Peirce, the distinguished mathematician, Judge Hoar, eminent at the bar and in the cabinet, Dwight, the leading musical critic of Boston for a whole generation, Sumner, the academic champion of Freedom, Andrew, "the great War Governor" of Massachusetts, Dr. Howe, the philanthropist, William Hunt, the painter, with others not unworthy of such company. And with these, generally near the Longfellow end of the table, sat Emerson, talking in low tones and carefully measured utterances to his neighbor, or listening and recording on his mental phonograph any stray word worth remembering.

Holmes later recalled: "The vitality of this club has depended in a great measure on its utter poverty in statutes and by-laws, its entire absence of formality, and its blessed freedom from speech-making." Representing and cross-pollinating a broad range of the sciences and liberal arts, the Saturday Club's diverse membership gave Holmes ample opportunity to field-test the themes aired by his fictional personas.[14]

Although Holmes stepped down from his deanship at Harvard Medical School in 1853, he kept up his high profile in the medical profession through his lectures and publications, including a new (1855) edition of his essay on puerperal fever. By the eve of the Civil War he thus enjoyed notoriety, indeed celebrity, in two diverse fields. His was a household name, and he was possibly the most photographed person in the United States. However, despite his genial nature, he was a target for ire from several directions. Physicians resented accusations of over-drugging and transmitting a deadly disease to their patients.[15] Orthodox Calvinists resented his polemics against the doctrine of Original Sin and his increasing bent toward religious latitudinarianism. And abolitionists resented his failure to openly support their cause (few Boston physicians did, with the notable exception of Holmes's friend, Henry Ingersoll Bowditch, who as a result was shunned in polite society,[16] but the abolitionists especially coveted the high-profile Holmes). More immediately, a civil war brewed in his household.

Holmes's frenetic activities as teacher, writer, public speaker, and dinner companion left too little time for his wife (who supported abolition) and their three children. Especially smarting were his sons, Wendell and "Neddie" (Edward Jackson Holmes). They resented their father's absenteeism,

---

[14]Oliver Wendell Holmes, *Ralph Waldo Emerson*, in *Ralph Waldo Emerson, John Lothrop Motley* [The Works of Oliver Wendell Holmes, Standard Library Edition, Volume XI] (Boston: Houghton, Mifflin and Company, 1892 [1884]), 171–2; and Holmes, "The Saturday Club," Appendix A in ibid., 497–9. Persons mentioned here include: Louis Agassiz, Harvard scientist best remembered today as an important opponent of Darwin; John Lothrop Motley, American historian; Richard Henry Dana, Jr., lawyer, politician, and author of *Two Years Before the Mast*; Ebenezer R. Hoar, politician and lawyer; John Sullivan Dwight, Unitarian minister and America's first influential classical music critic; Charles Sumner, lawyer, politician, and statesman; John Albion Andrew, politician and force behind the creation of the all-black 54th Massachusetts Infantry; Samuel Gridley Howe, physician and advocate for the mentally disabled and for the education of the blind; and William Morris Hunt, leading painter of mid-nineteenth-century Boston.

[15]In addition, Holmes had offended some physicians by decrying much of the American medical literature as putting "English portraits of disease on American frames" and by referring to the "inferior schools wrongly located" in the South and Southwest. See Holmes et al., "Report of the Committee on Medical Literature," *American Medical Association Transactions* 1 (1848): 249–88, quoted in Richard Harrison Shryock, "Medical Sources and Medical History," in *Medicine in America: Historical Essays* (Baltimore: The Johns Hopkins Press, 1966), 294; and Holmes, quoted in "Medical Practice in the Old South," in ibid., 61.

[16]See Eugene Perry Link, *The Social Ideas of American Physicians (1776–1976): Studies of the Humanitarian Tradition in Medicine* (Selinsgrove: Susquehanna University Press, 1992), 39–61.

did not care for his jokes, and disliked being called "Dr. Holmes's sons." The frostiness that characterized the relationship between Holmes and his namesake came to a head in September 1862 after Holmes Senior received a message that Wendell had been "wounded shot through the neck thought not mortal at Keedysville" as one of the 23,000 casualties in the bloodiest single-day battle in American history, generally known as Antietam. Holmes set out at once by train. He passed through New Jersey, Philadelphia, Baltimore, and Frederick, Maryland, describing along the way the agony of the wounded, the fatigue of the unwounded "with more spirit than strength," the crowded field hospitals, the piles of corpses, the landscape littered with dead horses, and the eternal folly of flaming men's passions by demonizing the enemy. Arriving at Keedysville, Maryland, several miles from the main battlefield, he met a "beady-eyed, cheery-looking ancient woman" named Margaret Kitzmuller who told him that his son had left the previous day in a milk-cart bound for Hagerstown, the terminus of the Cumberland Valley Railroad. Holmes raced ahead to Harrisburg, Pennsylvania, met a train from Hagerstown, and found his son in "the first car, on the fourth seat to the right." There ensued the following conversation:

"How are you, Boy?"

"How are you, Dad?"

Adding to Wendell's resentment was his father's literary exploitation of the episode as "My Hunt after 'The Captain.'"[17] William James, the future philosopher-psychologist who became from 1864 onwards one of the future justice's closest friends, recorded the extreme tension between father and son, and it was to James that the younger Holmes expounded on his theory that that "each generation strangles and devours its predecessor."[18]

Holmes taught at Harvard Medical School until 1882, when he retired to devote full time to writing.[19] He had kept up his Breakfast Table series

---

[17]Oliver Wendell Holmes, "My Hunt after 'The Captain,'" in *Pages from an Old Volume of Life* [The Works of Oliver Wendell Holmes, Standard Library Edition, Volume VIII] (Boston: Houghton, Mifflin and Company, 1892 [1862]), 16–77.

[18]Robert D. Richardson, *William James: In the Maelstrom of American Modernism* (Boston: Houghton Mifflin Company, 2006), 77.

[19]Holmes's biographers attribute his retirement to the encouragement of his publisher, but one wonders whether the directions Harvard's president Charles W. Eliot was taking the medical school had something to do with it. Holmes and the surgeon Henry Jacob Bigelow had been the major "old guard" professors who strenuously opposed Eliot's ambition to control what had been *de facto* a largely proprietary medical school and to make medical education more rigorous and scientific. By 1882, Eliot was beginning to get his way. See Kenneth M. Ludmerer, *Learning to Heal: The Development of American Medical Education* (New York: Basic Books, Inc., Publishers, 1985), 47–71.

in *The Atlantic* despite the Autocrat's marriage to the Schoolmistress and departure from the fictional boarding house. Succeeding *The Autocrat* were *The Professor at the Breakfast-Table* (1859), the central figure of which is, like Holmes, a Paris-trained physician, and *The Poet at the Breakfast-Table* (1872), built around Holmes's artistic persona. Somewhat apologetically, Holmes completed his quartet of conversational writings with *Over the Teacups* (1890), telling readers in the preface that "The morning cup of coffee has an exhilaration about it which the cheering influence of the afternoon cup of tea cannot be expected to reproduce."[20] In the meantime, he had completed his trilogy of "medicated novels" with *A Mortal Antipathy*. Holmes's later writings touch a wide range of interests but find a unifying thread in his 1870 Phi Beta Kappa address at Harvard on "Mechanism in Thought and Morals." Holmes, through his fiction, was exploring and interrelating psychology, psychiatry, theology, and philosophy. He was, in the broadest sense, pondering some of the issues now being addressed in such rapidly-developing disciplines as neuropsychology, neurophilosophy, neuroethics, and neurotheology.

Affecting the philosophical bent of Holmes's later writings were personal losses. "Neddie" died in 1884, leaving a widow and Holmes's only grandchild, Edward Jackson Holmes, Jr. Then Holmes's wife, Amelia, died in 1888, and their daughter, Amelia, died the following year. Holmes's son Wendell and his wife, Fanny, moved into the house to care for him. Holmes died on October 7, 1894, in the presence of Fanny and Wendell. Holmes had eerily become the subject of one of his earliest published poems, "The Last Leaf" (which may have been written as early as 1831, when Holmes was but 22 years of age):

> And if I should live to be
> The last leaf upon the tree
> In the spring,
> Let them smile, as I do now,
> At the old forsaken bough
> Where I cling.

Holmes had himself been the last leaf in Boston's reign as the unrivaled epicenter of American intellectual life. As his favorite newspaper, the Boston *Transcript*, put it, Holmes's death extinguished "the last lingering

---

[20]Oliver Wendell Holmes, *Over the Teacups* [The Works of Oliver Wendell Holmes, Standard Library Edition, Volume IV] (Boston: Houghton, Mifflin and Company, 1892 [1890]), 6.

star of what was a constellation of American genius."[21] And the two surviving members of Harvard's Class of 1829 had lost their poet.

An Afterlife

Is Holmes still relevant, and, if so, to what extent? And why is Holmes, once
so famous in two disparate fields, so little-known today, especially compared
to his namesake, the jurist? Subsuming these questions is a much larger one:
Do the humanities matter anymore for the practice of medicine? The eminent French medical historian Danielle Gourevitch recently opined that we
will soon witness widespread replacement of doctors by technicians, and
that there is nothing to be gained from "the pretense of teaching literature
to first-year medical students." She called William Osler "the last *maître à
penser* for a noble-minded general medicine."[22] Likewise, the ethicist Robert
M. Veatch, commenting on "the collapse of physician-humanist communication," treats Osler as the last of a long train of physicians who "almost"
confronted the humanities.[23] As a nineteenth century American physician at
home in the humanities, Holmes is not unique; others included Silas Weir
Mitchell, Hiram Christopher, Lawrence Irwell, Edward Waldo Emerson
(son of the transcendentalist), and Lawson Tait.[24] However, to return to
where we started, Holmes remains unsurpassed for major contributions to
both fields, even if judged only by his essay on puerperal fever and *The Autocrat of the Breakfast-Table*. It should perhaps comfort us that his originality in
the two disciplines did not occur simultaneously. In 1872 he wrote Weir
Mitchell: "I have missed you in the field of letters recently. I supposed you
are working in the mine of practice for I have heard that you have become a
great doctor."[25] Holmes, like Osler, would have us tell medical students and
young physicians that responsibility for their patients transcends any and all
outside interests apart from their families.

A common explanation for Holmes's posthumous assignment to his
son's penumbra holds that Holmes Senior spread his time and talent too

---

[21]Hoyt, *The Improper Bostonian*, 11.

[22]Danielle Gourevitch, "The History of Medical Teaching," *Lancet* 354 (Supplement,
December 1999): SIV33.

[23]Robert M. Veatch, *Disrupted Dialogue: Medical Ethics and the Collapse of the Physician-
Humanist Communication (1770–1980)* (New York: Oxford University Press, 2005), 122–44.

[24]John S. Haller, Jr., *American Medicine in Transition, 1840–1910* (Urbana: University of Illinois Press, 1981), 280.

[25]Oliver Wendell Holmes to S. Weir Mitchell, 16 April 1872, Mitchell Papers, Trent Collection, Duke University. Quoted in Charles E. Rosenberg, *The Care of Strangers: The Rise
of America's Hospital System* (New York: Basic Books, Inc., 1987), 384 n. 60.

thinly. Holmes Junior was among the first to level the charge of dilettan-
tism, and indeed one biographer alternately calls Holmes Senior a "master
dilettante," an "inestimable dilettante," and "a perfect dilettante."[26]
Holmes would probably not have minded, given his fervent opposition to
excessive specialization. Among his most vivid characters was "The
Scarabee," the obsessed entomologist in *The Professor at the Breakfast-Table*
who stakes his entire identity and self-worth on his ability to prove that a
tiny bee parasite represents the larval form of a certain beetle. Besides medicine, poetry, and creative fiction, Holmes wrote several popular hymns,
developed and popularized a stereoscope (a device using two eyeglasses to
create an illusion of depth, or "3-D"), and explored photography. He was
perhaps the last great American generalist. He would no doubt object to the
rampant specialization, subspecialization, and sub-subspecialization that
now characterize medicine and other disciplines. He was an intellectual
omnivore; indeed, Henry James, Sr., once told him: "Holmes, you are
intellectually the most alive man I ever knew."[27]

A second explanation for Holmes Senior's relative obscurity today
consists of his having made no provision to extend his personal influence
beyond nineteenth-century Boston. Except for his two years in Paris and
an 1886 trip to Europe with his daughter, he seldom left New England.
Although seasickness and lifelong asthma explain in part an aversion to
travel, he seemed to find in the greater Boston area everything he needed.
It was of course Holmes who nicknamed Boston "the Hub," short for
"hub of the universe," with the Boston State House being the center of the
solar system. The nickname lives on in New England and occasionally
draws wider attention as in the title to John Updike's paean to Ted Williams,
"Hub Fans Bid Kid Adieu." Likewise it was Holmes who coined the term,
Boston "Brahmin."[28] Yet, broadly interested in humanity as he was, it is
difficult to charge Holmes with excessive provincialism or elitism. More
importantly, and in contrast to Osler, he did not cultivate a devoted coterie
of protégées and other followers to perpetuate his memory.[29]

---

[26]Hoyt, *The Improper Bostonian*, 171, 177, 185.
[27]Gibian, *Oliver Wendell Holmes and the Culture of Conversation*, 49.
[28]Holmes, "The Brahmin Caste of New England," chapter 1 in *Elsie Venner*, 1–6.
[29]Osler commonly receives credit for popularizing bedside teaching in the United States, but
it was Holmes who wrote the seminal nineteenth-century essay on the subject. Osler made
bedside teaching a major focus and once said that he desired no other epitaph than his having
taught medical students in the wards. Holmes, on the other hand, tells us more than halfway
through his essay that "I myself have nothing to do with clinical teaching" ("Scholastic and
Bedside Teaching," in *Medical Essays, 1842–1882*, 291). Small wonder, then, that Osler had
numerous medical disciples to perpetuate his memory whereas Holmes did not.

Peter Gibian suggests a third reason for Holmes's relative obscurity today: his representation of a mindset and conversational style typical of mid-nineteenth-century Americans, as opposed to those of the Progressive Era (roughly, from the 1890s to the 1920s). Holmes Senior epitomized a generation of Americans who probed life's larger questions, struggled with the issues leading up to the Civil War, grappled with the implications of Darwinism, and thrived on talk for talk's sake irrespective of where the conversation might lead. Holmes Junior epitomized a more pragmatic generation, the can-do children of the Industrial Revolution who sought answers, results, judgments, and, above all, closure to the issues before them. It is largely for this reason, Gibian suggests, that Holmes Junior towers above his father in posthumous reputation as he did physically during life (the jurist stood 6 feet 3 inches, while Holmes Senior stood 5 feet 2 inches without his elevator shoes). The new generation lacked the patience necessary to enjoy the rambling discursiveness of "the amiable Autocrat."[30] Hence Holmes's creative fiction lacks appeal outside of English departments and—with certain exceptions such as "Old Ironsides," "The Chambered Nautilus," and "The Deacon's Masterpiece; or The Wonderful 'One-Hoss Shay'"—few spend much time with Holmes's poems, nor indeed with those of his fellow "fireside poets" (notably, William Cullen Bryant, Longfellow, Lowell, and John Greenleaf Whittier).

Yet it behooves us to acknowledge the fickleness of posthumous reputations. Holmes Junior, justly renowned for pithy opinions from the bench of the United States Supreme Court, now draws derision for such legal gems as "three generations of imbeciles are enough" (in *Buck v. Bell* [1927], upholding compulsory sterilization for the mentally retarded). Meanwhile, Holmes Senior finds his medical essays affirmed on a daily basis by those who deal with, for example, infection control, patient safety, rational drug use, medical education, and the "technological imperative" to focus more on the disease than on the sufferer. And Holmes Senior the writer finds his creative fiction affirmed by those fascinated by how our brains work.

Michael Weinstein and William C. Dowling aver that Holmes may yet be recognized as a major philosopher.[31] Dowling suggests that Holmes's time in Paris fostered optimism that science might be a new form of divine revelation. At the same time, Holmes, like his one-time medical student William James, never surrendered the pragmatic utility of religious

---

[30]Gibian, *Oliver Wendell Holmes and the Culture of Conversation*, 313–40.
[31]Weinstein, *The Imaginative Prose of Oliver Wendell Holmes*; Dowling, *Oliver Wendell Holmes in Paris*.

belief, including the possibility of an afterlife. Holmes can be seen as the nineteenth century's equivalent to the seventeenth century's Sir Thomas Browne: a physician who met his generation's challenge of science to faith with a gentle Christian (really, ecumenical) humanism that left lots of room for both. We might also observe that Holmes's literary device in the Breakfast Table series—that is, exploring issues through conversational dialogue around a strong personality—evokes not Browne but Plato.

Finally, we must ask whether Holmes on the bicentennial year of his birth would really care much about these appraisals. In all likelihood, he would not. He speculated on rare occasion whether future generations might find his writings of any interest—posthumous reputation concerns us all—but by and large he sublimated by keeping himself busy, useful, and interested in nearly everything around him. He lived fully, for and among his contemporaries, celebrating life and the human condition wherever and however he might find it. Osler, in his essay "An Alabama Student" about a physician who went to Paris to study under the great French clinicians only to die of tuberculosis upon return, begins his concluding paragraph: "The saddest lament in Oliver Wendell Holmes's poems is for the voiceless, 'for those who never sing/But die with all their music in them.' "[32] Oliver Wendell Holmes sang often and well. Might we do likewise!

[32]Osler, "An Alabama Student," in *An Alabama Student*, 1–18.

Oliver Wendell Holmes's 1842 Lectures on "Homœopathy and Its Kindred Delusions"

A Retrospective Look

JOHN S. HALLER, JR.

Such is the pretended science of Homœopathy, to which you are asked to trust your lives and the lives of those dearest to you. A mingled mass of perverse ingenuity, of tinsel erudition, of imbecile credulity, and of artful misrepresentation, too often mingled in practice, if we may trust the authority of its founder, with heartless and shameless imposition. Because it is suffered so often to appeal unanswered to the public, because it has its journals, its patrons, its apostles, some are weak enough to suppose it can escape the inevitable doom of utter disgrace and oblivion.

> —Oliver Wendell Holmes, "Homœopathy and
> Its Kindred Delusions" (1842)

WHEN HUMORIST MARK TWAIN DELIVERED an after dinner speech at the John Greenleaf Whittier birthday event in the Hotel Brunswick in Boston on December 17, 1877, he told the story of three drunken prospectors who visited his cabin in Nevada using the pseudonyms of "Mr. Longfellow, Mr. Emerson, and Mr. Oliver Wendell Holmes."

With intended good fun, the three men—all present at the dinner—were described: Mr. Emerson as "a seedy little bit of a chap"; Mr. Holmes as having "double chins all the way down to his stomach"; and Mr. Longfellow with "his nose . . . like a finger with the end joint tilted up." Judging from the effect on the audience and on subsequent speakers at the dinner, Twain's indiscretion set off a flurry of responses from the city's literati, few of whom were willing to take his remarks lightly. However, unlike Emerson, whose bruised feelings were unassuaged by Twain's apology, Dr. Oliver Wendell Holmes (1809–1894), Parkman professor of anatomy and physiology at Harvard Medical School, chose to treat the satire as harmless fun. Perhaps his decision was due to a similar public response he himself had received thirty-five years earlier to two lectures titled "Homœopathy and Its Kindred Delusions" given before the Boston Society for the Diffusion of Useful Knowledge.[1]

Holmes used the 1842 forum provided by the society to attack not only the foundations of homeopathic theory that were infiltrating the ranks of Boston's medical elite and their patrons, but to accuse its advocates of perpetuating the worst forms of medical charlatanism. Delivered when Holmes was still in private practice, the lectures were intended to treat homeopathy "not by ridicule, but by argument [and] with good temper and . . . peaceable language . . . with no desire of making enemies." Notwithstanding these laudable intentions, Holmes stirred a puddle of hurt and resentment that surfaced both in an out of print in subsequent years. Unlike Twain, who tried earnestly to turn a new page, Holmes chose instead to republish the unvarnished lectures in his *Currents and Counter-Currents in Medical Science*, in 1861, and again in 1883 and 1891 in his *Medical Essays, 1842–1882*.[2]

---

[1]http://www.neh.gov/news/humanities/2008-11Twain_Toast.html (1-6-09). During the heyday of the so-called "lecture-habit," Massachusetts was the cradle of the Boston Lyceum and the Boston Society for the Diffusion of Useful Knowledge, both organized in 1829. Ten years later came the Lowell Lectures. Together their platform speakers included Holmes, William Ellery Channing, Ralph Waldo Emerson, Rufus Choate, Wendell Phillips, Theodore Parker, and a host of others. The lecture circuit became the stomping ground for mesmerists, phrenologists, abolitionists, spiritualists, botanics, and all fashion of reformers. See Edwin P. Hoyt, *The Improper Bostonian: Dr. Oliver Wendell Holmes* (New York: William Morrow and Company, 1979), 100; and Carl Bode, *The American Lyceum: Town Meeting of the Mind* (Carbondale: Southern Illinois University Press, 1968).

[2]See Oliver Wendell Holmes, "Homœopathy and Its Kindred Delusions," and "Some More Recent Views on Homœopathy," in *Currents and Counter-Currents in Medical Science. With Other Addresses and Essays* (Boston: Ticknor and Fields, 1861), 51–188. The latter essay was a review of Joseph Hyppolyte Pulte's *Homeopathic Domestic Physician: Containing the Treatment of Diseases, With Popular Explanations of Anatomy, Physiology, Hygiene and Hydropathy; a Treatise on Domestic Surgery, and an Abridged Materia Medica* (London: James Epps, 1857). See also Oliver Wendell Holmes, "Homœopathy and its Kindred Delusions," in *Medical Essays, 1842–1882* [The Works of Oliver Wendell Holmes, Standard Library Edition, Volume IX] (Boston: Houghton, Mifflin and Company, 1892), 1–102.

HOLMES'S ARGUMENT

Incensed by homeopathy's duplicity and false reasoning, Holmes intended to deal a deathblow to the "delusion" and "emptiness of its pretensions." He began, in his first lecture, by identifying previous incarnations of apparently analogous medical "delusions." Recalling the Royal Cure of the King's Evil, or Scrofula; the Weapon Ointment (*Unguentum Armarium*) and Sympathetic Powder (a mixture made from the victim's blood-stained garments); the Tar-Water Cure of Bishop George Berkeley; and the Metallic Tractors of Elisha Perkins, he recounted the motivations of their originators, the breadth of their supposed preventive or curing capacities, and the effects of imagination on popular belief. Holmes reserved his severest criticism for the learned clergy, almshouse supervisors, military officers, attorneys, politicians, and university professors who were too often flattered into providing glowing tributes to the originators and their improbable doctrines.[3] There was, he lamented, a "class of minds" whose qualities were no doubt bright but who were nonetheless "aimless and fickle as the butterfly [and] settle upon every gaily-colored illusion as it opens into flower, and flutter away to another when the first has dropped its leaves, and stands naked in the icy air of truth!"[4]

As an example of prior charlatanism, Holmes offered physician Elisha Perkins (1741–1799) of Norwich, Connecticut, who received a fourteen-year patent on February 19, 1796, for his Metallic Tractors. Perkins's tractors, consisting of two four-inch metal rods, one of steel, the other of brass, were designed to draw pain and disease from the body by redirecting the body's electrical energy. The instrument and its theory derived from earlier experiments by Italian physician and physicist Luigi Galvani (1737–1798), whose theory of "animal electricity," as explained in his *De viribus electricitatis in motu musculari commentaries* (1791), described the effect of a metal scalpel on the exposed sciatic nerve of a frog. By analogy, drawing the pointed end of his rods across the diseased portion of the body for several minutes, Perkins claimed the ability to draw off the electrical fluid, and thus remove the affliction.[5] Although Holmes pronounced Perkinism "dead and gone," he viewed it as a valuable lesson for understanding the diffusion of its beliefs, the respectability and credulity of its advocates, the nature of its public and private face, and its contrivances to acquire public support.

---

[3]Holmes, "Homœopathy and Its Kindred Delusions [1892]," 22–5.
[4]Holmes, "Homœopathy and Its Kindred Delusions [1892]," 29.
[5]Jacques M. Quen, "Elisha Perkins, Physician, Nostrum-Vendor, or Charlatan?" *Bulletin of the History of Medicine* 37 (1963): 159–66. See also Luigi Galvani, *De viribus electricitatis in motu musculari commentaries* (Bologna: Ex Typographia Instituti Scientiarum, 1791).

As Holmes observed, Perkinism "was not the first nor the last hobby-horse [that enthusiasts] rode furiously." He also felt that homeopathy would suffer a similarly quick demise.[6]

In the second of his two lectures, Holmes directly addressed the subject of homeopathy (from the Greek *homios*, meaning similar or analogous; and *pathos*, meaning suffering), prefacing his remarks with the promise to treat it dutifully with arguments, not with ridicule. He failed in this endeavor, striking out almost immediately on an unusually vitriolic course. He noted that homeopathy had long held views hostile toward the regular medical profession and that he was therefore more than justified in choosing any method, however harsh, in self-defense. Exemplary of homeopathy's hostility, he pointed to the term *allopathy* (from the Greek *alloion*, meaning different; and *pathos*, meaning suffering), which Samuel Hahnemann (1755–1843), the founder of homeopathy, had coined to show that so-called medical orthodoxy had no better claim upon the public trust or a court of law than any other class of healers. Holmes took exception to the invented title, knowing that it was intended to diminish the full weight of medical knowledge from Hippocrates to his own day.[7]

In making his case, Holmes laid out Hahnemann's doctrines of homeopathy as explained in *Organon of Homeopathic Medicine* (1810), the four-volume *Materia Medica Pura* (1811), and the five-volume *Treatise on Chronic Diseases* (1828). Beginning with the basic principle of *similia similibus curantur*, or like cures like, Hahnemann had argued that the appropriate medicine for any group of symptoms was one capable of producing a symptom complex similar to the original disease in a person in good health. Achieving this required homeopaths to build elaborate repertories containing catalogs of symptoms produced by different drugs. Rather than prescribing a given drug for a specific disease, homeopaths worked with their patients to identify a long list of symptoms which were then matched with the symptom complex listed in their repertories. Once a match was made, the homeopath prescribed the specific medicine.[8]

---

[6]Holmes, "Homœopathy and Its Kindred Delusions [1892]," 28.

[7]Although Holmes was justified in his indignation over the use of the term allopathy as a catch-all designation for regular medicine, one should be mindful of Abraham Flexner's remark that "prior to the placing of medicine on a scientific basis, sectarianism was, of course, inevitable. . . . Allopathy was just as sectarian as homeopathy." See Abraham Flexner, *Medical Education in the United States and Canada* (New York: The Carnegie Foundation for the Advancement of Teaching, 1910), 156.

[8]See Samuel Hahnemann, *Organon of Homeopathic Medicine* (Allentown, Pennsylvania: Academical Bookstore, 1836); Hahnemann, *Materia Medica Pura* (4 volumes; New York: Radde, 1846); Samuel Hahnemann, *The Chronic Diseases: Their Specific Nature and Homeopathic*

Holmes took issue with Hahnemann's claim that so-called allopathic medicine was based on the principle of *contraria contrariis curantur*, or prescribing medicines known to produce an effect opposite to the disease. To reduce regular medicine's armamentarium to such a narrow range of options represented a colossal misrepresentation of western medicine and its advances over the centuries. Regular doctors had long employed derivative, revulsive, and counter-irritant methods to address disease (i.e., attacking internal pain using a warm poultice or mustard plaster on the body's surface) and palliative regimens such as opium for pain, purgatives for constipation, and cold water for burns. But just as likely, regular physicians were apt to rely on the self-help aspects of nature, or *vis medicatrix naturae*, and even the principle of *similia*.[9]

Holmes informed his listeners that Hahnemann himself had given little credence to the curative aspects of nature, believing that nature's resources brought only temporary relief, little more than palliative. For Hahnemann, nature's efforts were "highly imperfect" because the vital power was without intelligence. "What reflecting man would copy the efforts of nature in curing disease?" Hahnemann once asked. For Holmes, this attitude spelled a degree of indifference, if not ignorance, of the basic substratum of the universe and its life forces. Having learned from his years in Paris the importance of *méthod expectante* and reliance upon the *vis medicatrix naturae*, or the healing power of nature as fundamental to sound therapeutic practice, Holmes was eager to support what Hahnemann was so anxious to reject.[10]

Holmes found equally absurd Hahnemann's second doctrine, i.e., that highly attenuated medicines increased rather than reduced their pathogenetic or symptom-producing power. Not surprisingly, he delighted in explaining the fractional divisions implied by the principle of potentization

---

Treatment (5 volumes; New York: William Radde, 1845–46). The original 1810 edition of the *Organon* was not translated into English until 1913 by C. E. Wheeler. It was published as a historical document for Everyman's Library by J. M. Dent and Sons in London and E. P. Dutton and Company in New York. This translation is often used to explain Hahnemann's earliest thinking. But the first American edition was published in 1836, translated by Robert F. Dudgeon and prepared from the 1833 British translation of the fourth German edition. Other editions include the eighth American edition (1923) translated from the fifth edition by Dudgeon, and the sixth edition translated into English in 1922 by William Boericke.

[9]In his review of Pulte's *Homeopathic Domestic Physician* (1857), Holmes enlarged upon his view of regular medicine. "The only unconditional principle ever recognized by medical science has been, that diseases are to be treated by the remedies which experience shows to be useful. The universal use of both *cold* and *hot* external remedies in various inflammatory states puts the garrote at once on the babbling throat of the senseless assertion of the homeopathists, and stultifies for all time the nickname 'allopathy.'" See his "Some More Recent Views on Homœopathy," 186.

[10]Hahnemann, *Organon of Homeopathic Medicine* (1836), 34–5.

or dynamization—terms that could not be understood in chemico-physical language but which resounded among those impressed by the vitalistic ideas of the Romantic school of *Naturphilosophie*.[11]

> Swallowers of globules, one of your little pellets, moistened in the mingled waves of one million lakes of alcohol, each two miles in circumference, with which had been blended that one drop of Tincture of Camomile, would be of precisely the strength recommended for that medicine in your favorite Jahr's Manual, against the most sudden, frightful, and fatal diseases![12]

Hahnemann's third doctrine on chronic diseases stated that most of the ailments identified by distinct names were really the outcome of three miasms: *psora*, *syphilis*, and *sycosis*. Psora, the oldest of the three, had infected all of humankind and represented seven-eighths of all chronic maladies, manifesting itself in the common itch. This, Holmes found to be the most bizarre of all Hahnemann's claims, pointing out that few contemporary homeopaths were willing to subscribe to the principle.[13]

Holmes regarded homeopathy's crass reasoning as no substitute for rigorous clinical empiricism. A case in point was homeopathy's comparisons of bills of mortality and claims that their treatment had been superior to regular medicine for cholera and yellow fever victims. Having attended the École de Médecine in Paris between 1833 and 1835 in the company of Harvard colleagues James Jackson Jr., Jonathan Mason Warren, and Henry I. Bowditch, where they walked the wards at La Charité, Hôtel Dieu, and La Pitié under the tutelage of Gabriel Andral (1797–1876), Philippe Ricord (1800–1889), and Pierre C. A. Louis (1787–1872), Holmes learned to appreciate the fundamentals of pathological anatomy and dili-

---

[11]Ibid., 143–5.

[12]Holmes, "Homœopathy and Its Kindred Delusions [1892]," 53–4.

[13]Ibid., 45–48. The full measure of Hahnemann's miasm doctrine would become the life's work of Dr. James Tyler Kent (1849–1916), who taught at the Homeopathic Medical College of Missouri from 1881 to 1888 and later became dean and professor of materia medica at the Hahnemann Medical College of Chicago. He was responsible for moving homeopathy away from clinically-based empirical medicine to a metaphysical integration of homeopathic doctrines with Swedenborgian philosophy. Kent's integration of the two involved his expounding on the interior and external worlds of man and the dependence of the whole on the Divine. Kent's Swedenborgian bias drove homeopathy far beyond its historical boundaries and into the hands of followers who would transform homeopathy from a school of medical science into one that was predominantly faith-based. See James Tyler Kent, *Lectures on Homeopathic Philosophy* (Berkeley: North Atlantic Books, 1979 [1900]); and James Tyler Kent, *The Art and Science of Homeopathic Medicine* (Mineloa, New York: Dover Publications, 2002 [1900]).

gent record-taking.[14] An admirer of Louis's numerical method of validity testing, he pointed to investigations that had occurred as early as in 1832 at the Hôtel Dieu de Lyon by Jacques A. Guerard and Victor Baillie, and in 1834, at the Hôpital de la Pitié in Paris by Gabriel Andral. After a year of experimentation using aconite, arnica, belladonna, cinchona and sulfur, Baillie reported to the Academy of Medicine that homeopathic medicines had produced no visible effect. Baillie's investigations were significant because he had invited two homeopathic practitioners, Léon Simon and Paul Francis Curie, to treat patients over a period of five months, using medicines from the same pharmacy that supplied Hahnemann. Drawing also from Andral and similar tests carried out by Louis Fleury, F. J. Double, and M. Bonnet, President of the Royal Society of Medicine of Bordeaux, Holmes concluded that the repertories used to identify and explain the action of homeopathic drugs upon healthy persons failed to produce the results claimed by Hahnemann.[15]

For Holmes, homeopathy's explanations for lower mortality in its hospitals had been an *argumentum ad ignorantiam*. "An honest man should be ashamed" to make such claims, he wrote, given that the mortality in hospitals depended not only on the particular form of treatment but on the class of patients received and accepted by the hospitals. At La Pitiè, for example, Pierre Louis preferred to admit only those patients in the last stages of consumption. Not acknowledging this fact in their comparative data, homeopaths had foolishly made "a miserable appeal to the thoughtlessness of the vulgar."[16] Using the best King's English, Holmes concluded that homeopathy was little more than "a mingled mass of perverse ingenuity, of tinsel erudition, of imbecile credulity, and of artful misrepresentation."[17] He predicted that once the novelty of this fanciful system wore off, most believers would either lose confidence in its claims and "return to visible doses," or "embrace some newer and if possible equally extravagant doctrine."[18]

---

[14]See William C. Dowling, *Oliver Wendell Holmes in Paris: Medicine, Theology, and the Autocrat of the Breakfast Table* (Hanover, N.H.: University Press of New England, 2006); Ephraim Fischoff, *Oliver Wendell Holmes: Physician and Humanist* (Springfield, Illinois: The Pearson Museum Monograph Series, 1982).

[15]Holmes, "Homœopathy and Its Kindred Delusions [1892]," 77–82.

[16]Ibid., 73.

[17]Ibid., 101.

[18]Ibid., 99. See also Erwin H. Ackerknecht, *Medicine at the Paris Hospital, 1794–1848* (Baltimore: Johns Hopkins University Press, 1967).

Homeopathy's Persistence

To his credit, Holmes provided accurate descriptions of Hahnemann's principal doctrines and derivative beliefs. Where he erred was in believing that homeopathy would follow trajectories similar to those taken by Berkeley's tar water and Perkins's tractors as they rose quickly to prominence and then dropped just as quickly into obscurity. Holmes savored information that indicated a precipitous decline in homeopathic literature and was confident that reports from abroad recounting the school's falling numbers spelled the beginning of the end. He concluded his second lecture by stating that homeopathy was a "lifeless delusion, rolling its shapeless bulk into the path of a noble science it is too weak to strike or to injure."[19] Yet nearly fifty years later in the preface to the 1891 edition of his *Medical Essays*, Holmes was forced to admit: "Homeopathy has proved lucrative, and so long as it continues to be so will surely exist, as surely as astrology, palmistry, and other methods of getting a living out of the weakness and credulity of mankind and womankind."[20]

Both institutional and conceptual factors were at play in the changing dynamics of homeopathy. Institutionally, while Hahnemann certainly had made derisive claims regarding the foundations of orthodox medical knowl-

---

[19]Holmes, "Homœopathy and Its Kindred Delusions [1892]," 102.

[20]Oliver Wendell Holmes, "Preface," *Medical Essays, 1842–1882*, xiii. The first (and unpublished) of the three lectures (of which "Homœopathy and its Kindred Delusions" represented the final two lectures) presented in February of 1842 before the Boston Society for the Diffusion of Useful Knowledge had actually been entitled "Astrology and Alchemy." Therein Holmes had stated: "Enough of this long history of miscalled Science [i.e., astrology and alchemy]. We might even question how far it is profitable to search the records of so much folly long displaced by better knowledge. Cunning and arrogance and credulity will never again tread this deserted path in company, and as old folios drop to pieces and the eating bookworm destroys that which the writing bookworm does not replace, the once precious legends of antiquity will pass out of the memory of men. Every age must have its own growth of errors and the scholar may guard himself against those of his own time by calmly reviewing those of the past. The dead weeds that have been mown down look very differently it is true from the tall growing ones that hang out their gaudy flowers in his path. Let us all endeavor according to our capacities to keep back every noxious thing that would intrude into the fair fields of knowledge. Astrology and alchemy are dead—so far as the mere outward shape is concerned—but do not suppose that the nineteenth or twentieth or the hundredth century will witness the extinction of the thirst which lived under their deceitful features and now lurks under a mask as fair and as false as they were. Whatever the names of the demon who plays his fantastic tricks upon successive generations—whether it be Mephistopheles or Maurmon, let us be warned against the new deceptions by old stories. As one phantom after another passes by on the shades of his magic lantern, let it be our province to persuade all agitated children and their nurses that the show is but painted glass, and will come out of the blaze in a little while to be laid in the same heap with so many others."(In the Houghton Library, Harvard University, MS Am. 1234.7, pp. 124–5.)

edge (and was still making them at the age of eighty-seven from his home and office at No. 1 Rue de Milan in Paris), this was by no means the case of his followers in the United States. And surely not in New England where, in the absence of their own medical schools, the earliest students with homeopathic inclinations were taking instruction in regular medical colleges, sitting side by side with regular medical students. Indeed, the underlying objective of American homeopathy throughout the nineteenth and first half of the twentieth century was to become recognized as a specialty within regular medicine. With most having come from the ranks of regular medicine, homeopaths hoped to secure a special place within its fold.

Illustrative of homeopathy's incursion into New England, members of Holmes's own medical society had met two years before his lectures to form an association which they named the Homeopathic Fraternity and which subsequently became the Massachusetts Homeopathic Society. Article II in the fraternity's constitution required its fellows to be members in good standing (or eligible for membership) in the Massachusetts Medical Society.[21] In 1844, two years after Holmes's lectures, the American Institute of Homeopathy was founded with an initial membership of two hundred and fifty. The institute had originated at a July 1843 meeting of the New York Homeopathic Physicians' Society, which invited all homeopaths to meet in New York City the following year to form a national society. The association thus became the third oldest national medical association in the United States, following the Reformed Medical Society of the United States, organized in 1829, and the Friendly Botanic Society of the United States (Thomsonian), organized in 1832. The American Medical Association (regular) did not organize until 1846, followed by the National Eclectic Medical Association in 1849.[22]

Disputing Holmes's prediction of the death of homeopathy, the Massachusetts Homeopathic Hospital was chartered in 1855 and the Homeopathic Medical Dispensary in 1856. In 1855, Boston's homeopathic community celebrated the birthday of Hahnemann. The festivities, held at

---

[21]John L. Coffin, "Annual Oration Before the Massachusetts Homeopathic Medical Society, April, 1915," *New England Medical Gazette*, 50 (1915): 277–78; "Proceedings of the American Institute of Homeopathy," *Philadelphia Journal of Homeopathy*, 1 (1852): 140. The members included Josiah F. Flagg of Boston, Charles Wilde of Brookline, and J. P. Spooner of Dorchester. In 1851, the members changed their name to the Massachusetts Homeopathic Medical Society. See I. T. Talbot, "Homeopathy in Massachusetts," *Transactions of the World's Homeopathic Convention, Held at Philadelphia, Under the Auspices of the American Institute of Homeopathy, at Its Twenty-Ninth Session, June 26-July 1, 1876*, Volume II: *History of Homeopathy* (2 vols., Philadelphia: Sherman and Company, 1880), 644–52.
[22]Talbot, "Homeopathy in Massachusetts," 641.

the Tremont Temple and Faneuil Hall, included the lieutenant governor, members of the General Assembly, the mayor of Boston, editors, clergy, and numerous members of the regular medical profession including Dr. Samuel Gregg of Boston, anatomist Jeffries Wyman of Harvard Medical College, and Winslow Lewis, president of Boylston Medical School.[23]

As for homeopathy's persistent claims of success, it is clear that the earliest applications of quantitative methods to issues of public health had often been carelessly recorded, if not highly selective, for all parties. To be sure, Louis's numerical methodology became the engine of authority for regular medicine; but it also became the method of choice among the century's sectarians as well. For better or worse, Thomsonians, eclectics, physio-medicals, homeopaths and other groups embraced the new methodology to justify their particular theories and claims of lower mortality. As James Cassedy explained in *American Medical and Statistical Thinking, 1800–1860*, the data of early nineteenth-century medicine "were often carelessly collected, frequently representative of selected cases only, and rarely differentiated as to variables." This resulted in a war of words between regular and sectarian medicine with the combatants coming to metaphorical blows over their competing claims and statistical outcomes.[24]

Notwithstanding these legitimate criticisms, between the republication of Holmes's lectures in *Currents and Counter-Currents* (1861) and *Medical Essays* (1883), several insurance companies in both England and the United States, which heretofore had disregarded therapeutic differences among the competing schools of medicine, concluded that the medicines prescribed on the basis of homeopathic theory did less injury to the body. With this information, stockholders approved changes that allowed company directors to charge a lower premium for those treated homeopathically. The Atlantic Mutual Life Insurance Company of Albany, New York, even promised additional discounts as comparative rates of mortality became statistically determined. In all, ten companies offered lower premiums to persons adhering to the homeopathic system. According to company records, the practice ended around 1880 when it was discovered

---

[23]"Celebration of the Centennial Birthday of Dr. Samuel Hahnemann in Boston," *North American Journal of Homeopathy* 4 (1855): 150–2.
[24]James Cassedy, *American Medicine and Statistical Thinking, 1800–1860* (Cambridge: Harvard University Press, 1984), viii, 25–119.

that many policy owners misrepresented themselves in their applications in order to receive the discount.[25]

HOLMES'S BOSTON

In the aftermath of Holmes's two lectures, which pressed heavily on the tender consciences of Boston's homeopathic community, rebuttals were prepared by Charles Neidhard of Philadelphia, followed by Robert Wesselhoeft of Cambridge, Massachusetts, and Abraham H. Okie, of Providence, Rhode Island. The publisher for Wesselhoeft and Okie was Otis Clapp, a prominent Swedenborgian and retail druggist in Boston's Back Bay, who was a purveyor of homeopathic and Swedenborgian books, homeopathic medicine chests, and single homeopathic remedies. Clapp came from an illustrious family; his father was a professor of chemistry and a prominent New York physician, and his son, James Wilkinson Clapp, would become a homeopathic professor at the Boston University School of Medicine.[26]

The rebuttals written by Wesselhoeft and Okie are significant for their *ad seriatim* reply to Holmes's none-too-subtle criticisms; but it is their connection to Clapp, their publisher, and to the broader Swedenborgian community, that blunted the full effect of Holmes's lectures on Boston society. The religious and intellectual movement known as Swedenborgianism, with its Church of the New Jerusalem, was a variation on Christianity that included newer revelations and emphasized the connection between individual intelligence and the Divine Mind. Initiated by the writings of Swedish scientist, philosopher, and religious thinker Emanuel Swedenborg (1666–1772) and introduced into Boston society as early as 1818 by Harvard graduates Sampson Reed and Thomas Worcester—and

---

[25]"A London Life Assurance Office Converted to Homeopathy by the Evidence of Statistics," *American Homeopathic Observer* 2 (1865): 246–48; "Homeopathic Mutual Life Insurance Company of the City of New York," *North American Journal of Homeopathy* 17 (1868): 143–44; "Atlantic Mutual Life Insurance Company," *North American Journal of Homeopathy* 16 (1867): 624–25; "The Atlantic Mutual Life Insurance Company," *North American Journal of Homeopathy* 16 (1867): 319.

[26]See Dr. Charles Niedhard, *Answer to the Homœopathic Delusions, of Dr. O. W. Holmes* (Philadelphia: J. Dobson, 1842); Robert Wesselhoeft, *Some Remarks on Dr. O. W. Holmes's Lectures on Homœopathy and its Kindred Delusions; Communicated to a Friend* (Boston: Otis Clapp, 1842); and Dr. Okie, *Homœopathy with Particular Reference to a Lecture by O. W. Holmes, M.D.* (Boston: Otis Clapp, 1842). See also http://homeopathy.wildfalcon.com/archives/2008/03/21/otis-clapp-and-homeopathy/ (1-10-09).

popularized through the pages of the *New Jerusalem Magazine* (1827–72) and Emerson's 1845 essay on "Swedenborg, or the Mystic," which he later published in his *Representative Men* (1850)—Swedenborgianism was both contemporary and complementary to the rising popularity of homeopathy.[27]

Another of Clapp's authors, James John Garth Wilkinson (1812–1899), was introduced to homeopathy through Henry James, Sr. (1771–1832), and underwent a gradual conversion to Hahnemann's doctrines. Attracted as well to Swedenborg, Wilkinson edited and translated many of the Swede's works from Latin into English, subsequently published by Clapp. Wilkinson likened Hahnemann's laws and doctrines to Swedenborg's understanding of the self and soul. Swedenborg's Law of Correspondences (i.e., that the natural world was obedient to the spiritual world and actions of worldly bodies became omens, instructions, or warnings of the other-worldly) was used to explain the virtues of *similia similibus curantur*, drug and disease effects, the connection between the physical and the psychological, and the bridge between the brain, body, and soul. "The things which are in nature," wrote Swedenborg, "are mere effects, their causes are in the spiritual world, and the causes of those causes, which are ends, are in the interior heaven."[28] Hahnemann's infinitesimal medicines, particularly those from the third to the 200th dilution, represented different levels of spirituality; and his miasm theory (sycosis, syphilis, and psora) became for Swedenborgians the moral taint passed along through generations as Original Sin.[29]

For homeopaths who sought to justify their belief in the vital or spiritual power of medicines unlocked through dynamization and high dilutions, Swedenborgianism provided a set of beliefs that fit wonderfully into their mindset and their laws on *similia* and infinitesimals. Instead of diseases being affected by changes in the body's material structures, they were

---

[27]Clarence Paul Hotson, "A Background for Emerson's Poem 'Grace,'" *New England Quarterly* 1 (1928): 124–32; Octavius Brooks Frothingham, *Transcendentalism in New England* (New York: G. P. Putnam's Sons, 1880 [1876]), chapter 9.

[28]Emanuel Swedenborg, *Arcana Coelestia. The Heavenly Arcana Contained in the Holy Scriptures or Word of the Lord Unfolded Beginning with the Book of Genesis Together with Wonderful Things Seen in the World of Spirits and in the Heaven of Angels* (10 vols.: American Swedenborg Printing and Publishing Society, 1870–73), §5711; Clyde W. Broomell, *Divine Healing: The Origins and Cure of Disease as Taught in the Bible and Explained by Emanuel Swedenborg* (Boston: George H. Ellis and Company, 1907), 20.

[29]J. J. Garth Wilkinson, *Swedenborg Among the Doctors; A Letter to Robert T. Cooper, M.D.* (London: James Speirs, 1895), 18–19. Another example of this collaboration was the publishing house of Francis E. Boericke (1826–1901) and Adolph J. Tafel (1839–1895) of Philadelphia, homeopathic manufacturers and publishers, whose company also became a popular publishing house of Swedenborgian literature.

affected by dynamic changes to the body's spiritual existence. Both disease and sin had a common ancestry—the result of a system thrown out of balance, of the mind falling prey to disbelief in God and misdirected energies. Both homeopathy and Swedenborgianism appealed to an educated audience which yearned to escape the staid formality of the Enlightenment by inspiring a mystical world view that appealed to the spiritual and religious side of the American psyche.[30]

Holmes was a man with close connections to the intellectual currents of New England Unitarianism and Transcendentalism, whose representatives included Ralph Waldo Emerson, Henry David Thoreau, William Ellery Channing, George Ripley, Nathaniel Hawthorne, and Henry James, Sr. As a member of the Saturday Club, a frequenter of the Old Corner Bookstore on Washington Street, and as a writer for the *Atlantic Monthly*, he could hardly be anything less than a key architect of Boston's intellectual culture. As New England's educated classes became more liberal in their view of man, sin, and salvation, Holmes, along with his fellow intellectuals, chose to reengineer literature, religion, society, and even medicine to their liking. The same year Holmes was mounting his attack on homeopathy, the stockholders of Brook Farm were transforming their communal experiment in West Roxbury into a utopian oasis of Fourierism and Swedenborgianism. Holmes, however, remained aloof from those who allowed themselves to be transported to a mystical world-view in order to reestablish their own inner harmony.[31]

Rooted in and celebrating the growing trend toward reductionism in regular medicine, Holmes held his beliefs separate from those metaphysical breezes that circulated through the parlors of Boston's Back Bay under the shibboleths of Eclecticism, Mesmerism, Phrenology, Spiritualism, Mind-cure, Homeopathy, Fourierism, Transcendentalism, and Swedenborgianism. As a Paris-trained physician and a spiritual libertarian (King's Chapel Unitarian), he remained an unremitting opponent of proscriptive doctrines, whether Puritan orthodoxy, homeopathic pseudo-science, or Swedenborgian dogma. This explains how Holmes could be so opposed to the homeopathic ideas current among fellow Bostonians and yet conform so closely to the comment of Caroline Ticknor, editor of *Dr. Holmes's Boston*

---

[30]Kent, *The Art and Science of Homeopathic Medicine*, 126–52.
[31]See Anne Rose, *Transcendentalism as a Social Movement, 1830–1850* (New Haven: Yale University Press, 1981); Tamara Plakins Thornton, *Cultivating Gentlemen: The Meaning of Country Life Among the Boston Elite, 1785–1860* (New Haven: Yale University Press, 1989); Van Wyck Brooks, *The Flowering of New England, 1815–1865* (Boston: E. P. Dutton and Co., 1936), 343–58; Carl J. Guarneri, *The Utopian Alternative: Fourierism in Nineteenth Century America* (Ithaca: Cornell University Press, 1991).

(1915), that Boston "was not merely a place, it was also a very individual 'state of mind,' and the immortal Autocrat not only voiced that mental attitude, but did much to influence its trend and shape its course."[32] Like Emerson, whom he admired beyond measure, not the least of which because of his preference to teach from the lyceum rather than from the pulpit, Holmes insisted that each individual have the right to "weigh the universe, its laws and its legends, in his own balance, without fear of authority, names, or institutions." Holmes was not about to transfer the authority of New England's intellectual traditions to anything bearing the image of obtrusive dogma or vested orthodoxy. Describing Emerson's faith in the same manner that he would have chosen to describe his own, Holmes wrote: "His faith was too large and to deep for the formulæ he found built into the pulpit, and he was too honest to cover up his doubts under the flowing vestments of a sacred calling."[33]

Holmes declined to accept the more esoteric elements of metaphysical thinking that were making inroads among his circle of friends and acquaintances. Within the natural processes that formed the material universe, he was willing to postulate the consciousness of the individual mind, unbounded by the laws of physics. This, as Holmes's biographer William Sloan Kennedy explained in 1883, represented the limits of his *Religio Medici*. A theist at heart, Holmes could accept a feeling of uncertainty that would forever challenge the human spirit, but dogmatism, however defined, failed to explain the persistent mystery of consciousness in a world of unconscious matter.[34]

In the preface to his 1861 edition of *Currents and Counter-Currents in Medical Science*, Holmes admitted to having received hostile criticism to his earlier lectures but felt that his predictions had stood the test of time. He continued to downplay the numbers of homeopathic practitioners in Europe and the United States, although he admitted that in America homeopathy "has undoubtedly proved more popular and lucrative." Holmes reported that homeopathy was now a shadow of its former self and that infinitesimal doses were being replaced by fuller doses, which suggested to him that homeopathy was now "merely a name, an unproved theory, and a

---

[32]Caroline Ticknor, ed., *Dr. Holmes's Boston* (Boston: Houghton Mifflin Company, 1915), vi.
[33]Oliver Wendell Holmes, *Ralph Waldo Emerson*, in *Ralph Waldo Emerson, John Lothrop Motley* [The Works of Oliver Wendell Holmes, Standard Library Edition, Volume XI] (Boston: Houghton, Mifflin and Company, 1892 [1884]), 305–6, 324.
[34]William Sloane Kennedy, *Oliver Wendell Holmes: Poet, Littérateur, Scientist* (Boston: S. E. Cassino and Co., 1883), 257–61; Dowling, *Oliver Wendell Holmes in Paris*, 126–7. See also John S. Haller, Jr., *Healing at the Intersection of Mind and Body: The Competing Worlds of Mesmer and Swedenborg* (forthcoming).

box of pellets pretending to be specifics, which, as all of us know, fail igno-
miniously . . ."[35] In the preface to the 1891 edition of his *Medical Essays*, he
added a further clarification, noting that while homeopathy no longer had
pretensions to being a science, it "may be looked upon by a scientific man
as a curious object of study among the vagaries of the human mind."[36] It
would appear that Holmes knew full well that homeopathy had undergone
transformations due to the influence of Swedenborgian ideas. Holmes inti-
mated that the fads of Mind-cure and faith-cure were now "encroaching"
on homeopathy's territory and might well take possession of the field. How
prescient were his remarks![37]

Looking Forward

In considering the impact of homeopathy on American society in the
period between the initial delivery of Holmes's lectures in 1842 and their
subsequent republications, it is hard to ignore the fact that homeopathy
had used its time wisely to marshal both economic and political forces in
support of its schools, hospitals, and dispensaries. Despite Holmes's dire
predictions, two broad classes of homeopaths came to exist. One group
intended for homeopathy to follow in the path of regular medicine as it
moved toward an empirical and laboratory-based science. Even as late as
1965, when the president of the American Medical Association was a guest
speaker at the national convention of the American Institute of Homeopathy, the medically-trained leaders within American homeopathy were
seeking a level of accommodation and acceptance within regular medicine.
Only when the AMA refused to consider such an accommodation, and
only after America's homeopathic associations became increasingly metaphysical in their belief system did homeopathy's position change to one of
greater hostility.[38]

---

[35]Holmes, *Currents and Counter-Currents in Medical Science*, vi–viii. Over the course of the
nineteenth century, sixty-four homeopathic schools were established in the United States.
By far, the majority of them were proprietary in nature, with the remainder affiliated with
state-funded or private universities. Approximately a third of the schools were founded in
Maryland, Massachusetts, New York, Pennsylvania, and the District of Columbia. The
remaining two-thirds opened in California, Colorado, Illinois, Iowa, Kentucky, Michigan,
Minnesota, Missouri and Ohio. By 1900, twenty-two schools remained with a combined
enrollment of about 2,000 students.
[36]Holmes, "Preface," *Medical Essays, 1842–1882*, xiii.
[37]Ibid., xiv.
[38]W.W. Young, "The Perpetuation and Propagation Program," *Journal of the American Institute of Homeopathy* 60 (1967): 200. See also John S. Haller, *The History of American Homeopathy: The Academic Years, 1820–1936* (New York: Taylor and Francis, Inc., 2005), chapter 6.

The other group insisted that homeopathy was a therapeutic system of exclusive laws and doctrines as unchanging as the law of gravity. Unrecognized by Holmes in his 1883 and 1891 republication was the formation in 1880 of the International Hahnemannian Association, dedicated to advancing the teachings of so-called classical homeopathy in medical therapeutics, that is, symptomatology, single remedies, high dilutions, and the law of *similia* based on a strict interpretation of Hahnemann's *Organon of Homeopathic Medicine*. Having forged a connection between the human mind and the cosmic order, this latter group drifted first to the siren calls of the Swedenborgians in the years contemporary with Holmes, and much later to concepts of field theory, quantum theory, and relativity theory in the writings of theoretical physicist Albert Einstein (1879–1955), and to the ideas of systems theorist Fritjof Capra, author of *The Tao of Physics* (1975). Having escaped the hegemony of materialistic science, these homeopaths had expanded their metaphysical boundaries to include intuitive and contemplative energy systems.[39]

Grounded in the clinical medicine of the Paris hospitals, Holmes found too many differences between the competing worlds of matter and spirit for him to accept the metaphysical formula provided by homeopathy and its Swedenborgian interpreters. For Holmes, the die had been cast with the 1810 publication of Hahnemann's *Organon of Homeopathic Medicine* and nothing had occurred since then to change his mind. Homeopathy and regular medicine for him remained—and would continue to remain—irreconcilable.

---

[39]See Fritjof Capra, *The Tao of Physics: An Exploration of the Parallels Between Modern Physics and Eastern Mysticism* (Berkeley: Shambhala, 1975); Robert C. Fuller, *Alternative Medicine and American Religious Life* (New York: Oxford University Press, 1989); and Menas Kafatos and Robert Nadeau, *The Conscious Universe: Parts and Wholes in Physical Reality* (New York: Springer, 2000).

A Private Pestilence

Holmes and Puerperal Fever

AMALIE M. KASS

The disease known as Puerperal Fever is so far contagious as to be frequently carried from patient to patient by physicians and nurses.

—Oliver Wendell Holmes, "The Contagiousness of Puerperal Fever," (1843)

WHEN OLIVER WENDELL HOLMES READ his essay *The Contagiousness of Puerperal Fever* at a meeting of the Boston Society for Medical Improvement in February 1843, he was addressing a critical medical issue that had baffled physicians for centuries.[1] Few people were better qualified to compose the essay than Holmes. A member of the younger generation of Boston physicians, he had the capacity to look at medical questions with a new eye. He had spent three years in Paris, a Mecca for American and European medical students eager to learn the new ways of thinking about disease that had emerged in post-revolutionary France.[2] Self-confident and ambitious, he had already written three prize-winning medical essays. Most significantly, Holmes had the literary skills and the passion to write a paper destined to become a "medical classic." At the time it had little

---

[1] Oliver Wendell Holmes, "The Contagiousness of Puerperal Fever," *New England Quarterly Journal of Medicine and Surgery* 1 (1843): 503–30.
[2] Erwin H. Ackerknecht, *Medicine at the Paris Hospital, 1794–1848* (Baltimore: The Johns Hopkins University Press, 1967), 44. See also John Harley Warner, *Against the Spirit of System: The French Impulse in Nineteenth-Century American Medicine* (Princeton: Princeton University Press), 32–75.

impact. Indeed, its classic quality derives more from a retrospective view than from its contemporary effect.

A Scourge Second Only to the Plague

Maternal deaths from puerperal fever (also known as childbed fever, puerperal sepsis and puerperal peritonitis) have been part of medical literature since Hippocrates, but the disease did not receive wide attention in Europe until the seventeenth and eighteenth centuries, when the establishment of maternity hospitals for poor women created an environment where fever flourished. Death rates ran as high as 80 to 90 percent in some European lying-in hospitals during epidemic years.[3] In the United States, maternity hospitals were rare and almost all babies were born at home; but there, too, this devastating affliction was the leading cause of maternal mortality. One physician called it a scourge second only to the plague.[4]

In the developed nations of the twenty-first century, where puerperal fever is practically unheard of and childbirth is anticipated with confidence and joy, it is difficult to appreciate the fear with which nineteenth-century women faced childbirth. Physicians were equally distressed when a woman who had been safely delivered might suddenly develop alarming symptoms that could be erratic in their development and sometimes subsided, but often led to a painful death. Ominous warnings might appear before or during delivery, within twenty-four hours after delivery, or a week later.

Usually, but not always, the disease began with a severe chill followed by high fever, rapid pulse, headache, and acute pain in the pelvic area. The abdomen would swell and become exquisitely tender to the slightest touch. The pulse beat more rapidly, breathing was difficult, and the woman often became restless and dissociated from her surroundings. Sometimes a rash appeared. Nausea and vomiting, usually of the most repugnant contents, frequently occurred. Uncontrollable diarrhea could make the situation even more unpleasant. Death might come within a few days or after several weeks. At autopsy, evidence of disease might be limited to the uterus, found in the peritoneum, or seen in other parts of her body. Too often the newborn was also afflicted and the tragedy doubled.

---

[3]Irvine Loudon, *Childbed Fever, A Documentary History* (New York: Garland Publishing, 1995), xxxvi.

[4]Walter Channing, Lecture Notes, Lecture 36, Walter Channing Papers II, Massachusetts Historical Society. See also Amalie M. Kass, *Midwifery and Medicine in Boston: Walter Channing, M.D.* (Boston: Northeastern University Press, 2002), 156–67.

By the end of the eighteenth century, European physicians had enough experience with puerperal fever to assert that it did not fit the traditional nosological description of fever, but was a specific disease common only to parturient women. They also suspected that it might have some relation to erysipelas because the two diseases sometimes occurred simultaneously in a family or as epidemics.[5] They also recognized that it occurred in the private practices of midwives and physicians as well as in maternity hospitals and that it could be sporadic as well as epidemic.

But there was little agreement on the etiology of puerperal fever. Was it endogenous, caused by something within the woman's body such as retained lochia (blood, mucus and tissue that was not fully expelled from the vagina following birth of the child), by migration of milk to the pelvic area, by inflammation of the peritoneum, or by infection from the bowels? Many believed it was exogenous, caused by environmental conditions such as filth, bad sewage or other effluvia that poisoned the air. Some physicians attributed puerperal fever to atmospheric phenomena such as violent storms or extreme temperatures. And there were a few who held that parturient women might be predisposed to disease because of poor diet, lack of exercise or emotional states peculiar to their sex.

Additionally, there were many unanswered questions about the contagiousness of puerperal fever. Was it transmitted directly from person to person as were other infectious diseases such as smallpox or syphilis? It seemed unlikely, since it was always a consequence of childbirth, and did not spread to other members of a family or community. On the other hand, it could spread like wildfire from patient to patient in an urban maternity ward. In small towns and rural areas, it seemed to occur spontaneously in the practice of an individual doctor or midwife, but even there it sometimes reached epidemic proportions. Moreover, a birth attendant might encounter puerperal fever in a single case or several cases but not every case within a specific time period.

A DISCUSSION INVOLVING A CERTAIN SUPPOSED CAUSE OF DISEASE

Boston physicians had long been troubled by the dangers of puerperal fever. Obstetrics was not a medical specialty and all doctors could expect to deliver babies as part of their general practice.[6] Puerperal fever was a

---

[5]Erysipelas is a skin infection usually caused by *Streptococcus pyogenes* (group A streptococcus); it can become life-threatening and occasionally fatal.
[6]There were a few midwives in Boston whom some women preferred to a male physician.

frequent topic in the *New England Journal of Medicine and Surgery* and its successor, the *Boston Medical and Surgical Journal*, and had been discussed at meetings of the Boston Society for Medical Improvement since its initial meetings in 1828. This organization combined professional interests with collegiality and sociability, meeting twice monthly to report interesting cases, discuss topics of common concern, and listen to prepared papers on medical topics.[7] Holmes became a member shortly after he returned to Boston from Europe and attended his first meeting on May 25, 1838.[8] At the following meeting, Dr. Francis Higginson reported a fatal case of puerperal fever, but the minutes do not give any details.[9]

In subsequent years, Walter Channing, Professor of Midwifery at the Massachusetts Medical College[10] and Boston's most eminent obstetrician, described occasional cases of puerperal peritonitis, and in June of 1842 he read his notes regarding 13 fatal puerperal fever cases he had recently attended.[11] Discussion among the members revealed two cases of puerperal peritonitis and a "good deal" of erysipelas in Pembroke, a town 27 miles southeast of Boston, as well as the prevalence of puerperal fever in New York City. Two weeks later, Channing spoke about his more recent cases and announced that, contrary to his previous report, every patient had done well. In August, he described a woman who had suffered "profuse scarlet eruption within the second 48 hours following confinement, no chills or sore throat but great heat." And on October 10, he told of a recently confined woman who had developed puerperal fever "which would probably prove fatal," adding that there was severe typhus fever in her home.[12]

It was at that same meeting, with Holmes presiding, that Dr. John Fisher related a particularly disturbing tale. A colleague, Dr. Whitney, and two of his medical students had become severely ill following the autopsy of a puerperal fever victim. When examination of the body was complete,

---

[7]Boston Society for Medical Improvement Records (cited henceforth as BSMI), vol. 1, Constitution and ByLaws, Francis A. Countway Library of Medicine.

[8]Holmes became a member on May 9, 1836, less than six months after he returned to Boston. BSMI, vol. 1, List of Members; vol. 2, Minutes, 9 May 1836 and 25 May 1836.

[9]BSMI, vol. 2, Minutes, 13 June 1836.

[10]"Midwifery" and "obstetrics" were used interchangeably in reference to medical care for women in pregnancy, childbirth, and the postpartum period. At this time, Harvard Medical School was called the Massachusetts Medical College. See Henry K. Beecher and Mark D. Altschule, *Medicine at Harvard, the First 300 Years* (Hanover, NH: University Press of New England, 1977), 30.

[11]BSMI, vol. 3, Minutes, 24 April 1837, p. 35; 13 July 1840, pp. 310–1; 27 July 1840, p. 314; vol. 4, Minutes, 27 June 1842, pp. 167–8.

[12]BSMI., vol. 4, 11 July 1842, p. 170; 22 August 1842, p. 182; 10 October 1842, pp. 190–1.

Whitney noticed that one of his fingers was bleeding, an incident he attrib-uted to a hangnail not previously troublesome. The student who sewed up the body did not have a wound on his hands though he did have a scar from a recent burn. Whitney developed worrisome symptoms over several days: chills, fever, faintness, and a strange red spot half way up his arm with a red line extending to the thumb. The upper part of his arm eventually swelled to the size of his thigh. He suffered great soreness and pain through-out his body and became delirious. Dr. Fisher, who had been called to the case, was fearful of the worst. By the time Fisher told the story, the swollen arm had begun to subside but the patient remained "in a very equivocal state."

As for the students, they did not become ill as rapidly but after a few days the first young man also developed frightening symptoms, including great soreness and erysipelas-like markings on his side. He died a few days later. When the other student began to feel badly, he chose to go home and no further information was available.[13]

Toward the end of the evening there was more talk of puerperal fever. Dr. J.S.C. Greene reported a fatal case in East Boston and that of another woman, still in his care, who had recovered. Five weeks later her illness reappeared with a scarlet eruption that covered her body. Greene called it "a case of eczema."[14] On November 28th, Drs. Solomon Townsend and Channing each reported a fatal case. With such a long litany of varied and sometimes contradictory reports all related in some way to puerperal fever, it is easier to understand the quandary physicians were in regarding this mysterious disease. Holmes described it as "a discussion involving the sub-ject of a certain supposed cause of disease, about which something was known, a good deal suspected, and not a little feared."[15]

A FULLER KNOWLEDGE OF THE FACTS

It was at this point that Holmes began to investigate puerperal fever.[16] As he later wrote, "it was plain that a fuller knowledge of the facts relating to the subject would be acceptable to all present."[17] There is no evidence that he had ever seen a case of puerperal fever, even in the Paris hospitals, but

---

[13]Ibid., pp. 191–2.
[14]Ibid., pp. 193–4.
[15]Oliver Wendell Holmes, *Puerperal Fever as a Private Pestilence* (Boston: Ticknor and Fields, 1855), 1. Henceforth cited as *Private Pestilence*.
[16]Eleanor M. Tilton, *Amiable Autocrat, a Biography of Dr. Oliver Wendell Holmes* (New York: Henry Schuman, 1947), 170.
[17]Holmes, *Private Pestilence*, 1.

he was not a complete neophyte. As a medical student he had attended Channing's midwifery lectures and received tutorial instruction at a private medical school led by Channing and Dr. James Jackson when formal classes at the medical college were not in session.[18]

Channing's lectures emphasized the extreme seriousness of the disease and included references to the teaching of many European physicians on its nature and treatment. One of the authors he highlighted was Alexander Gordon, a Scottish physician whose 1795 treatise about a puerperal fever epidemic in Aberdeen clearly pointed to physicians, midwives and nurses as the agents of infection.

> I arrived at that certainty in the matter, that I could venture to foretell what women would be affected with the disease, upon hearing by what midwife they were to be delivered, or by what nurse they were to be attended during their lying-in; and, almost in every instance, my prediction was verified. . . . It is a disagreeable declaration for me to mention, that I myself was the means of carrying the infection to a great number of women.[19]

Gordon's treatise prefigured Holmes's essay written nearly fifty years later.

Under Channing's direction, Holmes had also read Thomas Denman's *Introduction to the Practice of Midwifery*, wherein as early as 1801 the British obstetrician had stated:

> There is another consequence of an epidemic, or even a sporadic puerperal fever, on which it would be criminal to be silent. This is the contagious nature of these fevers; it having been long suspected, and being now fully proved, that they may be, and often have been conveyed by midwives or nurses, from one patient to another.[20]

---

[18]List of Pupils with Drs. Jackson & Channing & time of entrance, Francis A. Countway Library of Medicine. Harvard required student attendance at two four-month sessions and a three-year apprenticeship with a reputable physician. In 1825, Channing and James Jackson started a private school where students had access to their medical books, supervised reading, and instruction, as well as clinical experience at the Massachusetts General Hospital.

[19]Alexander Gordon, *A Treatise on the Epidemic Puerperal Fever of Aberdeen* (London: printed for G.G. and J. Robinson, 1795), 3. Gordon had conducted a simple epidemiological study of 77 cases with dates of delivery, name of midwife or physician who delivered the baby or the nurse present during the lying-in period, location and outcome. The relationships were clear. See also Walter Channing, Lecture Notes, Lecture 36, Walter Channing Papers II, Massachusetts Historical Society. For Gordon's priority regarding the contagiousness of puerperal fever, see George W. Lowis, "Epidemiology of Puerperal Fever: The Contributions of Alexander Gordon," *Medical History* 37 (1993): 399–410.

[20]Thomas Denman, *Introduction to the Practice of Midwifery*, from the last London edition, revised by the author and with notes and emendations by John W. Francis (New York: E. Bliss and E. White, 1825), 589.

News of puerperal fever continued to attract Holmes's attention and that of the Society. On January 9, 1843, Dr. John Jackson reported the death of another physician from a dissecting wound incurred in the autopsy of a puerperal fever case. Coupled with the previous report about Whitney and his students, the assembled doctors must have become quite anxious, for it was clear that they too might be in danger if called upon to perform a puerperal fever post-mortem.[21] On January 23, Jackson "asked the opinion of the Society as to the contagion of Puerperal Fever, and the probability of Physicians communicating it from one patient to another."[22] A lively discussion followed, though none of the remarks were recorded.

The pace of Holmes's research became more intense, for he intended to respond affirmatively to these critically important questions.[23] The medical essays that had already won him three Boylston Medical Prizes were good preparation for the task, honing his ability to find the information he needed in medical publications and providing an opportunity to gather additional information from conversations and correspondence with local physicians.[24]

Now, he thoroughly investigated the medical literature, giving special attention to British reports of puerperal fever epidemics, for the British had been writing on the topic for half a century and there were several, in addition to Gordon and Denman, who referred to the contagiousness of the disease.[25] He also searched American journals for information and sent inquiries to local physicians asking about the incidence of puerperal fever in their practices. No one had ever cast so wide a net on the topic.

As he later recalled, "This paper was written in a great heat and with passionate indignation . . . I could not if I had tried, have disguised the feelings with which I regarded the attempt to put out of sight the frightful facts which I brought forward and the necessary conclusions to which they led."[26] Within three weeks he was ready to respond to the original query:

---

[21]BSMI, vol. 4, Minutes, 9 January 1843, pp. 218–9.
[22]Ibid, 23 January 1843, p. 221.
[23]Tilton, *Amiable Autocrat*, 170, 409 nn. 40, 44.
[24]Oliver Wendell Holmes, *Boylston Prize Dissertations for the Years 1836–7* (Boston: Charles C. Little and James Brown, 1838). The topics of Holmes's previous essays were the use of external instruments in diagnosis, malaria in New England, and neuralgia.
[25]Included were Charles White, Robert Collins, Nathaniel Hulme, Thomas West, Robert Gooch, John Haighton, James Blundell, John Ramsbotham, John Roberton, and Edward Rigby.
[26]Oliver Wendell Holmes, "Preface to the New Edition," *Medical Essays, 1842–1882* [The Works of Oliver Wendell Holmes, Standard Library Edition, Volume IX] (Boston: Houghton Mifflin, 1892), xvi.

Is puerperal fever contagious and is there a probability of physicians communicating it from one patient to another? His unequivocal answer: Yes, puerperal fever is contagious and yes, it is communicated from patient to patient by the physician, midwife, or nurse who attended them, either directly with their hands or indirectly on their clothing or instruments. And he had plenty of evidence to prove it.[27]

There is no record of comments from his colleagues. Perhaps the audience was too stunned to respond but "it was voted that Dr. Holmes be requested to publish the paper which he had just read."[28] The list of puerperal fever deaths grew longer that very evening when Dr. Storer announced recent cases that had occurred in the practices of Dr. Thaxter of Dorchester and Dr. Flint of Boston. This depressing news must have increased the anxiety of his colleagues, since Holmes had just placed blame for the transmission of puerperal fever squarely on them and their associates.

THE ESSAY

Holmes's essay appeared in the next issue of the *New England Quarterly Journal of Medicine and Surgery*, a new publication launched by two members of the Society for Medical Improvement.[29] It presents a carefully constructed argument for contagion that begins with the uncompromising assertion that the question was no longer debatable:

> In collecting, enforcing and adding to the evidence accumulated upon this most serious subject, I would not be understood to imply that there exists a doubt in the mind of any well-informed member of the medical profession as to the fact that puerperal fever is sometimes communicated from one person to another, both directly and indirectly. . . . No negative facts, no opposing opinions, be they what they may or whose they may, can form any answer to the series of cases within the reach of all who choose to explore the records of medical science.[30]

---

[27]The minutes were very brief, i.e., "Dr. Holmes read a paper upon the contagion of Puerperal Fever."

[28]BSMI, vol. 4, Minutes, Feb. 13, 1843, p. 223. The minutes were equally terse in this regard.

[29]The journal was edited by Charles Eliot Ware and Samuel Parkman, members of the Society for Medical Improvement, who saw a need for publishing longer articles than could be accommodated by the *Boston Medical and Surgical Journal*. BSMI, vol. 4, 27 February 1842, p. 137; "Advertisement for the *New England Quarterly Journal of Medicine and Surgery*," *Boston Medical and Surgical Journal* 27 (1842–43): 28.

[30]Holmes, "Contagiousness of Puerperal Fever," 503.

Holmes was so certain he was right that he did not hesitate to suggest that the authors of two of America's most widely read midwifery texts should explore the records of medical science. William Dewees's *Treatise on Diseases of Females* had dismissed contagion. "In this country, under no circumstance that puerperal fever has appeared hitherto, does it afford the slightest ground for the belief which would lead the reader to suspect that the idea of contagion had ever been entertained."[31] Charles D. Meigs's *Philadelphia Practice of Midwifery* had simply ignored contagion as a possible explanation. Holmes was determined to remedy the ignorance encouraged by such renowned teachers.

In defense of his thesis, Holmes quoted extensively from British authors, acknowledging first "the *treatise* of Dr. Gordon, of Aberdeen, being among the earlier special works upon the disease. . . . His expressions are so clear . . . that it may be quoted as a model which might have been often followed with advantage."[32] The midwifery text of Charles White, written several years prior to Gordon's was also cited, for he too had found a correlation between the incidence of disease and particular physicians' practices. Numerous midwifery treatises and articles from the *London Medical Gazette*, the *Lancet* and other British medical journals provided examples of physicians and midwives in whose practices sequential cases of puerperal fever had occurred. Two of them were known to have withdrawn from practice, so convinced were they of conveying the contagion. Many had begun to pay attention to cleanliness, fumigating their clothing or changing it when it appeared they might be the agent of disease, and some had begun to wash their hands before attending a birth. British experience in maternity hospitals showed the effectiveness of fumigating, ventilating, and whitewashing the wards to contain epidemics.[33]

> The recurrence of long series of cases like those I have cited, reported by those most interested to disbelieve in contagion, scattered along through an interval of half a century, might have been thought sufficient to satisfy the minds of all inquirers that here was something more than a singular coincidence. But if on a more extended observation, it should be found that the same ominous groups of cases, clustering about individual practitioners, were observed in a remote country, at different times, and in widely separated regions, it would seem incredible that any should be found too prejudiced or indolent to accept the solemn truth knelled into their ears by

---

[31]Dewees quotation, in ibid., 504.
[32]Ibid., 506.
[33]Charles White, a Manchester surgeon, is often credited with being among the first to insist on cleanliness. See Loudon, *Childbed Fever*, 9–12.

the funeral bells from both sides of the ocean—the plain conclusion that the physician and the disease entered, hand in hand, into the chamber of the unsuspecting patient.[34]

There was equally damning testimony from American journals, though of more recent vintage than their British counterparts since the growth of the medical profession on this side of the ocean lagged behind them. Dr. Peirson of Salem, Massachusetts confessed to twenty consecutive cases with four fatalities in his practice, adding "I am not informed that a single case had occurred in the practice of any other physician."[35] A particularly egregious example was that of a Philadelphia physician, Dr. Rutter, who over several weeks encountered "puerperal fever in nearly every female he attended in confinement." Cognizant that he might be responsible, Rutter abandoned his practice and left the city for a week. When he returned, he was careful to thoroughly cleanse himself and wear new clothing. Yet one of the very first cases he attended resulted in a fatal attack of puerperal fever, leading him to conclude that "transmission of the disease from female to female, in the person or clothes of the physician" could not be true. Consequently he continued to practice obstetrics and by the end of the year had delivered 70 women who developed puerperal fever.[36]

The unnecessary suffering and death caused by Rutter's inability to accept contagion infuriated Holmes. He could not refrain from mentioning a comment made by Charles D. Meigs, Professor of Midwifery at Jefferson Hospital in Philadelphia and author of one of the texts mentioned above. Regarding the unusually high number of puerperal fever cases in Rutter's practice, Meigs had explained that his obstetrical practice "was greater than that of any other gentlemen, which was probably the cause of his seeing a greater number of the [fatal] cases."[37] Holmes's inclusion of Meigs's ridiculous opinion was the first in a series of nasty exchanges between the two men.

The essay included many "gloomy facts" showing that contagion was not limited to direct transmission by the medical attendant himself. There was evidence that instruments such as catheters and forceps could spread disease.[38] Nurses were known to become ill, and some to die, after laundering clothing or bed linen used by the patient.

---

[34]Holmes, "Contagiousness of Puerperal Fever," 511.

[35]Ibid., 512

[36]Ibid., 512–3.

[37]Ibid., 513.

[38]The argument can be made that the obstetric care provided by physicians contributed to increased rates of puerperal fever because of the interventions that they were trained to provide and that their patients desired. Female midwives were not trained to use obstetrical instruments.

Erysipelas was shown to be part of the picture. "Seven females, delivered by Dr. Jackson in rapid succession were all attacked with puerperal fever, and five of them died. . . . When the first case occurred, he was attending and dressing a limb extensively mortified from erysipelas and went immediately to the accouchement."[39] In another situation, "there were also many cases of erysipelas in town at the time of the fatal puerperal cases which have been mentioned."[40]

The relationship between post-mortem examinations and disease was undeniably clear. One example among many is the statement of a doctor who had assisted at an autopsy of puerperal peritonitis "in which he laded out the contents of the abdominal cavity with his hands." Five women whom he delivered shortly afterward "were attacked with what is commonly called puerperal fever" and two died.[41]

Holmes was deeply concerned by the effect of dissection wounds, which had led to the deaths of two Boston doctors and provided the initial impetus for his investigations. He wondered why autopsies of puerperal fever patients led to such serious consequences when dissection wounds incurred in post-mortems of all other diseases were extremely rare. "The conclusion is irresistible that a most fearful morbid poison is often generated in the course of this disease. Whether it is *sui generis*, confined to this disease, or produced in some others, as for instance erysipelas, I need not stop to inquire."[42]

By the time of Holmes's essay, some doctors who were aware that puerperal fever might be contagious had adopted precautionary practices. "While I attended these women in their fevers, I changed my clothes, and washed my hands in a solution of chloride of lime after each visit," wrote Dr. David Storer, and others echoed his report.[43]

Holmes was a strong proponent of prevention, proposing eight rules for physician conduct he deemed justified by the evidence he had presented.[44] The first three urged extreme caution following post-mortem examinations. He warned that it is "highly inexpedient" for a physician

---

[39]Ibid., 514. This was Dr. Samuel Jackson of Northumberland, rather than either of the two Drs. Jackson of Boston mentioned above.
[40]Ibid., 515.
[41]Ibid., 513–4.
[42]Ibid., 524–5.
[43]Ibid., 518.
[44]Ibid., 529–30. Holmes's rules for physicians' conduct were similar to those already published in Britain by Robert Lee and James Copeland. See Irving S. Cutter and Henry R. Viets, *A Short History of Midwifery* (Philadelphia, W.B. Saunders Co., 1964), 133–4; Harold Speert, *Obstetrics and Gynecology in America, a History* (Chicago: The American College of Obstetricians and Gynecologists, 1980), 132. Alexander Gordon had included some of the same preventive measures in his *Treatise*, 97–8.

who practices obstetrics to engage in an autopsy or surgical treatment of an erysipelas patient. If a physician has a single case of puerperal fever in his practice he must consider the next woman he attends to be in danger of being infected by him and take "every precaution to diminish her risk of disease and death." If he has two cases in a short period of time and there are no others in the neighborhood, he should not practice obstetrics for at least a month. Three or more cases in the practice of one individual and no others occurring in the neighborhood, must be considered *prima facie* evidence that he is "the vehicle of contagion."

Holmes ended his essay with a stern warning to physicians who might have to curtail their practice:

> Whatever indulgence may be granted to those who have heretofore been the ignorant causes of so much misery, the time has come when the existence of a *private pestilence* in the sphere of a single physician should be looked upon not as a misfortune but a crime; and in the knowledge of such occurrences, the duties of the practitioner to his profession should give way to his paramount obligations to society.[45]

Holmes had written a powerful essay. The coincidence attested to by so many observers "that one man or woman should have ten, twenty, thirty, or seventy cases of this rare disease, following their footsteps with the keenness of a beagle, through the streets and lanes of a crowded city, while the scores that cross the same paths on the same errands know it only by name," would seem to have settled the question of contagion.[46]

Holmes's eloquence, coupled with his passionate concern for women in childbirth, added to the persuasiveness of his argument.

> The woman about to become a mother, or with her new-born infant upon her bosom, should be the object of trembling care and sympathy wherever she bears her tender burden, or stretches her aching limbs. The very outcast of the streets has pity upon her sister in degradation when the seal of promised maternity is impressed upon her. The remorseless vengeance of the law, brought down upon its victim by a machinery as sure as destiny, is arrested in its fall at a word which reveals her transient claim for mercy. The solemn prayer of the liturgy singles out her sorrows from the multiplied trials of life, to plead for her in the hour of peril. God forbid that any member of the profession to which she trusts her life, doubly precious at that eventful period, should hazard it negligently, unadvisedly or selfishly.[47]

---

[45]Holmes, "Contagiousness of Puerperal Fever," 530.
[46]Ibid., 521–2.
[47]Ibid., 528–9.

It is unlikely that any other medical man in America had the ability to play on the heartstrings of his readers so dramatically.[48]

CONTINUED UNCERTAINTY AND
ADDITIONAL EVIDENCE

Yet the immediate impact of his efforts was limited. There must have been considerable conversation about his paper in Boston's medical community, but none was recorded. The *New England Quarterly Journal of Medicine and Surgery* attracted few subscribers; thus copies were limited and it ceased publication after one year. The *Boston Medical and Surgical Journal* ignored it, but an abstract of the original article appeared in the *American Journal of the Medical Sciences*.[49] This journal had a national reputation and was widely read, although the abstract could not convey the full force of the multitudinous cases cited by Holmes and lacked the urgency of his prose. In the following years, the *American Journal* published several articles and notices regarding puerperal fever and erysipelas that supported Holmes's thesis; and in January 1846 it featured a long piece, "On the Contagiousness of Puerperal Fever," written by Dr. Samuel Kneeland of Boston, which reprised much of Holmes's essay and gave him full credit.[50] Thanks to the *American Journal*, news of Holmes's essay also traveled

---

[48]For a study of Holmes's medical writings as a reflection of his Parisian training and as preparation for his literary achievements, see William C. Dowling, *Oliver Wendell Holmes in Paris: Medicine, Theology and the Autocrat of the Breakfast Table* (Hanover, New Hampshire: University Press of New England, 2006), especially 83–109.

[49]"Contagiousness of Puerperal Fever," *American Journal of the Medical Sciences* 6 (1843): 260–4. The *AJMS* was published in Philadelphia.

[50]Tilton, *Amiable Autocrat*, 172–3; Charles Hall and George J. Dexter, "Account of the Erysipelatous Fever, as it Appeared in the Northern Section of Vermont and New Hampshire, in the Years 1842–3," *American Journal of the Medical Sciences* 7 (1844): 13–27; "Epidemic Erysipelas, Known by the Popular Name of 'Black Tongue,' which recently Prevailed in Ripley and Dearborn Counties, Iowa," *American Journal of the Medical Sciences* 7 (1844): 247–52; "Contagiousness of Puerperal Fever," *American Journal of the Medical Sciences* 7 (1844): 487–8; F.W. Sargent, "Report of Three Cases of Puerperal Peritonitis, which Occurred in the Wards of the Pennsylvania Hospital," *American Journal of the Medical Sciences* 10 (1846): 287–96; Samuel Kneeland, "On the Contagiousness of Puerperal Fever," *American Journal of the Medical Sciences* 11 (1846): 45–63; "On the Contagious Effects of Puerperal Fever on the Male Subject; or on Persons not Child-bearing," *American Journal of the Medical Sciences* 11 (1846): 245–8; "Contagiousness of Puerperal Fever and its Connection with Erysipelatous and Phlebitic Inflammation," *American Journal of the Medical Sciences* 11 (1846): 513–6; See also "Erysipelas and Puerperal Peritonitis," *Boston Medical and Surgical Journal* 29 (1844): 489–91.

across the Atlantic and was acknowledged by the noted statistician and Registrar-General of Britain, William Farr, in his Fifth Annual Report, as well as by James Copland, of Edinburgh, in his *Medical Dictionary*.[51]

At the meetings of the Medical Improvement Society, reports of puerperal fever continued but contagion was not discussed. In March 1844, Channing read a paper "containing several facts to show that puerperal fever is not always contagious." Although he had recently been a consultant in a series of fatal cases, in his own practice he had not had a single case of puerperal fever.[52] Despite the persuasiveness of Holmes's data, the contrarian experience of individual physicians continued to make acceptance of his conclusions difficult.

That difficulty was compounded by the unwillingness of many doctors to accept responsibility for spreading disease to their patients. How could men who had dedicated their professional lives to healing be agents of disease? Even more compelling was the intellectual difficulty that stemmed from not knowing exactly what it was they might be transmitting to their patients since no one had identified a specific cause for the disease. Though Holmes had accumulated abundant data to convincingly demonstrate the correlation of puerperal cases and attendant, as well as the probable connection with erysipelas and autopsies, he could not explain *what* was carried from patient to patient, or from cadaver to dissector to patient. Holmes's reference to a "morbid poison" was not an answer; it was just as easy to believe in the putrid effect of effluvia or miasmas.

It was Ignaz Semmelweis, an assistant physician in the maternity wards at the Vienna General Hospital, who provided definitive empirical evidence of the contagiousness of puerperal fever and of effective preventive medical practices. In 1847, Semmelweis ordered the medical students who had performed autopsies of puerperal fever patients to wash their hands with chloride of lime before examining women in labor. Within a month, maternal fatalities were reduced from more than 10 percent to less than 2 percent. However, Semmelweis was no closer than Holmes to the correct explanation. He attributed the disease to "cadaveric poisons" and later to "decomposing animal organic matter" and "harmful things." This made it difficult for his colleagues to accept the implications of his discoveries, and

---

[51]Holmes acknowledged those publications as well as an addition to the *Medical Dictionary* by Robert Lee, also of Edinburgh, at the beginning of *Puerperal Fever as a Private Pestilence*. See also Tilton, *Amiable Autocrat*, 172–3.
[52]BSMI, vol. 4, Minutes, 11 March 1844, p. 329.

their resentment was a contributing factor to his dismissal from the hospital in 1849.[53]

Neither Holmes nor Semmelweis knew of the other's work, but the contagionist theories of each were condemned by some of the most prominent medical scientists and obstetricians of the time. Rudolf Karl Virchow, the renowned German pathologist, thought Semmelweis's theory was based on false premises. Wilhelm Friedrich Scanzoni, one of Europe's leading obstetricians, rejected Semmelweis's theory and continued to insist the disease was caused by atmospheric or miasmatic influences. On the other hand, James Young Simpson, Professor of Medicine and Midwifery in Edinburgh, thought Semmelweis had not said anything new.[54]

A Private Pestilence

Despite the unconscionable sickness and fatalities that continued among women in childbirth, Holmes might have accepted the slow response to his essay, hoping that in time his colleagues would agree with the logic of his contagionist view. However, he was unable to disregard the vehement opposition of two influential Philadelphia professors of midwifery, Hugh L. Hodge of the University of Pennsylvania and Charles D. Meigs of Jefferson Medical School, whom Holmes had criticized in the essay.

Hodge lambasted contagion in a lecture titled *On the Non-contagious Character of Puerperal Fever*. He reminded his students "of the value and dignity of our profession" and sought to remove the fear that they could ever be ministers of evil, "especially to woman under the extremely interesting circumstances of gestation and parturition." He was certain they could never convey, "in any possible manner, a horrible virus, so destructive

---

[53]Ignaz Semmelweis, *The Etiology, Concept, and Prophylaxis of Childbed Fever*, trans. and ed. K. Codell Carter (Madison: University of Wisconsin Press, 1983); Cutter and Viets, *Short History*, 139; Loudon, *Childbed Fever*, xliv–xlix; K. Codell Carter and Barbara R. Carter, *Childbed Fever, A Scientific Biography of Ignaz Semmelweis* (Westport, Connecticut: Greenwood Press, 1994); and Sherwin B. Nuland, *The Doctors' Plague* (New York: W.W. Norton, 2003). Many factors contributed to Semmelweis's dismissal from the hospital, his unhappy return to Budapest, and tragic last years.

[54]Semmelweis, *Etiology*, Introduction, 32–4, 42. Scanzoni believed puerperal fever could also be caused by emotional trauma. Other naysayers included the noted French obstetrician Paul-Antoine Dubois (1795–1871). For studies of anti-contagionist ideas, see Edwin H. Ackerknecht, "Anticontagionism Between 1821 and 1867," *Bulletin of the History of Medicine* 22 (1948): 562–93; Gail Pat Parsons, "The British Medical Profession and Contagion Theory: Puerperal Fever as a Case Study, 1830–1860," *Medical History* 22 (1977): 138–50.

in its effects, and so mysterious in its operations as that attributed to puerperal fever." In his opinion, Holmes's thesis was only a supposition without any real proof.[55]

Meigs's attacks were more scathing and more personal. Outraged that a young man with no obstetrical experience should dare to insult respectable men (such as he), Meigs urged his students to

> disregard the jejune and fizenless dreamings of sophomore writers, who thunder forth denunciations, and would mark, if they might, with a black and ineffaceable spot, the hard-won reputation of every physician, who in the Providence of God, is called upon to contend with the rage of one of the most destructive of epidemics.

To the implication that doctors' hands were not clean, Meigs responded that doctors are gentlemen and a gentleman's hands are clean. As for the cause of puerperal fever, Meigs preferred "to attribute them to accident, or Providence, of which I can form a conception, rather than to a contagion of which I cannot form any clear idea, at least as to this particular malady."[56]

Holmes was incensed by these criticisms, particularly by the influence they would have on medical students who might accept the lofty professors' views. He was also eager to have his own views receive wider attention from his professional colleagues. Thus, in 1855 he reprinted the essay with a new title, *Puerperal Fever as a Private Pestilence*, a lengthy introduction, and three additional pages of references and cases. Holmes could no longer be attacked as a "jejune and fizenless sophomore," for he designed the title page to include "Parkman Professor of Anatomy and Physiology in Harvard University" beneath his name.

The corpus of the publication was a verbatim reproduction of the original essay, but the introductory remarks were even more assertive. He rejected "medical theorists" who thought his thesis should conform to their preconceived notions of contagion or with "alleged laws of contagion deduced from other diseases." To rule out the possibility that chance

---

[55]Hugh H. Hodge, *On the Non-contagious Character of Puerperal Fever: An Introductory Lecture, 11 October, 1852* (Philadelphia: T.L. and P.G. Collins: 1852), 26–7. "Virus" was not used in the modern microbiological sense but more generally as a poisonous substance that can invade the body and cause disease.

[56]Charles D. Meigs, *On the Nature, Signs, and Treatment of Childbed Fevers; in a Series of Letters addressed to the Students of His Class* (Philadelphia: Blanchard and Lea, 1854), 113; Meigs, *Obstetrics: The Science and the Art*, second edition, revised (Philadelphia: Blanchard and Lea, 1852), 631. For a defense of Meigs written by his great-great grandson, see J. Wister Meigs, "Puerperal Fever and Nineteenth-Century Contagionism: The Obstetrician's Dilemma," *Transactions and Studies of the College of Physicians of Philadelphia* 42 (1975): 273–80.

rather than logical deduction could explain the coincidence of disease in one doctor's practice, Holmes strengthened the moral argument of his revised essay by revealing the calculations of an actuary to prove that chance could not be the explanation.[57]

Holmes mercilessly dissected the most offending paragraphs in Meigs's book, specifically mentioning the errors and adding new facts to support his original text. Meigs had included another defense of Dr. Rutter, whom Holmes had exposed in the original essay for carrying puerperal fever from patient to patient (see above). Holmes responded acerbically that if Meigs had his way, physicians would not warn a colleague with puerperal fever patients to cease obstetrical practice but allow him "to go on not to seven, or seventy only but to seventy times seventy if [he] could find patients."[58] To Meigs's idea of Providence as the cause of puerperal fever, Holmes scornfully replied, "We do not deny that the God of battles decides the fate of nations; but we like to have the biggest squadrons on our side, and we are particular that our soldiers should not only say their prayers, but keep their powder dry."[59]

Puerperal Fever as a Private Pestilence did not lack any of the eloquence of the original version. Indeed, having been criticized for his views, Holmes was even more insistent on the righteousness of his cause.

> The teachings of the two Professors in the great schools of Philadelphia are sure to be listened to, not only by their immediate pupils but by the Profession at large. . . . I do entreat those who hold the keys of life and death to listen to me also for this once. I ask no personal favor; but I beg to be heard in behalf of the women whose lives are at stake . . . it is a question whether or not the "blackdeath" of child-bed is to be scattered broadcast by agency of the mother's friend and adviser. Let the men who mould opinions look to it; if there is any voluntary blindness, any interested oversight, any culpable negligence, even, in such a matter, and the facts shall reach the public ear; the pestilence-carrier of the lying-in chamber must look to God for pardon, for man will never forgive him.[60]

This time, the essay was well received. *The Boston Medical and Surgical Journal* gave it an enthusiastic review as did *The American Journal of the*

---

[57]Holmes, *Private Pestilence*, 13. See also James S. Cassedy, *American Medicine and Statistical Thinking, 1800–1860* (Cambridge: Harvard University Press, 1984), 82–3. Holmes's appreciation of the value of statistics was one result of his medical studies in Paris.
[58]Holmes, *Private Pestilence*, 20.
[59]Ibid., 22.
[60]Ibid., 23–4.

Medical Sciences, and the American Medical Association added it to its list of recommended publications. Meigs lost much credibility, and the next edition of his book was criticized for ignoring Holmes's doctrine.[61]

At last, Walter Channing abandoned his earlier skepticism, whole-heartedly agreeing with Holmes about contagion and endorsing his preventive measures. Nonetheless, Channing could not refrain from asking the fundamental question that had troubled him and many other physicians for decades. "Whence the FIRST CASE?" The second, third and fourth cases could be explained by transmission from patient to patient but what initiated the string of cases?

"A contagious disease is a specific disease, depending for its existence on a specific cause, which is nothing else, and can be nothing else than itself." The answer, wrote Channing, "has in it the whole history of a contagious disease."[62]

Not until the advent of bacteriology in the 1860s and 1870s could this question be answered and the etiology of puerperal fever be clearly understood. In 1879, Louis Pasteur identified the streptococcus as the cause of puerperal fever as well as of erysipelas and of the dangerous blood poisoning that frequently resulted from a wound infection. At last, puerperal fever could be explained as a bacterial infection originating from the internal wounds women suffered during the birth process, especially from separation of the placenta. All the other explanations—miasmas, effluvia, climate changes, idiosyncrasies of the female body or emotions, and inflammation of other parts of her anatomy—were useless. Furthermore, as Gordon, Holmes, Semmelweis and others had warned, the relation between puerperal fever and erysipelas made sense, as did the transmission of disease from the autopsy room to the bedside of the parturient woman.

However, knowing the cause of disease does not ensure prevention or cure. Joseph Lister must be credited for introducing the concept of antisepsis in 1867 that went far beyond the chlorine handwashing Semmelweis had prescribed.[63] But established practices do not disappear quickly and

---

[61]"Biographical Notices," *Boston Medical and Surgical Journal* 52 (1855): 25–7; "Puerperal Fever as a Private Pestilence," *Boston Medical and Surgical Journal* 52 (1855): 95–101; "Review of Puerperal Fever as a Private Pestilence," *American Journal of the Medical Sciences* 29 (1855): 459–62; Tilton, *Amiable Autocrat,* 176. For criticism of Meigs's book, see "Bibliographical Notices," *Boston Medical and Surgical Journal* 55 (1857): 489–93.
[62]Walter Channing, "On the Contagiousness of Puerperal Fever," *Boston Medical and Surgical Journal* 52 (1855): 297. Carter suggests that Semmelweis's contribution to medical science lies in his methodology, which required a "necessary cause" for all cases of puerperal fever. See K. Codell Carter, "Semmelweis and his Predecessors," *Medical History* 25 (1981): 57–72.
[63]The importance of antisepsis played a significant role in the transfer of childbirth from home to hospital in the early years of the twentieth century.

large numbers of women continued to die from puerperal fever until the 1930s, when German chemists under the direction of Gerhard Domagk discovered the sulfonamides.[64] The effectiveness of the synthetic drug Prontosil against puerperal fever, erysipelas, septicemia and other strepto-coccal infections ushered in the antibiotic revolution that has saved millions of lives and freed women from the fear of death in childbirth.

Why then is Holmes a medical icon? He was not the first to claim that puerperal fever is contagious. Gordon had done that fifty years earlier with a primitive epidemiological study, whereas Holmes read the literature and logically derived his thesis from other men's experience. He had no scientific proof, whereas Semmelweis showed empirically that the unwashed hands of doctors coming from the autopsy room carried contagious matter. Pasteur discovered the cause, Lister introduced an effective method of prevention, and Domagk developed the cure.

The initial adulation came from men who had known him and who appreciated "the genial humor, the refined wit, the pathos, the tender sensitiveness to the lights and shadows of life" of the literary Holmes. For William Osler, himself a highly esteemed physician, Holmes was "the most successful combination the world has ever seen of the physician and man of letters," adding that "so far as this country is concerned, the credit of insisting upon the great practical truth of the contagiousness of puerperal fever belongs to Dr. Holmes." *American Medical Biographies* (1920) describes his essay "as a truly great contribution to medical science." The editor of *Medical Classics* (1936) considered it "a masterpiece of medical literature which every physician should know." A late twentieth-century text on obstetric infections (1993) calls the essay "a major event in nineteenth-century medicine."[65]

As should be expected, Holmes has the last word. In his later years, asked about his role in the elucidation of puerperal fever, he gave the following explanation:

[64]Irvine Loudon, "Puerperal Fever, the Streptococcus, and the Sulphonamides, 1911–1945," *British Medical Journal* 295 (1987): 485–90; David Charles and Bryan Larsen, "Streptococcal Puerperal Sepsis and Obstetric Infections: A Historical Perspective," *Reviews of Infectious Diseases* 8 (1986): 411–22.

[65]William Osler, "Oliver Wendell Holmes," *Bulletin of the Johns Hopkins Hospital* 5 (October 1894): 85–8; Howard A. Kelly and Walter L. Burrage, eds., *American Medical Biographies* (Baltimore: The Norman, Remington Co., 1920), 542–5; Emerson Crosby Kelly, ed., *Medical Classics*, vol. 1, no. 3 (Baltimore: Williams and Wilkins, 1936), 208; David Charles, *Obstetric and Perinatal Infections* (St. Louis: Mosby Year Book, 1993), 62.

I do not know what others have done since my efforts; I do know that others had cried out with all their might against the terrible evil, before I did and I gave them full credit for it.

But I think I shrieked my warning louder and longer than any of them, and I am pleased to remember that I took my ground upon the existing evidence before the little army of microbes was marched up to support my position.[66]

---

[66]Osler, "Oliver Wendell Holmes," 88.

Medical Therapeutics and Its Kindred Delusions

Oliver Wendell Holmes on Drugs, Disease, and Rational Care

CHARLES E. ROSENBERG

E VEN THE MOST CASUAL STUDENT of America's medical history is familiar with Oliver Wendell Holmes's wry dismissal of mid-nineteenth-century therapeutics. "I firmly believe," he contended in 1860, "that if the whole materia medica, *as now used*, could be sunk to the bottom of the sea, it would be all the better for mankind,—and all the worse for the fishes."[1] It is almost certainly the single most-quoted sentence fragment in America's medical history.

It is quoted because it is quotable. Holmes could always turn an attention-getting phrase and that skill (along with the fame of a supreme

---

[1] Oliver Wendell Holmes, "Currents and Counter-Currents in Medical Science," in *Medical Essays, 1842–1882* [The Works of Oliver Wendell Holmes, Standard Library Edition, Volume IX] (Boston: Houghton, Mifflin and Company, 1892), 203. (Cited hereafter as "Currents and Counter-Currents"). This was originally an 1860 address to the Massachusetts Medical Society. Holmes was fond of such modest proposals. "It would be better if the patient were allowed a discount from his bill for every dose he took," Holmes suggested on another occasion, "just as children are compensated by their parents for swallowing hideous medicinal draughts." In Holmes, "Valedictory Address delivered to the Medical Graduates of Harvard University, at the Annual Commencement, Wednesday, March 10, 1858," in *Currents and Counter-Currents in Medical Science. With Other Essays and Addresses* (Boston: Ticknor and Fields, 1861), 389.

court justice son) explains his continued name recognition. But Holmes's critique of mid-nineteenth-century drugging is memorable not only because of its colorful language, but because the words fit nicely into a narrative of beneficent progress. The intimidating arsenal of purges and vomits, of mercury and arsenic, of the bleeding and blisters that had been the everyday practice of medicine in George Washington's era represents in retrospect an object of whimsy or disdain—a grim and often dangerous reality from which medicine has gradually evolved. Holmes was not just a minor literary figure, the story follows, but a self-conscious reformer in service of Western medicine's larger movement toward a more efficacious and scientifically-based therapeutics.

The rationale for this shift in bedside practice has become an historical commonplace. This change in outlook was based on a critical empiricism and justified in terms of a newly-emphasized respect for the body's innate healing powers. The great majority of ailments ended in recovery— whether or not a physician ever appeared at the bedside. The physician needed to identify those ills that were "self-limited" and then pursue an appropriately diffident therapeutic course—while following a similarly cautious and minimally intrusive strategy in ills whose natural trajectory ended in death. In either case, dramatic interventions might only cause discomfort without altering the patient's experience for the better. Understanding these "natural" trajectories of illness was key to effective doctoring. It implied skill in diagnosis and prognosis, and in devising a treatment plan. To twenty-first century readers familiar with such arguments, Holmes and such like-thinking critics of mid-nineteenth-century clinical practice as Jacob Bigelow in the United States and Sir John Forbes in England, seem heroes in a narrative of laudable progress.[2] They are easily cast in the role of clear-headed and forward-looking critics of mindless, sometimes mercenary, and often brutal routinism in therapeutic practice. This generation of Anglo-American critical spirits applied the insights and experience of Parisian wards and autopsy rooms—the French emphasis on clinical-pathological correlation, medical statistics, and clinical observation—to evaluate medical practice in the light of a novel understanding of dis-

---

[2]Jacob Bigelow, *Brief Expositions of Rational Medicine, to which is Prefixed the Paradise of Doctors, A Fable* (Boston: Phillips, Sampson and Company, 1858); Bigelow, *Nature in Disease: Illustrated in Various Discourses and Essays* (Boston: Phillips, Sampson and Company, 1859); John Forbes, *Of Nature and Art in the Cure of Disease* (London: John Churchill, 1857). For Holmes's honorific references to Bigelow and Forbes, see Holmes, "Currents and Counter-Currents," 182.

ease.[3] It is a comforting and conventional story of medicine freeing itself from millennia of speculative pathologies and turning to an observation-based view of clinical practice and a lesion-based understanding of disease entities. Mid-nineteenth-century competition from homeopathic practitioners with their highly-diluted drugs and emphasis on diet and lifestyle only underlined the market handicap embodied in a traditional practice that featured bleeding and blisters, emetics, and cathartics.

But the story is not quite so simple. To begin with, Holmes did not disavow all contemporary medicines; they had a place if used prudently. Even his whimsical consignment of drugs to the fishes did not include opium, wine "which is a food," a few specifics, ". . . and the vapors which produce the miracle of anæsthesia." And he was careful to italicize the phrase "as now used." A "*presumption against*" a particular group of drugs was not the same as a categorical prohibition.[4] Even toxic metals such as antimony and mercury might be helpful in experienced hands and in the appropriate clinical circumstances. Both death and recovery could be managed and smoothed along their predetermined way. "Some diseases are curable by art, and others are not;" as Jacob Bigelow explained, "yet, in the treatment of all diseases there is a right method and a wrong. . . . A good shipmaster or pilot could often navigate his vessel in safety, though he could not cure the storm."[5]

---

[3]John Harley Warner has provided the most detailed and insightful account of these events: Warner, "'The Nature-Trusting Heresy': American Physicians and the Concept of the Healing Power of Nature in the 1850's and 1860's," *Perspectives in American History* 11 (1977–78): 291–324; Warner, *The Therapeutic Perspective: Medical Practice, Knowledge, and Identity in America, 1820–1885* (Cambridge: Harvard University Press, 1986); Warner, *Against the Spirit of System: The French Impulse in Nineteenth-Century American Medicine* (Princeton: Princeton University Press, 1998). Two now classical studies remain valuable for understanding these developments: Max Neuburger, *The Doctrine of the Healing Power of Nature Throughout the Course of Time*, trans. by Linn J. Boyd (New York: American Institute of Homeopathy, 1932); Erwin H. Ackerknecht, *Medicine at the Paris Hospital, 1794–1848* (Baltimore: Johns Hopkins University Press, 1967).
[4]Oliver Wendell Holmes, "Border Lines of Knowledge in Some Provinces of Medical Science [1861]," in *Medical Essays, 1842–1882*, 254–5. "Specifics" almost certainly refers to quinine in malaria and mercury in syphilis. Holmes was, in fact, well aware that bleeding and "the traditional idea of always poisoning out disease, as we smoke out vermin" were already on the wane in 1861. In ibid., 257.
[5]Bigelow, *Brief Expositions*, p. 19. John Forbes employed a similar metaphor, likening disease to a horse and the physician to its rider. Remedies, no matter how effective, Forbes explained, are no more than the rider's voice, hand, whip, or spur in relation to the horse's forward movement. In Forbes, *Nature and Art*, 35.

PERFORMING AUTHORITY

Holmes was well aware that his language was more inflammatory and polarizing than the middle-of-the-road practices he actually endorsed. The platform pyrotechnics were necessary, however: "To hold the attention of an audience is the first requisite of every such composition; and for this a more highly colored rhetoric is admissible than might please the solitary reader."[6] It was written, he explained of one of his influential addresses, as an "*Oration*, a florid rhetorical composition, expressly intended to secure the attention of an audience not easy to hold as listeners."[7] His elegant essays, in their oral and written versions, were performance—and performance in a variety of ways. He was not only performing the role of public commentator—whether speaking to Harvard medical graduates, the Massachusetts Medical Society, or a general audience—he was speaking in a particular voice. It was a voice embodying reason, critical distance, and respect for empirical—numerically-expressed and evaluated—evidence. Holmes saw it as the spirit of the age.

> The two dominant words of our time are *law* and *average*, both pointing to the uniformity of the order of being in which we live. Statistics have tabulated everything,—population, growth, wealth, crime, disease. We have shaded maps showing the geographical distribution of larceny and suicide. Analysis and classification have been at work upon all tangible and visible objects. The Positive Philosophy of Comte has only given expression to the observing and computing mind of the nineteenth-century.[8]

Nothing was to be accepted on faith; everything was to be observed, tabulated, evaluated. Medical statistics were to medicine as quantitative analysis was to chemistry. Holmes was also acting out a role, demonstrating through language and reference his social authority and that of like-thinking intellectuals in invoking the ideal of a new and un-compromising—evidence-based—truth.

Not all of his contemporaries accepted that authority or his conclusions. And some of them experienced Holmes's Brahmin style not as urbane

---

[6]Oliver Wendell Holmes, "Mechanism in Thought and Morals [1870]," in *Pages from an Old Volume of Life* [The Works of Oliver Wendell Holmes, Standard Library Edition, Volume VIII] (Boston: Houghton, Mifflin and Company, 1892), 260.

[7]Oliver Wendell Holmes, "Preface," in *Currents and Counter-Currents in Medical Science*, iv.

[8]Holmes, "Currents and Counter-Currents," 180. Holmes could refer admiringly to the "calm statisticians of the Insurance office" or the merchant balancing his accounts in endorsing the numerical method in medicine. In ibid., 195. Compare this remark to similar references in Holmes, "The Contagiousness of Puerperal Fever [1855 reprint with additions]," in *Medical Essays, 1842–1882*, 126; Holmes, "The Position and Prospects of the Medical Student [1844]," in *Currents and Counter-Currents in Medical Science*, 301.

and ironic, but as condescending and at the same time out of touch with the realities of practice. The Boston poet and anatomist had in fact ceased to practice medicine when he delivered his most uncompromising attacks on contemporary therapeutics—and could be pictured by skeptical contemporaries as irresponsibly removed from the day-to-day realities of bedside care. At least some physicians were also indignant at his much-discussed contention that childbed fever was spread by physicians themselves. Both his very public criticism of therapeutics and his emphasis on the transmissibility of childbed fever seemed to his critics to undermine the confidence patients and their families needed to invest in their physicians.[9]

Holmes was accurate indeed when he described Massachusetts—and Boston in particular—as the "American head-quarters of the nature-trusting heresy."[10] Like a number of his Boston contemporaries, Holmes opposed both hard-edged Calvinism and nationalistic bravado; he referred after visiting Salem to the Puritans as "old Judaizing witch-hangers" and used Benjamin Rush as an embodiment of both a naively self-confident nationalism and a brutally energetic therapeutics. How could those bold, hearty, and innovative Americans who had "contrived the Bowie-knife and the revolver," Holmes asked, "be content with any but 'heroic' practice? What wonder that the stars and stripes wave over doses of ninety grains of sulphate of quinine, and that the American eagle screams with delight to see three drachms of calomel given at a single mouthful?"[11] Rush's boasted guidelines for success in treating yellow fever in 1793 seemed not to have helped those many scores who had died sixty years later of outbreaks in Norfolk and Portsmouth and New Orleans.[12]

---

[9]Holmes, "The Contagiousness of Puerperal Fever," 105–12; Warner, *Therapeutic Perspective*, 32–6.

[10]Holmes, "Currents and Counter-Currents," 183.

[11]Ibid., 193. On the term "heroic medicine," see Robert B. Sullivan, "Sanguine Practices: A Historical and Historiographic Reconsideration of Heroic Therapy in the Age of Rush," *Bulletin of the History of Medicine* 68 (1994): 211–34. Holmes shared the casual anti-Catholic bias of the vast majority of his Protestant contemporaries. He characterized Homeopathy, for example, as "image worship, relic-wearing, holy-water-sprinkling, transferred from the spiritual world to that of the body." In "Some More Recent Views on Homœopathy [1857]," in *Currents and Counter-Currents in Medicine*, 187.

[12]"Where was it [Rush's therapeutic legacy] when the blue flies were buzzing over the coffins of the unburied dead piled up in the cemetery of New Orleans, at the edge of the huge trenches yawning to receive them?" In Holmes, "Currents and Counter-Currents," 192. For contemporary yellow fever accounts, see: William S. Forrest, *The Great Pestilence in Virginia; Being an Historical Account of the Origin, General Character, and Ravages of the Yellow Fever in Norfolk and Portsmouth in 1855* (New York: Derby & Jackson, 1856); New Orleans Sanitary Commission, *Report of the Sanitary Commission of New Orleans on the Epidemic Yellow Fever of 1853* (New Orleans: The Picayune Office, 1854).

Disease in Nature

But Holmes did have faith in his own understanding of disease and in the generations of systematic investigation that separated his generation from Rush's. If rational medicine was based in a trust in nature's healing power, prognosis implied an understanding of disease and its clinical course. Here too Paris had reshaped medical notions of what constituted disease. The insights accumulated at countless post-mortems, allied with growing skills at physical examination (palpation, auscultation and percussion), challenged traditional non-specific disease concepts and instead created pictures of discrete disease entities configured around the associations between lesions after death and clinical findings observed and reported during life.[13] Holmes found the case of what we now call tuberculosis particularly instructive.

> The diseases now known as tuberculous were for a long period scattered and concealed under various disguises, which prevented their real identity from being recognized. In the lymphatic glands tubercule was known as scrofula, in the bones as white swelling, in the lungs as phthisis, in various other internal organs by no distinctive name whatever. Thus, the tuberculous affections were separated at their natural point of union, and became joined to various other diseases, with which their relations were wholly accidental.[14]

The newly-construed unity of tuberculosis—its "real identity"—was based not on the presence of a microorganism, as a twenty-first century reader might assume, but on post-mortem findings.[15] It is no wonder that Holmes referred to a thorough physical exam as "an autopsy performed before death." Advances in microscopy and an even more novel emphasis on the cellular basis of life and disease seemed only to clarify and intensify such views of disease as having an essential and characteristic specificity. It is no

---

[13]Holmes was an ardent admirer of Marie François Xavier Bichat and his tissue-oriented General Anatomy. "Anatomy, Physiology, and Pathology have received a new light from this novel method of contemplating the living structures, which has a vast influence in enabling the practitioner at least to distinguish and predict the course of disease." In Holmes, "Border Lines in Medical Science," 222–3.

[14]Holmes, "Position and Prospects of the Medical Student," 292.

[15]It is striking how little attention Holmes paid to the nature of the mechanism that might explain the contagiosity of such diseases as smallpox, and how little attention he paid to the problem of epidemic disease generally—even though his retrospective fame rests so much on his discussion of the transmissibility of childbed fever. He was careful, in fact, to make allowance for factors other than personal transmission in the spread of puerperal fever, "especially for epidemic influences." In Holmes, "The Contagiousness of Puerperal Fever," 107.

wonder that it became increasingly natural to think of diseases as entities; Holmes once likened them to the occupants of a menagerie with open doors. The beasts varied a great deal, with some dangerous and others relatively benign—though even the strongest human being would eventually fall victim to one or another of these creatures.[16] Such metaphors expressed a rather different conceptual world from that traditional view in which diseases were individual and shape-shifting, in which a cold might drift into bronchitis, bronchitis into tuberculosis. A knowledge of this bestiary of disease entities was a necessary guide to prognosis and therapeutic choice.[17] "A just classification," Holmes explained, "like the lens in an optical instrument, converges and brings into a clear image the scattered and refracted rays of individual observation."[18]

Holmes's ideas were at the same time—and at first thought paradoxically—traditional, holistic, and non-specific. He saw both health and disease as aggregate products of the same constitutive processes.[19] The body was constantly renewing itself through nutrition, digestion, assimilation; it needed proper food, clean air, water, and a proper mixture of rest and exercise. Sickness was the result of that life-constituting and sustaining process gone awry. To prescribe for a patient "without insuring favorable hygienic conditions," Holmes contended, "is like amputation without ligatures."[20] The body was always becoming, always shedding its old fabric and recreating itself. From this perspective, the use of drugs such as mercury and antimony had to be regarded with suspicion—they were not part of the body's normal components and could not be assimilated. Yet scurvy, a devastating systemic illness, could be cured by the simple provision of fresh fruit and vegetables—part of a normal diet. It was no more than logical that Holmes should have emphasized sanitation, ventilation, and adequate

---

[16]Holmes, "Some More Recent Views on Homœopathy," 182. "A physician," Holmes extended his metaphor, "is one who has lived among these beasts, and studied their aspects and habits. He knows them all well, and looks them in the face, and lays his hand on their backs daily."

[17]For an overview of this trend toward disease specificity and some of its implications, see Charles E. Rosenberg, "The Tyranny of Diagnosis: Specific Entities and Individual Experience," *Milbank Quarterly* 80 (2002): 237–60; Rosenberg, "Managed Fear," *Lancet* 373 (2009): 802–3.

[18]Holmes, "Position and Prospects of the Medical Student," 295.

[19]"Disease, being always an effect," Holmes explained, "is always in exact proportion to the sum of its causes." In "Currents and Counter-Currents," 198.

[20]Ibid., 203. Holmes referred here to his youthful excursions into his city's slums as a Boston Dispensary physician. Skilled nursing was one such healing necessity that was often lacking. In ibid., 203–4.

nutrition, along with careful nursing. "The bills of mortality," Holmes preached from his generation's Book of Sanitary Reform, "are more obviously affected by drainage, than by this or that method of practice."[21]

The body's normal physiological processes constituted both sickness and health; ongoing metabolic process explained pathology and healing, the abnormal and the normal. This was a traditional view, but one Holmes refreshed by casting it in the language of currently fashionable cell theory. Every healthy cell "performs its functions properly so long as it is supplied with its proper materials and stimuli. But if originally sound and subsequently diseased, there has certainly been some excess, deficiency, or wrong quality in the materials or stimuli applied to it." The physician's task was clear: he had to identify and remove the "injurious influence and substitute a normal one."[22] In retrospect, this holistic and plastic view of disease might seem inconsistent with an acceptance of the notion of specific disease entities. But to a well-educated physician of Holmes's generation, both ways of conceptualizing disease seemed consistent. And both could be used to undercut a traditional, interventionist approach to therapeutics. The unnatural might be unnecessary as well as dangerous.

But all cells are not created equal. Not everyone started on a level physiological playing field. Constitution as well as individual life course helped explain disease—and especially its chronic forms. Holmes warned against immoderate expectations.

> When an oil is discovered that will make a bad watch keep good time; when a recipe is given which will turn an acephalous fœtus into a promising child; when a man can enter a second time into his mother's womb and give her back the infirmities which twenty generations have stirred into her blood, and infused into his own through hers, we may be prepared to enlarge the National Pharmacopoeia with a list of specifics for everything but old age,—and possibly for that also.[23]

---

[21]Holmes, "Border Lines in Medical Science," 259. Holmes noted sardonically that insurance companies didn't set different rates for patients of different physicians.
[22]Ibid., 253.
[23]Oliver Wendell Holmes, "Notes to the Address on Currents and Counter-Currents in Medical Science," in *Medical Essays, 1842–1882*, 443. Holmes expressed what might be called proto-eugenic views, characterizing the medical profession, for example, as working not only for the moment, "but for the race and the future." In Holmes, "Homœopathy and its Kindred Delusions [1842]," in *Medical Essays, 1842–1882*, 102. Like many of his socially-oriented contemporaries, Holmes was concerned about the "racial" consequences of social change. Some races, he warned, "are breeding down and tending to run out," while others were "breeding up, or accumulating vital capital." In Holmes, "Currents and Counter-Currents," 198–200. The language cited is on p. 198.

Humility was a necessary and proper component of the prudent physician's clinical tools. Watching and waiting, easing pain and providing comfort were sometimes the most efficacious and appropriate prescriptions.

HOLMES ON THE SOCIOLOGY OF MEDICINE

Holmes was a shrewd and prescient observer of medical practice as well as the sickness around which it was organized. Like the body, medical thought and practice was labile, ever-changing; Holmes observed in his usual worldly style that whatever was believed about therapeutics in one generation would be displaced in the next. Medical ideas and practices were contingent, reflecting the particular social world in which they were learned. "The truth is," he argued, "that medicine, professedly founded on observation, is as sensitive to outside influences, political, religious, philosophical, imaginative, as is the barometer to the changes of atmospheric density."[24]

Some aspects of medical practice were enduring, however, rooted in human nature and the doctor-patient relationship. "Part of the blame for over-medication," Holmes argued, for example, must "rest with the profession, for yielding to the tendency to self-delusion, which seems inseparable from the practice of the art of healing."[25] Such "self-delusion"—the evidence-distorting need to witness efficacy, to reassure both patient and practitioner—was insidious and inescapable. It was all too easy to credit therapeutic inputs for positive outcomes. Patients were necessarily part of this system of belief, demanding treatment and sharing a traditional faith in "active drugs." Physicians, patients, and patients' families had seen patients recover after heroic treatment—had seen them "work." What we might today call the social efficacy of traditional therapeutics had been acted out for centuries in the bedside rituals of bleeding, vomiting, and purging.[26] The biological reality underlying this mutually assured illusion of efficacy lay in that very healing power of nature that—as Holmes argued—most physicians tended to ignore or discount. Drugs and bleeding had seemed effective for centuries because most ills were in fact self-limited.

Holmes was well aware that a consistent "therapeutic nihilism" was not a real option. Patients expected and in fact demanded "active" medical

---

[24]Ibid.,177.
[25]Ibid.,185.
[26]Charles E. Rosenberg, "The Therapeutic Revolution: Medicine, Meaning, and Social Change in Nineteenth-Century America," *Perspectives in Biology and Medicine* 20 (1977): 485–506. For a discussion of "social efficacy," see Rosenberg, *Our Present Complaint. American Medicine, Then and Now* (Baltimore: Johns Hopkins University Press, 2007), 9–10.

treatment (a reality not entirely historical). The public, as Holmes put it, "insists on being poisoned. Somebody buys all the quack medicines that build palaces for the mushroom, say rather, the toadstool millionaires."[27] Lay people had assimilated and come to depend on outmoded theories drawn from previous centuries; they were co-conspirators in their own mistreatment. "A French patient complains that his blood heats him, and expects his doctor to bleed him. An English or American one says he is bilious, and will not be easy without a dose of calomel."[28] How was the physician to respond? Holmes was particularly vexed by what he referred to as "the detestable old superstitious presumption in favor of whatever is nauseous and noxious as being good for the sick."[29]

It is not surprising that homeopathy was such an object of discussion and contempt for Holmes and his generational colleagues in the "regular" medical profession. It was, of course, a source of competition in a world of sharp elbows and intense competition for a limited number of paying patients. Holmes himself reminded Harvard medical graduates in 1858 of the professional commandment: *"Though shalt not covet thy neighbor's patients."*[30] Equally significant, homeopathy undercut the legitimacy of mainstream practice in a more fundamental yet paradoxical way. Homeopathy's success clearly depended on "imagination," what might today be called the placebo effect (since homeopathic drugs were, it seemed to regulars, ludicrously diluted). "So long as the body is affected through the mind," as Holmes summed up this consensus, "no audacious device, even of the most manifestly dishonest character, can fail of producing occasional good to those who yield it an implicit or even a partial faith."[31] Every physi-

---

[27]Holmes, "Currents and Counter-Currents," 186. Holmes's acid phrase provided the title for a classic study of the field: James Harvey Young, *The Toadstool Millionaires. A Social History of Patent Medicines in America before Federal Regulation* (Princeton: Princeton University Press, 1961).

[28]Holmes, "Currents and Counter-Currents," 188.

[29]Ibid. Holmes also believed that one of homeopathy's major appeals was its mild therapeutics—especially with children. "You may depend upon it," Holmes argued, "that half the success of Homœopathy is due to the sweet peace it has brought into the nursery. Between the gurgling down of loathsome mixtures and the saccharine deliquescence of a minute globule, what tender mother could for a moment hesitate?" In Holmes, "Valedictory Address," 405.

[30]Ibid., 398.

[31]Holmes, "Homœopathy and its Kindred Delusions," 2. Homeopathy might even be thought of as being useful, Holmes suggested, in teaching "us a lesson of the healing faculty of Nature." (In Holmes, "Preface," *Currents and Counter-Currents in Medical Science*, viii.)

cian accepted the reality of such mind-body interactions, but of course they could not be the legitimating basis for a profession that prided itself on learning and access to effective therapies. Physicians could hardly deny the role of faith or imagination in helping patients heal—but they could not rest too visibly on that assumption. The psychological effects of medical practice had to remain a kind of background noise, rather than signal, in the rational work of healing. Otherwise there would be no difference between the homeopath or other quack and the regularly educated physician.

Science increasingly seemed the key to that necessary differentiation; medicine could not be a species of faith healing. "We who are on the side of 'Nature,'" Holmes contended, "please ourselves with the idea that we are in the great current in which the true intelligence of the time is moving." Medicine must not lag behind the sciences, but should ideally "be at length brought fully to share, if not lead, the great wave of knowledge which rolls with the tides that circle the globe."[32] Therapeutics might change, with each generation renewed and recast. But it would not, Holmes argued, be random change. Science would come ever closer to an understanding of the natural world—even if the mid-nineteenth century was still in what Holmes called a "semi-barbarian" state.[33] Pathological anatomy, the achromatic microscope's insights, the growing knowledge provided by chemistry all pointed to a cumulative understanding of the body in health and disease—and thus an increasingly rational therapeutics. The "solemn skepticism of science" would provide an ever-more abundant stream of insights.[34] Although the growth of scientific knowledge was unpredictable, it was cumulative and necessarily in the direction of greater understanding and

---

[32]Holmes, "Currents and Counter-Currents," 183.

[33]Holmes, "Some More Recent Views on Homœopathy," 185.

[34]This phrase is taken from a particularly revealing passage: "These new tables of the law," Holmes observed, "placed in the hands of the geologist by the same living God who spoke from Sinai to the Israelites of old, have remodeled the beliefs of half the civilized world. The solemn skepticism of science has replaced the sneering doubts of witty philosophers. The more positive knowledge we gain, the more we incline to question all that has been received without absolute proof." In Holmes, "Currents and Counter-Currents," 180–1. Holmes sought to avoid a crude mechanism by routinely invoking the conventional language of natural theology; he was happy to cede ultimate if undefined power to a great Artificer: "To fear science or knowledge, lest it disturb our old beliefs, is to fear the influx of the Divine wisdom into the souls of our fellow-men; for what is science but the piecemeal *revelation*—uncovering—of the plan of creation, by the agency of those chosen prophets of nature whom God has illuminated from the central light of truth for that single purpose." In Holmes, "Border Lines of Knowledge," 251.

medicine would ultimately benefit in terms of clinical efficacy and social legit-imacy.[35] Science had its martyrs in Bruno and Servetus, its heroic innovators in Harvey and Newton, but they had—as many scores of medical school commencements and valedictory addresses emphasized—not struggled and died in vain.

[35]"Who can tell what mysteries are ready to burst into the flame of demonstration with the chance spark of any day of scientific labor?" In Holmes, "Position and Prospects of the Medical Student," 288.

Doctor Holmes

The Life in Conversation

PETER GIBIAN

"This business of conversation is a very serious matter."
—Oliver Wendell Holmes,
The Autocrat of the Breakfast-Table (1858)

A TINY, HYPERACTIVE, AND HYPER-LOQUACIOUS bundle of energy, Doctor Holmes wanted to play all the parts. His life (1809–1894) spanned most of the nineteenth century, and for much of that time he was recognized by his contemporaries as a national character, even a national institution. Preeminent in American medicine as well as in American literature, he was somehow able to combine the stances of grave scientist and light humorist, Sage and Jester, traditionalist and progressive, Voice of Reason and confirmed ironist. Crusading all his life against emerging specialization, the generalist Holmes produced lectures, essays, and poems that placed him at the center of national debates in a surprising range of fields: theology, psychology, and natural science, as well as medicine and literature. But it is clear that a key connecting thread, linking all of Doctor Holmes's multiple professional activities and speaking roles, his diverse forms of scientific and literary work, and his active social life, was always his fundamental interest in the workings of "conversation."

HOLMES'S CULTURE OF CONVERSATION:
CONVERSATION AND CRITICAL ANALYSIS

Holmes thus became both the best model and the best analyst of one of the dynamic activities most central to nineteenth-century social, intellectual, and literary life: intimate, interactive talk. When we think of eras defined by their conversation, we most commonly call up visions of the salons of eighteenth-century France or the coffee-houses of eighteenth-century England. But the mid-nineteenth century was America's "Age of Conversation." This was the era of the elite salon and the working-class saloon; of the drawing-room and the firemen's hall; of the literary society and the voluntary association; of metropolitan conversation groups on the celebrated model of the Saturday Club; of organized, solemn Public Conversations guided by professional conversationalists like Margaret Fuller and Bronson Alcott; and of a popular craze for print versions of the table-talk of great minds. And this was, after all, a culture that epitomized many of its ideals in the image of the Victorian parlor. Aptly named from the French—for *parler*—the "parlor," designed as a speech-space in the private home, became a necessary element in even very modest domestic designs of the mid-century. Even small mid-century towns with any pretensions also had their reading circles, tea tables, reform groups, or Shakespeare Clubs. Meeting and talking with others, then, became not only a fundamental aspect of everyday private life but also a dynamic central to the workings of a number of public activities at the heart of civil society.

A number of contemporary American authors, artists, and culture critics took the talk forms emerging in the era as crucial barometers of the dynamics of mid-century American life. And if one of the best ways in to the spirit of a culture is through its conversation, certainly one of the best ways in to the conversation of the mid-century household, club, boardinghouse, schoolroom, Lyceum, or doctor's office is through the life and writings of Doctor Holmes. Widely celebrated as one of the nation's most brilliant talkers, and recognized internationally for his experiments in conversational writing, the Doctor also emerged as one of the era's leading theorists of the implications of dialogue form, and one of the most probing analysts of conversational dynamics. For Holmes-the-virtuoso-talker, the parlor was a favorite stage for impromptu performances; for Holmes-the-scientist, it could serve as his laboratory for verbal experiments in a sort of "sentimental physics." Holmes-the-poet loved to play out the intoxicating dance of metaphor, but Holmes-the-psychologist would then want to study the patterns of such mental movements in conversation, to try to explain the "associations" between ideas or between people, the mechanical workings of our "trains" of thought or "currents" of feeling. For the Doctor, conversation became both a prime site and a prime vehicle for critical analysis.

Conversation and the Clinical Revolution in Medicine: "Freedom of Discussion"

The mid-century's best-known doctor, Holmes was one of the fathers of modern American medicine. A professor at and dean of the Harvard Medical School, and a major advocate of the revolutionary shift to Parisian "clinical" methods in North America, Doctor Holmes addressed and educated his countrymen as the leading spokesman for the medical field at a crucial transitional period in its development. But while he was a key promoter of the "clinical" revolution that worked to clear away the errors and myths of an earlier "heroic" medicine, he was also associated with many major developments—such as germ theory, antisepsis, and anesthesia—that would later lead beyond the impasse of the clinical method's "therapeutic nihilism," making possible key advances in nineteenth- and twentieth-century medical treatment.

Beginning two years of medical study in Paris in 1833, Holmes was among the first Americans to participate in the fervent theoretical debates that led to the birth of the "clinical method." As a follower of the modest clinician Pierre-Charles-Alexandre Louis, Holmes listened with great skepticism to the bombastic lectures of François Broussais, a leading representative of the older "heroic" medicine, which had posited visionary, holistic, monistic systems in diagnosis, usually advocating one cause and one cure for all ailments, and which then attempted to balance systemic tensions or humors through radical interventions such as purging, bleeding, or sweating (Broussais himself was convinced that all disease was a version of gastroenteritis, and his practice featured a lavish use of curative leeches). The party of Louis urged a paradigm shift, moving away from such extremely generalized systematic visions to an extremely localized pathology, focusing closely on particular diseases and particular parts of the body. But the real thrust of their teaching was negative. Stressing the need for careful physiological observation (using percussion, the stethoscope, and later the microscope and regularized autopsy), laboratory testing, and comprehensive numerical evaluation of the effectiveness of cures based on large samplings of patient histories at the new clinical research hospitals, the clinicians highlighted the imperfections in present diagnoses and therapy, frankly admitting that doctors often worked in ignorance. Their new studies pointed up Broussais's reliance on myth, superstition, and subjectivity, uncovering the cruelty of an insistence on purgative methods that were now proven to have no positive effects. This rational debunking of long-held medical myths, with an accompanying stress on the limits of medical knowledge and power, led to a profound pessimism about all current therapies and medical arts, and warnings about the dangers of hubris in "heroic" doctors— defining a new vision of "therapeutic skepticism" that could be caricatured, in the period, as "therapeutic nihilism."

In his role as America's leading spokesman for this "clinical" vision (or what he termed the "Nature-trusting heresy"), the Doctor took up the stance of "therapeutic skepticism," applying it very broadly not only in his medical work but in many other areas of his expanding interests. And certainly this unsettling skepticism becomes the ground and goal of Holmes's work in the verbal realm—fundamental to his theory and practice of critical, analytical conversation. But the young man Calvinists would call a "moral parricide" for the way he abandoned his father's theology first used his Parisian clinical training to join in the general revolt against one of the leading figures of the Revolutionary generation and one of the Founding Fathers of American medicine: Doctor Benjamin Rush. America's Broussais, a symbol of Enlightenment self-confidence, Rush had declared that there is but one disease and one type of treatment; every malady was traceable to an excess or lack of nervous stimulation, and, since Rush distrusted natural powers of healing, each problem should then be treated through special, sudden actions by a heroic doctor—usually with a single massive purging of blood. Playing maliciously on the eminent doctor's name, Holmes would suggest that Rush's obsession with nervous pressures could be traced to the "rush" of his own high-pressured blood and to the "rushing" of a Revolutionary spirit in the air—which then led him to "rush" into intervention before he knew what he was doing.[1]

In other medical writings, too, the Doctor's intentionally provocative pronouncements were meant to spark debate, and worked to place him at the active center of highly charged, polarized conversations within the medical community: "The history of medicine [is to a] great . . . extent a record of self-delusion"; or "I firmly believe that if the whole materia medica, *as now used*, could be sunk to the bottom of the sea, it would be all the better for mankind,—and all the worse for the fishes."[2] Even in medicine,

---

[1]Holmes's most extended discussion of Rush comes in "Currents and Counter-Currents in Medical Science [1860]," in *Medical Essays, 1842–1882* [The Works of Oliver Wendell Holmes, Standard Library Edition, Volume IX] (Boston: Houghton, Mifflin and Company, 1892), 192–3.

[2]Holmes, *A Mortal Antipathy* [The Works of Oliver Wendell Holmes, Standard Library Edition, Volume VII] (Boston: Houghton, Mifflin and Company, 1892 [1885]), 172; "Currents and Countercurrents," 203.

then, Holmes was an advocate of conversation. His central purpose was to promote the freedom of discussion that might open up a healthy questioning of old systems and remedies and perhaps also pave the way for the emergence of the new. Always testing for telling responses, Holmes analyzed the verbal resistances to his interventions in these debates the way a medical "percussionist," or later a psychoanalyst, would. During one argument with Medical Society members, for example, he offered a physician's diagnosis of the pulses, pressures, and reflexive responses revealed through the dynamic of dialogue: "A loud outcry at a slight touch reveals a weak spot in a profession, as well as a patient."[3]

And the Doctor's own medical writings are often surprisingly dialogical themselves, alternating between specialized medical discourse and a highly literary language. "The Contagiousness of Puerperal Fever" (1843) was written in the hope that it would announce Holmes's entrance as a major voice in American medicine. But it was highly controversial in its day, triggering virulent counterattacks from the medical establishment for its overall message—which is directly in the line of a French "clinical" vision. Here again, Holmes's unusually strong, polemical assertions are framed as provocations to dialogue, necessary to open up a free, rational "exchange of opinions" in a profession stubbornly resistant to critical thought, and to counter the harsh words of dogmatic believers that "might well put a stop to all scientific discussions."[4] He urges physicians to talk, and to think, before they act. Challenging the medical profession and the authority of doctors, Holmes's essay concludes that the infection of childbed fever had its source not in the affected women themselves but in "heroic" male physicians (and some nurses and midwives), whose unconsidered movements within the hospital or between cases—rushing directly from the sick chamber of a woman with puerperal fever to the birth chamber of a woman in labor, or even from performing a puerperal fever autopsy to assisting at a birth, without changing their clothes, replacing or sterilizing their medical tools, or washing their hands—had in fact made them carriers of the contagion they meant to cure. This early study anticipates Pasteur's germ theory by over fifteen years and Lister's stress on sterilization and antisepsis by a quarter century. Surprisingly, though, Holmes arrives at these speculative, breakthrough insights not by rigorously adhering to a "clinical" language and logic but by managing the collisions of discourse in a strange, hybrid text. The essay is fascinating for the way in which the

---

[3]Holmes, "Preface," *Medical Essays, 1842–1882*, vii–viii.
[4]Holmes, "The Contagiousness of Puerperal Fever [1843, 1855]," in *Medical Essays, 1842–1882*, 110.

doctor/writer Holmes here combines the neutral, rational, abstract, statistical language of an emerging modern medicine with impassioned, sentimental, imagistic literary language, turning to tones of stirring myth and melodrama to drive home his main point: doctors themselves, blind to their own ignorance, have in these cases served as dark "ministers of evil," committing not only "irreparable errors" but a "crime," bringing "heartbreaking calamity" and death to what should be the scene of birth, and poisoning the purity of innumerable chambers of sacred maternity.[5]

As Freud did, Holmes moved in his later medical career from neurophysiological approaches to verbal and psychological ones, with an increasing emphasis on dialogic interactions between doctors and patients—speculating on the placebo effect, on therapeutic uses of humor and laughter, and on the importance of counseling, nursing, and bedside manner. Stressing microscopically intense monitoring both of a patient's bodily dynamics and of the pulses and image patterns in the patient's verbal exchanges with the physician, Holmes developed an experimental, conversational model for diagnosis, caring, and curing that anticipates the Freudian "talking cure" and is still suggestive to medical explorers today. Here the Doctor's work begins to verge on the new speculative psychology, and his most influential writings as a psychologist also reflect his grounding in the dynamics of talk. Studying the power of subconscious associations to shape or direct streams of consciousness in what he called "the underground workshop of thought,"[6] he introduced and explored notions of multiple personality, or of multi-voiced and multi-layered consciousness, becoming a prime theorist of the divided self (or of what his student William James would later term the "social self"), defining all mental process as an internal conversation.

From Social Conversation to Dialogic Writing: A Carnival of Talk

At the same time, Holmes earned a preeminent place among American literary figures for his work in a variety of verbal forms—from poetry, prose, and public speaking to what was perhaps his main expressive mode: witty, interactive social conversation. With his motto, "Every man his own

---

[5] Ibid., 108, 167–9.
[6] Oliver Wendell Holmes, "Mechanism in Thought and Morals [1870]" in *Pages from an Old Volume of Life* [The Works of Oliver Wendell Holmes, Standard Library Edition, Volume VIII] (Boston: Houghton, Mifflin and Company, 1892), 278.

Boswell,"[7] he made clear his desire to become the Doctor Johnson of America—a figure whose blunt or brilliantly witty off-the-cuff opinions would form the talk of the town and of the nation. This sense of life as an ongoing verbal performance—a carnival of talk—pervaded all of Holmes's public activities. In an era that placed a special value on spoken expression and modes of oral performance, Holmes was much in demand as a traveling public speaker, emerging as the most celebrated after-dinner toastmaster and versifier in his day. He was also one of the trail-blazers in opening up the lyceum lecture circuit at mid-century, becoming in that venue both widely popular as one of the first comic lecturers and widely controversial as a proselytizing, scientific Voice of Reason. Then, with a bustling social life centered around verbal exchanges in drawing rooms, salons, boarding-houses, and elite clubs, he came to be widely celebrated as the most brilliant conversationalist in America's "Age of Conversation." This view of Holmes was epitomized by his role as a presiding figure at Boston's renowned Saturday Club—where his sense of talk defined the verbal environment for those important monthly conversation meetings that brought together authors such as Ralph Waldo Emerson, Nathaniel Hawthorne, Henry Wadsworth Longfellow, James Russell Lowell, John Greenleaf Whittier, Henry James Sr., and Richard Henry Dana Jr.; scientists such as Louis Agassiz and Asa Gray; historians and scholars such as Francis Parkman, Charles Eliot Norton, William Prescott, and John Lathrop Motley; and many other prominent figures in business, politics, law, science, and intellectual life.

Holmes's best writing developed out of his explorations of talk form. Print versions of the light, elegant occasional verse he had performed at banquets and public functions brought him his first wide recognition as an author—and he eventually produced some four hundred such works. But Holmes also became known as one of the Fireside Poets for a series of more serious poems memorized by generations of schoolchildren—including "Old Ironsides" (1830), which gave voice to early stirrings of nationalist fervor; "The Chambered Nautilus" (1858), a haunting meditation on the ongoing motions of intellectual progress; and "The Deacon's Masterpiece: or The Wonderful 'One-Hoss-Shay'" (1858), a humorous romp that reduces Calvinist dogma to absurdity. Turning to prose fiction in later years, Holmes experimented with an early form of literary naturalism in a series

---

[7]Oliver Wendell Holmes, *The Autocrat of the Breakfast-Table* [The Works of Oliver Wendell Holmes, Standard Library Edition, Volume I] (Boston: Houghton, Mifflin and Company, 1892 [1858]), title page.

of what he called "medicated novels"—*Elsie Venner* (1861), *The Guardian Angel* (1867), and *A Mortal Antipathy* (1885). Combining his table-talk wit and personae with aspects of the clinical case history, these novels follow a series of anomalous life stories (involving multiple personalities, repetition compulsions, trauma-induced mental blocks, paralyzing erotic "antipathies," and so on) that pose severe problems of diagnosis for the central doctor/psychologist figures in each plot, raising questions about psychological and physiological determinism and generally challenging conventional thinking about the "normal." Although the physiological causes of the problems explored in these "medicated novels" make them appear incurable and intractable, in each case the main opening for diagnosis or therapy comes through the operations of a semi-confessional "talking exam" with one of Holmes's doctor figures. In *Elsie Venner*, for example, Elsie's inhuman coldness and her snake-like lisp emerge primarily as symptoms of a fundamental defect in her ability to speak: we are told that she has "never shaped her inner life in words" so that her emotion might "open the gate for itself into the great community of human affections." As Sophy, her nanny and companion, explains: "she kin' o' got the way o' not talkin' much." So the only hope is that perhaps the arrival at her bedside of the young, communicative Bernard, or the wise, sympathetic Doctor Kittredge, or later the nurse-like Helen, might draw Elsie out into some potentially cathartic conversational expression.[8]

THE *ATLANTIC* AND THE *AUTOCRAT*: THE CULTURAL WORK OF CONVERSATION

Certainly, though, Holmes's works of written table-talk remain his most important and still-vital verbal productions. The first of these works, *The Autocrat of the Breakfast-Table*, an utterly distinctive, landmark work of American non-fiction prose, was born out of the brilliant talk at a series of Boston dinner meetings in 1857. These dinners brought together a constellation of the most eminent representatives of the sudden mid-nineteenth-century "renaissance" of New England literature and culture—Emerson, Longfellow, Lowell, Motley, and Holmes, among others—to discuss the founding of an ambitious new journal. Finally, Lowell agreed to serve as editor if Holmes would sign on as the magazine's first regular contributor, and the result was the formation of *The Atlantic Monthly*, an enduring and

---

[8]Oliver Wendell Holmes, *Elsie Venner* [The Works of Oliver Wendell Holmes, Standard Library Edition, Volume V] (Boston: Houghton, Mifflin and Company, 1892 [1861]), 341–2, 419, 433.

extremely influential new organ for the development and promotion of American thought and writing—a journal that would serve as the nation's prime intellectual forum for many decades to come. The *Atlantic's* godfather, Doctor Holmes gave it its name and then also contributed to each issue the "breakfast-table" essay—beginning with the twelve monthly installments of *The Autocrat of the Breakfast-Table* for 1857–58—which quickly became the journal's most recognized feature, despite the contributions of such writers as Emerson, Longfellow, Hawthorne, Whittier, and Harriet Beecher Stowe. These enormously popular columns, that both recorded and shaped the talk of the town for a large public, also transformed Holmes's life—giving the dilettante doctor-writer his sobriquet, the "Autocrat," and making him a household name both in England and in the United States for more than a century.

The successful founding of the *Atlantic* seems to have confirmed Holmes in shifting his primary focus from medicine to literature. Drawing upon all of his past experiences in social talk at salons and clubs and lyceums, he launched himself seriously into writing by committing himself to an extended series of humorous essays presented as multi-voiced, interruptive conversations taking place among diverse characters gathered around a boardinghouse breakfast-table: after *The Autocrat* (1858) came *The Professor at the Breakfast-Table* (1860), *The Poet at the Breakfast-Table* (1872), and, near the end of his life, *Over the Teacups* (1891). Framing his "talk of the town" opinion columns as a series of quasi-theatrical spoken dialogues and encounters, and including verse interludes as well as some novelistic plotting in the relations between the speaking characters, Holmes transformed the English essay, giving it a new, dramatic, and dynamic rhetorical form.

Rooted in the table-talk of the elite dinner clubs or common boardinghouses of nineteenth-century America, just as the early essays of Joseph Addison and Sir Richard Steele had been rooted in the coffeehouse discussions of eighteenth-century England, Holmes's essays are less a form for lyrical reflection or sequential argument than a social experiment, a verbal laboratory for studies of the volatile "associations" between diverse people and diverse ideas. A spirit of "carnival" is central to this vision of written conversation. The Doctor often reminds us that he was born amidst the exploding noise and color of Cambridge's academic carnival (a multi-day celebration of graduation and the release from school); his sense of writing as riotous wordplay was then crucially formed by what he experienced as the "festive indulgences and gay license" of the "revelries" among other "young bacchanalians" in student groups like Harvard's Hasty Pudding Club (where mock debates, burlesque trials, and wildly costumed travesties

of solemn speeches burst apart the "sober habits" of his Calvinist upbring-
ing).[9] And Holmes's own written conversations take their place in a long
line of "dialogic" writing (analyzed most notably by Mikhail Bakhtin) that
developed out of thousand-year-old folk traditions of seasonal "carnival"—
public rituals of holiday feasting, masquerading, and merry-making in which
revelers act out a temporary release from the constraints of the current
order, turning the conventional world upside down through a saturnalian
logic that brings a general suspension of social and intellectual hierarchies.
Translating the dynamics of street saturnalia into literary form, writings
in the "carnivalesque" mode (epitomized in the bawdy, learned humor of
one of Doctor Holmes's main models—the doctor/writer François
Rabelais) develop as parodic versions of the philosophical dialogue, playing
out bloodless struggles among a wild mix of competing voices.[10] But
Holmes, in staging breakfast-table debates among a wide range of uncom-
prehending strangers speaking for divergent ideologies in divergent languages, presented his readers with a carnivalesque festival of verbal
pyrotechnics and comic misunderstandings that also developed as a minia-
turized, caricatural model of the national conversation in these troubled,
divisive years just before the Civil War. These debates thus played out the
rational and irrational forces shaping public opinion in this period, and made
possible some detached reflection on the explosive, interruptive, and multi-
voiced dynamics of the "public sphere" in mid-nineteenth-century America.

Just two years after Walt Whitman's "Song of Myself" (1855) had
introduced his giant Self as a public site in which to gather up the nation's
many languages, Holmes in the *Autocrat* introduced his giant Breakfast-
Table as the utopian site for a potential "conversation of the culture."
Though different in so many ways, both Whitman and Holmes, in working
to translate interactive social talk into written form, were responding to a
felt need to try to counter the ominous breakdown in mid-century discussions and debates by building texts that could work as print simulacra of an
ideal public sphere. This made it possible for readers to imagine themselves to be entering a national arena for dialogue—a dialogue that perhaps could only be realized through the mediation of a written, printed,
fictional construct. In an increasingly fragmented and privatized society,
Holmes's print replicas of Saturday Club table-talk generated a sense of
loyal fellowship and intimacy among a huge and diverse readership. Iso-

[9]Oliver Wendell Holmes, "The Autobiographical Notes," in John T. Morse, Jr., *Life and Letters of Oliver Wendell Holmes* (Boston: Houghton Mifflin, 1897), 1: 50–1.
[10]Mikhail Bakhtin, *Problems of Dostoevsky's Poetics*, trans. R. W. Rotsel (New York: Ardis, 1973), 88, 100–6; and Bakhtin, *Rabelais and His World*, trans. Helene Iswolsky (Cambridge: M.I.T. Press, 1968), 4–14.

lated citizens and alienated writers would have been especially receptive to this verbal mode that seems to create its own community, picturing speakers and readers in a close social relation—conversing easily as members of the same family or of the same convivial, urbane, metropolitan club.

But Holmes's breakfast-table is far from a model of easy cultural coherence. "I was just going to say, when I was interrupted . . ."—the famous first phrase in the first installment of *The Autocrat of the Breakfast-Table*—focuses our attention on the talk element most fundamental to his vision of conversational form: the dynamic moment of "interruption" that allows one speaker to take the floor from another and so makes possible constant changes of voice, tone, and topic.[11] Even the title of *The Autocrat of the Breakfast-Table* foregrounds a sense of conversation as an ongoing struggle between urges to "autocratic" monologism and periodic bursts of revolutionary interruption. Here the classic image of totalizing Old World authority—the Autocrat—meets the era's prime symbol of democratic decentralization: the American boardinghouse or hotel. And the cap is that even in this reduced realm—of just one small table—no Autocrat can hold much sway. At every turn in Holmes's table talk, the efforts of any figure of moral authority—whether the bluntly opinionated Autocrat, the Professor, the Master, or, in the 1880s, the Dictator—to monopolize the conversation, to define its terms or its tastes, to impose Robert's Rules of Order on its debates, or in any way to assert an ominously integrative centralizing power, will always soon be unsettled by explosive outbursts from the Babel of surrounding boardinghouse voices. Miming a sort of perpetual revolution, these conversations give the floor to a succession of "carnival kings"—not only to the title characters but also to the many more minor players speaking for the positions and experiences of diverse classes, genders, ages, regions, specialized professions, political factions, educational backgrounds, and so on. Each develops his or her own hobby-horse in an over-elaborate personal prose only to be quickly mocked and dethroned by the rabble constantly waiting on the fringes to interrupt.

While the *Autocrat* may then reflect a strongly felt desire for some unifying authority, it also speaks forcefully for antebellum America's central ambivalence to such authority. For Holmes, the literary conversation does not operate simply as a *tour de force* of cultural centralization, with a Boston Brahmin from the metropolis through his definition of "civility" subtly controlling and judging all peripheral languages. Rather, the conversation opens up as an arena of carnivalesque vocal diversity and of sometimes

---

[11]Holmes, *Autocrat of the Breakfast-Table*, 1.

explosive struggles for power. And though in the retrospective vision of the self-consciously "modern" twentieth century Holmes often came to be viewed as a social and cultural conservative, the dynamics of his character-istic talk form move in the opposite direction—opening the dogmas, cer-tainties, and habits of thought of the old authorities to a barrage of questions and impolite interruptions. Instead of epitomizing a monolithic vision of the mid-century cultural ideal—serving as the port of entry guiding read-ers into a newly prescribed bourgeois, polite "parlor culture"—conversa-tion for Holmes is built upon dialogical breaks, changes in voice and perspective, that take one out of the limits of one's provincial language and home, forcing recognition of the multiplicity of cultures, and also serving as a site for possible meetings between these cultures.

CONVERSATION AND COSMOPOLITANISM

Many of Holmes's dialogues turn on the question of provincialism. To be sure, his Autocrat voice often speaks as the epitome of regional chauvin-ism, having given Boston its still-current title as "Hub" of the universe, and having named and defined the "Brahmin caste" of intellectuals so often associated with that New England center. But the turns of talk at the breakfast-table finally explode that impulse, working to break down the bar-riers of atomistic individualism, social hierarchy, or local pride. The boos-terish slogan hailing Boston State-House as "the hub of the solar system," for example, is actually voiced by the deformed character Little Boston. Hardly an unambiguous defender of local pride, Little Boston, with his "whims and local prejudices," becomes a topic of study for many other speakers at the breakfast-table. And his mysterious dwarfism is finally diag-nosed by the Professor as the fatal, physiological result of a pathological provincialism: "It dwarfs the mind, I think, to feed it on any localism. The full stature of manhood is shriveled—."[12] The turns of Holmes's written table-talk are meant, then, to work like a tire-iron, helping to pry people out of their spherical self-involvement and expand their horizons. And Holmes's breakfast-table came to embody for many readers not localism but widely-shared national aspirations to sociability, civility, and a cos-mopolitan openness. Always the contrarian working in dialogic opposition to dominant trends in the era of the Common Man, the Autocrat advocates metropolitan urbanity in the face of contemporary rural provincialism;

---

[12]Holmes, *Autocrat of the Breakfast-Table*, 125; Oliver Wendell Holmes, *The Professor at the Breakfast-Table* [The Works of Oliver Wendell Holmes, Standard Library Edition, Volume II] (Boston: Houghton, Mifflin and Company, 1892 [1859]), 87, 310.

celebrates clubs and talk groups ("Mutual Admiration Societies") as the foundations of a vital culture; playfully mocks the very idea of the "self-made" man; and defends intellectual reflection as a counter to the pragmatic business values of a Bowie-knife civilization or to fixed conceptions of fact and truth based in law or hard science.

This is where Holmes's notion of the Boston Brahmin comes into play. When the "Brahmin Caste of New England" is first introduced and defined by Holmes, in the first chapter of *Elsie Venner*, his vision is far from the stereotype of "bloated aristocracy" that it would become for later generations. Clearly disengaged from any connections to economic, political, or social power, and making no claims to worldly leadership or aristocratic rule, his "Brahmin caste" is an "academic class," a community of "scholars," always pale-faced, white-linened, and usually physically weak, defined by book-learning and intellect alone. The realm of Holmes's Brahmin is the realm of reflective talk—the play of ideas in the back-and-forth, anti-foundational movements of free conversation. In *Elsie Venner*, the impoverished Bernard proves himself a Brahmin by his gift for conversation. This doctor-confessor-psychologist hero does not speak just a single genteel language in a single tone; he is marked by a special ability to understand a wide variety of professional and regional idioms, to be able to modulate his own language so as to engage easily with a range of interlocutors, and so to serve as a sort of moderator attempting to mediate among the diverse dialects of limited, provincial speakers. Against the backdrop of a deeply fragmented rural scene—a body politic divided by wars among social classes, churches, and chauvinistic boosters of each locality—Bernard enters to suggest the ideal alternative possibility of a cosmopolitan public man, without local or class or family affiliations, able to move comfortably among diverse strangers.

And Bernard's mentor, Doctor Kittredge, emerges as a doctor-talker epitomizing this conversational ideal. A sort of secular priest, Kittredge has apparently become a rival or replacement for area churchmen through his verbal ministry to townspeople of every race and rank—even in fact serving as an intimate minister to the ministers in a series of heartfelt dialogues with the heads of the local religious sects. In these one-on-one interviews (or interactions) between the area's various "doctors"—heads of the Catholic, orthodox Calvinist, and liberal Protestant churches, as well as Doctor Kittredge—the process of talk reveals that no beliefs are fixed, static, or final: each of the churchmen is seen to be in fact deeply uncertain, continually engaged in an anxious internal dialogue about his faith but unable to admit it. Several of these speculative, interpenetrative conversations then develop as experiences of conversion as each talker is led to change his initial position, or even to exchange positions with his inter-locutor: the Calvinist reveals his secular, humanitarian leanings; the Uni-tarian reveals his innermost desire for the security of Catholic ritual; and Kittredge himself reveals that in many ways his medical training has led him to Calvinist stances regarding the over-determining power of innate, hereditary, physiological predispositions to certain emotional or spiritual problems. From this perspective, those who remain set in their unchange-able beliefs are seen as weak or childish. By contrast, the speculative, Brah-min intellectuals who are at the "front ranks of thought" break away from the "spiritual dictatorship" of the "propagandist ready with his bundle of finalities," and are seen as voyagers who dare to depart from protected ports for the "free thought and free speech" that opens up through ongo-ing, ever-changing, oceanic talk.[13]

DIALOGUE VS. DOGMA: A CONVERSATIONAL APPROACH TO TRUTH

A main target of much of the talk at Holmes's breakfast-table is the rigid dogma of Calvinism, which the Autocrat and the Professor critique just as the Doctor himself challenged the rigid dogma of fixed "systems" of med-ical belief. In theology as in medicine, Holmes always positions himself in opposition to such systematic, universalizing visions. Just as he raised skeptical questions about the "rush" to diagnosis and heroic therapy in eighteenth-century medicine, so he questions the rush to judgment in the-ology, or in law. But the specific theological opposition to Calvinist doc-trine comes to define the general dynamics of Holmes's talk form. The light, airy verbal fireworks of humor here erupt in explosive opposition to antebellum forces of theological, scientific, and literary gravity, promoting the Rise of Man against a Calvinist stress on man's original Fall, centrifu-gal movements of "levitation" against the downward-tending, centripetal force stressed in science based on Newton's law of gravitation, and Shandyan digressiveness against a literary decorum of plain directness. (Along the same lines, the Doctor's medical writings promote the thera-peutic values of lightness, laughter, sociability, play, recreation, and exer-cise against the heavy weight of a Puritan moral seriousness and solemnity seen to be debilitating to natural life-forces.) If a dogmatic Calvinist stress on the Fall of Man is seen to permeate American culture, blocking spiritual development, intellectual progress, emotional growth, and even physical

---

[13]Holmes, *Elsie Venner*, 252–4, 417.

health, Holmes's speakers see the tendency of the talk at their breakfast-table talk as working in opposition to that—and in the process helping to break up all monological or monolithic notions of a single or final Truth.

Of course, Holmes's Autocrat is himself full of strong, bluntly expressed opinions. His pronouncements, though, tend to work not as *doxa* but as *paradoxa:* always playing with and against received, majority opinion, drawing it out, exposing its contradictions, turning it back on itself for some critical self-reflection. His startling, exaggerated opinions are intended to unsettle matters rather than to settle them, to start conversation rather than to stop it. And much of the Autocrat's talk is devoted to defending his realm of speculative dialogue from the conversational bullies who come toting the legalistic "facts" that are "intended to stop all debate, like the previous question in the General Court."[14] The site of freewheeling verbal improvisation and interaction seems always to be surrounded by hordes of such fact-bearers, who tend to turn talking into fighting: "The men of facts wait their turn [during a discussion] in grim silence, with that slight tension about the nostrils which the consciousness of carrying a 'settler' in the form of a fact or a revolver gives the individual thus armed."[15] The Autocrat utters his decrees against "facts" in talk full of the witty, multileveled "embellishments" of simile and metaphor sure to befuddle any Royal Society literalist:

> All generous minds have a horror of what are commonly called "facts." They are the brute beasts of the intellectual domain. Who does not know fellows that always have an ill-conditioned fact or two which they lead after them into decent company like so many bull-dogs, ready to let them slip at every ingenious suggestion, or convenient generalization, or pleasant fancy? I allow no "facts" at this table. What! Because bread is good and wholesome, and necessary and nourishing, shall you thrust a crumb into my windpipe while I am talking? Do not these muscles of mine represent a hundred loaves of bread? And is not my thought the abstract of ten thousand of these crumbs of truth with which you would choke off my speech?[16]

And he is always concerned, in defining the arena of talk at his breakfast-table, to differentiate conversational from absolute truth:

> Some persons seem to think that absolute truth, in the form of rigidly stated propositions, is all that conversation admits. . . . [But] conversation must have its partial truths, its embellished truths, its exaggerated

---

[14]Holmes, *Autocrat of the Breakfast-Table*, 28.
[15]Ibid., 142.
[16]Ibid., 5.

truths. . . . One man who is a little too literal can spoil the talk of a whole tableful of men of *esprit*.[17]

Indeed, the Autocrat often warns readers not to take his own axioms too literally, as *doxa* to be applied on any occasion: "The above remark must be conditioned and qualified for the vulgar mind. . . . The speaker disclaims all responsibility for its abuse in incompetent hands."[18]

Again and again, at Holmes' table, the singular Truth of theological dogma, the scientific fact, or the legal proposition confronts the multiple truths of conversational process. In a rising passage describing his highest ambitions for his own talk-based works, he brings us back to the carnival roots of all dialogues, to the "glorious license" of the Dionysiac symposium. Challenging the idea that any static, axiomatic "Truth" can stand outside of this festival intercourse, he hopes to return philosophy to its setting as a party, or a three-ring circus: "This truly intellectual banquet," says the Autocrat,

> calls upon Truth, majestic virgin! to get down from her pedestal and drop her academic poses, and take a festive garland and the vacant place on the *medius lectus*,—that carnival-shower of questions and replies and comments, large axioms bowled over the mahogany like bomb-shells from professional mortars, and explosive wit dropping its trains of many-coloured fire, and the mischief-making rain of *bons-bons* pelting everybody that shows himself.[19]

Talking Exams: The Self in Conversation

Enacting the back-and-forth movement of this "carnival-shower of questions and replies," Holmes's writings operate on many levels through what we might term a "carnivalization of judgment." If his talk form challenges conventional notions of a singular Truth, it can also work to challenge our conceptions of a singular selfhood. In many passages, the breakfast-table-divided becomes the Doctor's model of a mind divided: a model that undercuts any sense of a unitary, stable identity that could stand outside the multi-voiced committee-of-the-self and resolve its internal disputes. Holmes made a great deal of the notion that we have a bicameral brain, housed in right and left chambers, which struggles toward judgment—like the house divided of our bicameral legislatures—through the checks and balances of lengthy and often angry debate. In its most characteristic

---

[17]Ibid., 51–2.
[18]Ibid., 5.
[19]Ibid., 64.

scenes or recurring "plots," his table-talk is constantly putting before us pictures of committees that can't decide, debates that never end, and so on. If there is a point to all of this comic misrule, it is part of the Doctor's life-long crusade against over-certain and hasty judgment—a position that became the central point of contention in the Doctor's ongoing debate with his son, the future justice, Oliver Wendell Holmes, Jr.

Holmes's writings along these lines anticipate specific insights, and a general perspective, that we might term "psychoanalytic." In his table-talk books, both the Autocrat and the Professor often point to seemingly anomalous moments in their own experiences of social conversation—slips of the tongue, repetition compulsions, unconscious plagiarism, and so on—as case studies provoking speculation about the power of subconscious associations to shape or direct streams of thought in what Holmes called "the underground workshop" of the mind, and raising unsettling questions about the role of mechanism, automatism, or compulsion in thought and morals. In Doctor Holmes's medical writings, the same examples recur as points of departure for expanded study. *Mechanism in Thought and Morals*, Holmes's Harvard Phi Beta Kappa address for 1870, sets out, through a survey of the latest developments in psychiatry, to explore "unconscious cerebration" as an automatic, autonomic system, a purely physiological "reflex action of the brain." But Holmes's ground-breaking work then develops, characteristically, as a dialogue between opposed approaches to these speculative questions, alternating between neurophysiological (psychiatric) and verbal-rhetorical (psychoanalytic) conceptions of what he terms the "unconscious."[20]

When he turns to just-published research on aphasia (such as an 1870 article by T. W. Fisher, "Aphasia and the Physiology of Speech"), for example, he departs from an initial consideration of the implications of a nuts-and-bolts "somatic style" localization of certain speech functions in specific lobes of brain matter to find here support for his emerging sense of the mind as a dynamic system, a conversational interaction between two mobile, unlocalized, non-physiological, rhetorical "fields"—two tropics of the mind:

> The brain being a double organ, like the eye, we naturally ask whether we can think with one side of it, as we can see with one eye; whether the two sides commonly work together; whether one side may not be stronger than the other; whether one side may not be healthy, and the other diseased; . . . This is a subject ingeniously treated by Dr. Wigan in his work on the dual-

---

[20]Holmes, "Mechanism in Thought and Morals," 277.

ity of the mind. . . . The left half of the brain, which controls the right half of the body, is, he believes, the strongest in all but left-handed persons.

The resemblance of the act of intelligence to that of vision is remarkably shown in the terms we borrow from one to describe the other. . . . We have a field of vision; have we a field of thought?[21]

As the *Mechanism* lecture develops, verbal action takes precedence over the actions of nerves, organs, or muscles. The most extended and illuminating passages explore the workings of our "unconscious mental actions" not as they are opened up for static examination by the surgical scalpel but as they manifest themselves dynamically in everyday speech.[22] Holmes recalls his own experiences of social talk to explain why we forget or mispronounce names, or make revealing slips of the tongue. Apparently our ongoing mental processes involve diverse layers of consciousness, separate voices always engaged in their own murmuring background dialogue, and often the promptings of one unconscious inner voice can emerge to interrupt or derail the train of thought of another more conscious one. *Déja vu* would reflect such a disruption of our inner dialogue—the effect of a time lapse between two halves of the brain. Already in the *Autocrat* the Doctor—soon to play a major role in the development of the stereoscope, as well as render a lifetime of references to ideas of "parallax"—had sought to explain *déja vu* by speculating on "Dr. Wigan's doctrine of the brain's being a double organ, its hemispheres working together like the two eyes . . . the center of perception [being] double."[23] And Holmes's invention of one form of stereoscope grew out of this conception of a radically doubled, decentered viewing subject, as the bifocal illusion of depth here builds out of each viewer's own internal fusion of two slightly different, partial images before his eyes. Presenting the Doctor's most developed analysis of the divided self, and of mental process as fundamentally conversational, *Mechanism* finds bipolarity in every element of the human constitution: we have two eyes, which see the world in paired images and paired, complementary colors; we have hearts that work through a collaboration of two interactive ventricles; we have right and left hands which have different talents and orientations; and, most important, we have a bicameral brain. In one of the most cited *Mechanism* passages, Holmes asks us to picture all of the interacting influences in the "underground workshop" of our thoughts as the multiple voices of a House committee. And here again the two psychic economies are defined as distinct economies of conversation:

---

[21]Ibid., 267–9.
[22]Ibid., 285.
[23]Holmes, *Autocrat of the Breakfast-Table*, 74.

We all have a double, who is wiser and better than we are, and who puts thoughts into our heads, and words into our mouths. Do we not all commune with our own hearts upon our beds? Do we not all divide ourselves, and go to buffets on questions of right or wrong, of wisdom or folly? Who or what is it that resolves the stately parliament of the day, with all its forms and conventionalities and pretenses, and the great Me presiding, into the committee of the whole, with Conscience in the chair, that holds its solemn session through the watches of the night?[24]

Yet the Holmes passages that had the most documentable influence on the course of later thinking in psychology comes not in his scientific writings, but in the *Autocrat* (though it appeared originally in an 1857–58 lyceum lecture, "Our Second Selves"). Again arising out of the Doctor's central experience of the confusions and misunderstandings inherent in social conversation, the famous "Three Johns" scene that opens the third *Autocrat* paper develops a ground-breaking conception of the self in its social relations, defined not in its spherical or self-reliant singularity but in its polymorphousness:

It is not easy, at the best, for two persons talking together to make the most of each other's thoughts, there are so many of them.

[The company looked as if they wanted an explanation.]

When John and Thomas, for instance, are talking together, it is natural enough that among the six there should be more or less confusion and misapprehension.

[Our landlady turned pale;—no doubt she thought there was a screw loose in my intellects,—and that involved the probable loss of a boarder. . . . Everybody looked up; I believe the old gentleman opposite was afraid I should seize the carving-knife; at any rate, he slid it to one side, as it were carelessly.]

Before the boarders decide his talk has finally led him over the edge, the Autocrat then quickly outlines his "theory of the three Johns."[25] In any dialogue with Thomas, John will appear as the real John, John's ideal John, and Thomas's ideal John (paralleling the three Thomases):

I think, I said, that I can make it plain to Benjamin Franklin here, that there are at least six personalities distinctly to be recognized as taking part in that dialogue between John and Thomas. . . . Only one of the three Johns is taxed; only one can be weighed on a platform-balance; but the other two

---

[24]Holmes, "Mechanism in Thought and Morals," 289.
[25]See also pages 190–1.

are just as important in the conversation. . . . Of these, the least important, philosophically speaking, is the one that we have called the real person. No wonder two disputants often get angry, when there are six of them talking and listening all at the same time.

Just as he is making these remarks, though, the Autocrat is forced to confront another unexpected interruption; in the arena of actual table-talk, involving multiple responses from a diverse group, such "philosophical" points can be quickly countered or forgotten. Here, just as a basket of rare, luscious peaches that has been making its way around the table is about to be passed to the Autocrat, a boarder who happens himself to be named John makes "a very unphilosophical application" of the three Johns theory:

> [. . . He appropriated the three that remained in the basket, remarking that there was just one apiece for him. I convinced him that his practical inference was hasty and illogical, but in the mean time he had eaten the peaches.][26]

John's interruption makes the classic Holmesian turn, as speculative philosophy meets pragmatic action, verbal inflation meets materialist deflation. If the Autocrat takes more than his share of the conversational pie, John may be on one level "convinced" by the theory, but in the meanwhile he will also be sure to take more than his share of the peaches.

Whimsical as it is, the conversational theory of the self put into play in carnivalesque passages like this from the *Autocrat*, the *Professor*, and *Mechanism in Thought and Morals* seems to have served as an important stimulus to later theorists. Silas Weir Mitchell, who followed Holmes's example to center his practice on doctor-patient dialogue through his "rest cure," also produced a series of psychological novels that, like Holmes's, allowed him to delve into irregular areas of abnormal psychology (split personalities, thwarted passions, and so on); the main character in his first novel was named Dr. Ezra Wendell. He also found that the writing of semi-fictional "conversation novels" liberated him for speculative insight. One of these works, *Dr. North and His Friends*, a direct imitation of the *Autocrat* with a central character clearly modeled on Holmes, includes hypothetical asides on verbal associations, multiple personalities, and on case histories showing that the workings of table-talk can erupt in a wild humor that unsettles medical certainties about Will, Conscience, and a unified, responsible personal identity. Dr. North's joke about the dilemma posed by the "crisis of the somatic style" at the turn of the century harks back quite explicitly to the "three Johns" passage in Holmes:

---

[26]Holmes, *Autocrat of the Breakfast-Table*, 52–4.

If I am two people, and one can pop up like a jack-in-the-box, I may be six people, and how can I be responsible for the love affairs of five? Have I six consciences?[27]

Morton Prince, the "Boston School" neurologist and leader in the advancement of psychotherapy, also arrived at his most important contributions through an exploratory interest in the question of multiple personalities, or subconscious selves, as dissociated but interactive strata in our mental life. And his 1885 description of the power and action of a "subconscious" stratum was based not only on recent French and British experiments but also on the still-familiar formulations of Holmes.

But of all the leading American psychologists in these years, William James was the closest to the Doctor and his family: he studied medicine under Holmes, and was a lifelong friend of his son.[28] In codifying early conceptions of the unconscious, James pointed out that the discovery of the subconscious seriously challenged previous notions of the self as a unity, operating in one-dimensional clarity about its motives. James would certainly have been well aware of Holmes's theories of the self as a conversation between multiple personalities when he began to develop his own elaborate descriptions of the complex inner life of the "social self." And in *Over the Teacups*, written in 1890, the Doctor was happy to survey the new developments in psychology and find that his former student was carrying the earlier, literary speculations of the Autocrat and Professor much further:

> I have long ago noticed and referred to the fact of the stratification of the currents of thought in three layers, one over the other. I have recognized that where there are two individuals talking together there are really six personalities engaged in the conversation. But the distinct, separable, independent individualities, taking up conscious life one after the other, are brought out by Mr. James . . . as I have not elsewhere seen them developed.[29]

---

[27]Silas Weir Mitchell, *Dr. North and His Friends* (New York: Century Co., 1900), 294.
[28]See also page 16, n. 19. James was a frequent visitor in the Holmes household, but, judging from what we know about the close relationship between James and Holmes Junior, it's highly unlikely that Holmes Senior and James enjoyed a close mentor-protégé relationship.
[29]Holmes, *Over the Teacups* [The Works of Oliver Wendell Holmes, Standard Library Edition, Volume IV] (Boston: Houghton, Mifflin and Company, 1892 [1890]), 166.

An Age of Uncertainty

Like most jokes in Holmes, the humorous motto, "Every man his own Boswell," has its serious side.[30] It implies the basic self-doubling that would make the Doctor such an insightful participant in and observer of the talk of his day. For Holmes, the self-in-conversation plays the roles of both speaker and listener, writer and critic, poet and scientist, enthusiast and analyst. This seems to be what Holmes's English admirer Oscar Wilde recognized and valued in the "Boswell" motto, which he repeats near the opening of his "The Critic as Artist," thus placing his own self-reflexive dialogue on the duality of the artist, a defense of self-consciousness or "criticism," directly in the line of Holmes's conversations.

There is an undeniable joy and vitality in such models of intellectual freeplay, but, at the same time, the Doctor's destabilizing conversational dynamics are of a piece with his medical stance of "therapeutic skepticism"—implying an all-pervasive doubt that tends to challenge the solid certainties of any monolithic dogma and to undermine the basis for judgment, belief, or action. Working to clear a space for the development of new cures and new thought, Holmes's medical, literary, and philosophical skepticism raises questions more than it provides answers; it takes apart old intellectual systems rather than building new ones; it is most useful as a tool for critical analysis or diagnosis rather than for therapy. Overall, then, Holmes's talk-based works complicate our stereotyped vision of Victorian America as dominated by a settled culture of fixed beliefs and complacent optimism, leaving us with a very different sense of the spirit of the age and of its genteel culture. Developing out of a continual alternation between opposing voices, which means that every question opens into a multiplicity of possible responses in a process that unsettles fixed standards and involves an almost pathological avoidance of direct statements or conclusions, the multi-voiced table-talk writings that made Holmes a major cultural spokesman speak powerfully for the ambivalences of a self-divided nation at a major turning point in its history; they can be seen as representative expressions of the profound anxieties and indecisions of an "age of uncertainty."

---

[30]Holmes, *Autocrat of the Breakfast-Table*, title page.

Oliver Wendell Holmes's
Depth Psychology

A Reconstruction

MICHAEL A. WEINSTEIN

T HE FIELD OF DEPTH PSYCHOLOGY examines how the deep layers of our unconscious minds impact on how we think, behave, and interpret reality. Pioneers of depth psychology include (in order of their births) Sigmund Freud (1856–1939), Alfred Adler (1870–1937), Carl Jung (1875–1961), and Otto Rank (1884–1939). A small body of literature suggests that Oliver Wendell Holmes (1809–1894) anticipated by a generation much of what we now know as depth psychology, especially through his creative fiction. Clarence Oberndorf argued that Holmes in his three "medicated novels" anticipated much of Freudian theory. Charles Boewe suggested that Holmes is more appropriately understood as having generalized the physiologic reflex arc discovered by Marshall Hall to the psychology of conscious experience. More recently, Peter Gibian discusses how Holmes deployed the "talking cure" to relieve the discontents of some of his literary friends and characters. Although each of these approaches has merit and, taken together, they place Holmes's psychological writings in context, none of them centers upon what Holmes himself had to say about the ontology of mental life, which is the purpose of the following reconstruction.[1]

---

[1]Clarence Oberndorf, *The Psychiatric Novels of Oliver Wendell Holmes* (New York: Columbia University Press, 1944); Charles Boewe, "Reflex Action in the Novels of Oliver Wendell Holmes," *American Literature* 26 (1954): 303–19; Peter Gibian, *Oliver Wendell Holmes and the Culture of Conversation* (Cambridge: Cambridge University Press, 2001).

It is important to note at the outset that Holmes does not treat psychodynamics in isolation from physiological, metaphysical, and moral discourses. Psychology, which ranks among the youngest of the formally-recognized academic disciplines, was during Holmes's lifetime only beginning to differentiate itself as a distinctive set of discursive practices. To attempt a reconstruction of his psychological reflections, we must begin by abstracting elements from larger discussions. We can then piece these elements together into an intelligible order upon which Holmes probably did not consciously reflect. Although this method of reconstruction has its limits, it is nevertheless possible to identify in Holmes's writings the elements of a coherent reflection.

A Depth Psychology of Conscious Experience

In the broadest sense Holmes's psychology is phenomenological; that is, it is based on the close observation of conscious experience and, indeed, on pervasive experiences that are privy to all human beings should we care to acknowledge them. Unlike the depth psychologists who followed Freud's path, Holmes does not articulate a hidden grammar of motives that work within a repressed unconscious. Thus, Holmes does not offer a theoretical account of unconscious processes that would explain conscious experience in terms that are unfamiliar to ordinary language and often defy it.

The depth of Holmes's psychology is based on the propensity of humans to ignore or pass over that which is discomforting, inconvenient, or frightful. Individuals are, for Holmes, neglectful of their experience and prey to delusion, but the process of forgetfulness is not repression. Rather, it is a form of *suppression* that can be removed without resorting to a specialized language identifying motives that the individual has hidden so deeply that they could not be acknowledged by that individual without a second-order vocabulary.[2] That is not to say that any given individual has the strength to be "inwardly tolerant of life," as Holmes's onetime student

---

[2]Psychologists make an important distinction between "repression" and "suppression" as defense mechanisms used in everyday life. "Repression" refers to excluding thoughts, desires, and impulses from consciousness by subduing them to the subconscious mind. "Suppression" refers to the conscious (deliberate) attempt to exclude thoughts and impulses. "Suppression" is considered a healthy way to get through daily stresses—for example, by saying "I can't deal with this problem just now" rather than submitting to an impulse or another's request. "Repression" is considered unhealthy since it involves denial that the thought, desire, or impulse even exists. "Repressed" to the unconsciousness, the unwanted item can affect us in ways that we fail to consciously understand.

William James put it,[3] but only that the unconscious is accessible without an interpretative key or specialized cryptography.

The general thesis of Holmes's psychology is that we seldom estimate ourselves accurately. Rather, we endow ourselves with characteristics that we do not evince in practice and we exclude characteristics that we do evince. Except in cases of severe personality conflict described by Holmes in his "medicated novels"—*Elsie Venner* (1861), *The Guardian Angel* (1867), and *A Mortal Antipathy* (1885)—which can be understood from a psychological perspective as case studies of what Holmes calls "disordered volition," each of us has both an "official self" and a much wider mental life. The "official self" is a construction of who we believe we are. The wider mental life both supports and subverts the official self. Mental health, for Holmes, involves a process of achieving a self-estimation that augments the official self. This process entails both incorporating latent potentialities and also excising self-delusion. Through this process we work through conflicts and overcome them.

MENTAL BEDLAM

The founding insight of Holmes's depth psychology centers on the obvious and ubiquitous fact that we do not and cannot control our thoughts, not simply because of "misrecognition" proceeding from hidden psychodynamics, as the cogent follower of Freud, Jacques Lacan, has it, but by virtue of one's own simple inspection of one's experience that reveals directly our lack of control.[4] It is possible to read structuralist psychoanalytical theory and walk away with one's "imaginary" (one's "official" self-description, which according to Lacan is always inaccurate) fully intact, because the claims that it makes cannot be verified directly by personal

---

[3]See William James, "The Will to Believe," in James, *The Will to Believe and Other Essays in Popular Philosophy*, ed. Frederic H. Burkhardt. Fredson Bowers, and Ignas K. Skrupskelis (Cambridge, Massachusetts: Harvard University Press, 1979). James (1842–1910), the pioneering psychologist and pragmatic philosopher, became a close friend of Oliver Wendell Holmes, Jr., and indeed their discussions, joined by a few others, led to the formation in 1872 of the Metaphysical Club (1872), which is thought by some to have had a major impact on American intellectual thought for decades to come. See also pages 16, 91.

[4]See Jacques Lacan, *The Language of the Self* (New York: Dell, 1968). For Lacan (1901–1981), "misrecognition" begins early in life as the child interprets as "me" what is in reality only an image of itself. Such misrecognition creates the "ego," the "I" identity (as Holmes put it), which at least to some extent will always be a fantasy, an illusion of wholeness and integration, and an armor against assaults to one's identity.

observation; it is the opposite when reading Holmes, who simply points to what is always already present, constraining the reader to admit it or to pass over it or work to deny it if the insight proves to be unpalatable. After all, who would want to admit that a form of schizophrenia is ever present in conscious experience?

Holmes presents his insight in the second of his table-talk books, *The Professor at the Breakfast-Table*, where, writing as his professor-persona, he remarks that human beings know "something of the filmy threads of this web of life in which we insects buzz awhile, waiting for the old gray spider to come along."[5] Leaving aside the grim image of finitude, which would be essential to understanding Holmes in another context, those threads turn out to be the elements of the thought process, of which the professor says that he is "twirling on his fingers the key of a private Bedlam of ideals."[6]

To grasp Holmes's depth psychology, it would be enough to stop here and work out the consequences of his image of a "private Bedlam of ideas"—namely, that the substrate of conscious experience can be likened to a madhouse. Introspection is surely speculative in comparison with experimental science, but any of us would find it hard to deny that as the day goes by—and into the night in the form of dreams—we are aware, if only dimly, of a cascading flow of thoughts partaking of mania and depression, sadism and masochism, hope and despair, anxiety and contentment, goodness and evil, and any of a profusion of other familiar doublets. To dwell on this cascading stream of thought too intently and intensely is, of course, itself a sign of madness or at least a path to it, and most of us pass over it most of the time. We involve ourselves with immediate practical affairs, diverting ourselves with amusements, losing ourselves in obsessions, mounting attempts to narrow and focus our thoughts, and employing similar simplification mechanisms to keep our personalities relatively acceptable to ourselves and others.

Acquaintance with one's private Bedlam of ideals should be sufficient to cast doubt on the adequacy of the official self to account for the entire range of conscious experience, which is "brimming," as Holmes says, with pleasant and unpleasant surprises, as well as with all-too-familiar discon-

---

[5] Oliver Wendell Holmes, *The Professor at the Breakfast-Table* [The Works of Oliver Wendell Holmes, Standard Library Edition, Volume II] (Boston: Houghton Mifflin and Company, 1892 [1859]), 23.

[6] The term "bedlam," commonly used to denote uproar or confusion, derives from one of the names (Bedlam) by which the British psychiatric hospital, generally considered the world's oldest institution devoted exclusively to the mentally ill, has been known; other names for this hospital include St. Mary Bethlehem, Bethlehem Hospital, Bethlem Hospital, and Bethlem Royal Hospital.

tents and reassurances. Who knows what he or she will think next? Pondering that question too much is also a path to madness. It is possible to be fairly confident of what one will do in the short term, but it seems rash to pretend that one will be able to predict what one will be thinking and feeling as practical life proceeds. One can only trust that the stream of thought will be relatively canalized by habits or, alternatively, will be harnessed within a system of rationalizations. Towards the end of his life, in *Over the Teacups*, Holmes reached the conclusion that we do not know who we are.[7]

In a later chapter of *The Professor*, the Professor himself remarks on the temporal dimension of the substrate of thought. Observing that he often thinks of several things at once (what is now called "polyphasic thinking"), the Professor moves on to say that "the inner world of thought and the outer world of events are alike in this, that they are both brimful. There is no space between consecutive thoughts, or between the never-ending series of actions."[8] Here the relentless flow of thought comes into prominence; not only is mental life profuse, multiple, spontaneous, and unbidden, but it also cannot be stopped—a fact that is again accessible to immediate observation and destructive of any illusion that the official self is in any way essential or primary.

How, then, is it possible for humans to achieve the relative stability that is as much a part of mental life as is its irreducible diversity, complexity, and spontaneity? Eliminating the idea that there is a moment of suspension in which the willing ego emerges apart from the flow in the "interspaces of thought," of which there are none, the Professor offers another striking image, suggesting that the ego is similar to "a circus-rider whirling round with a great troop of horses." The rider cannot halt the movement of the horses, and is left only with the option of stepping from one saddle to another in a series of excursions; so the ego achieves the position of to some extent directing the flow of thinking by taking "his foot from the saddle of one thought" and putting it "in that of another."[9]

It is that process of leaping on a thought and letting it unfold its implications through free association and/or disciplined logic that allows a person to shut out Bedlam and believe that the self is structured around persistent themes, which, indeed it is in its higher strata, once the inherited physical constitution with its strengths and limitations ("breeding")

---

[7]Oliver Wendell Holmes, *Over the Teacups* [The Works of Oliver Wendell Holmes, Standard Library Edition, Volume IV] (Boston: Houghton, Mifflin and Company, 1892 [1890]), 312.
[8]Holmes, *The Professor at the Breakfast-Table*, 38.
[9]Ibid.

has been partially determined through socialization ("education") and the opportunities and obstacles presented by contingent events ("circumstance"), all of which are evinced in habits and enforced by memory.

Considered phenomenologically rather than through the conditions of development (the familiar triad of nature, nurture, and circumstance, which Holmes adopts), the capacity to take a ride on a passing thought and to follow out its consequences is what John Dewey, whose naturalistic philosophy is the most kindred to Holmes's in the American tradition, called "focal attention."[10] It is focal attention, which is just as pervasive as the mental Bedlam, that allows us to abstract a theme from the ongoing flow of heterogeneous thoughts and, therefore, to banish that flow from awareness so that it becomes, at the limits, unconscious. The experiences of plunging into a task and losing sight of any other concerns—of losing ourselves in contemplation, meditation, aesthetic engagement, response to an external disturbance, intimacy with another, or through an obsession (only to name a few of the ways of canalizing conscious experience, many of which Holmes describes in his rich imaginative prose)—are what we take to be life, until we are somehow driven to distraction and the flow of thoughts resurfaces.

Repeated rides that are reinforced positively or negatively by behavioral conditioning, or assail the person from the past as a result of some conflict or trauma, give the person what Justus Buchler, another American philosophical naturalist kindred to Holmes, called a "proceptive direction," which is a more or less coherent line of activity with associated sentiments that confer on the self a sense of continuity, whether or not it is affirmed.[11] The proceptive direction precipitates the official self, which guards against the eruption of mental Bedlam, often at the cost of blocking the person from access to latent enriching potentialities.

---

[10]See John Dewey, *Experience and Nature* (New York: Dover Publications, 1958). Dewey (1859–1952), now recognized as a pioneering psychologist, educator, and philosopher, wrote among other things: "We do not *know* what we are really after until a *course* of action is mentally worked out" (John Dewey, *Human Nature and Conduct: An Introduction to Social Psychology* [New York: Henry Holt and Company, 1922], 36–7). Of interest, Dewey wrote a paper on "The Reflex Arc Concept in Psychology" [*Psychological Review* 3 (1896): 357–70]—an idea derived from Marshall Hall's work and anticipated at least to some extent by Holmes.

[11]See Justus Buchler, *Toward a General Theory of Human Judgment* (New York: Columbia University Press, 1951). An interpreter of Buchler (1914–1991) defines Buchler's "proceptive direction" as "the result of the propulsions of the individual and the specific directions in which they lead; and it is, naturally, malleable by events and variable" (Victorino Tejera, "Buchler's Metaphysics: The Dimensions of Reflective Activity," in Tejera, *American Modern: The Path Not Taken. Aesthetics, Metaphysics, and Intellectual History in Classic American Philosophy* [Lanham, Maryland: Rowan and Littlefield, 1996], 124).

The unstoppable whirl of thoughts and the capacity to take a ride on one or another of them are the building blocks of Holmes's depth psychology. What focal attention leaps and fixes on and why it does so in particular are the contents of the psyche's form and the materials on which twentieth- and twenty-first century psychotherapists work.

MULTIPLE PERSONALITY

Yet it is an oversimplification to reduce the upper strata of conscious experience to the precipitate of an official self placed in a complex relationship with a brimming mental Bedlam that is mediated by strands of practicality, habit and memory conditioned by nature, nurture, and circumstance—as complicated by the mutually involved components as that account is. For Holmes, there is indeed an official self that the person takes to be the real one. But that conceit is delusive; conscious experience is populated by a multiplicity of selves, and the normal diversification of the substrate of mentality is paralleled by an equally normal condition of multiple personality at the higher strata that is accessible to anyone who is disposed to acknowledge it.

The title character of Holmes's novel *The Guardian Angel*, Byles Gridley, puts the matter succinctly in one of his philosophical writings: "This body in which we journey across the isthmus between two oceans is not a private carriage but an omnibus."[12] That conveyance, Holmes writes in his last work of imaginative prose, the table-talk book *Over the Teacups*, carries "I-My-Self & Co."[13]: that is, the observing and executing ego; the emotional and volitional physical person, including the official self-definition; and one or more other selves; or, as Holmes puts it in *The Guardian Angel*, "co-tenants" of the corporeal house. Here Holmes is on familiar ground for twentieth-century and contemporary theorists of the self. Part of Holmes's analysis of the self—the "I" and "myself"—was replicated by the philosopher-sociologist George Herbert Mead, who socialized the "me" and made the "I"-"me" interplay the foundation of the "symbolic interactionist" movement in sociology.[14] Mead, however, did not go as far as

---

[12]Oliver Wendell Holmes, *The Guardian Angel* [The Works of Oliver Wendell Holmes, Standard Library Edition, Volume VI] (Boston: Houghton, Mifflin and Company, 1892 [1867]), 23.
[13]Oliver Wendell Holmes, *Over the Teacups*, 166.
[14]See George Herbert Mead, "The Social Self," in Mead, *Selected Writings*, ed. Andrew Reck (Indianapolis: Bobbs-Merrill, 1964). Mead (1863–1931) is considered one of the founders of social psychology. The term "symbolic interactionism" was coined by Mead's student and interpreter Herbert Blumer. Derived from American pragmatism, this perspective holds that the *meanings* we assign to things, which are based on our social interactions and modified by our interpretations, determine how we act toward things.

Holmes, who added other me's (emotional and volitional selves) to the "company."

The multiplicity of the self was so conspicuous to Holmes that he made it the very basis of the conception of his table-talk books, in which he self-consciously adopted distinct personae to play the part of the major rhetor—the Autocrat, the Professor, the Poet, and the Dictator—each one evincing a different mentality and sensibility, though not so diverse that any one of them was alien to the others, as befits a mild and, indeed, productive condition of multiple personality. It is no stretch at all to claim that in deploying differentiated personae in his table-talk books Holmes is what today is called "postmodern"—not in the sense that he anticipated postmodernism, but that the latter has brought into high relief the phenomenon of "performance" that was always already present as a feature of mental life.

Indeed, performance is a staple—a necessity—of everyday social life, at least in the impersonal and specialized conditions of urban society. It is a commonplace of sociology that each of us plays several different roles that call forth distinct character traits and temperaments. Nearly everyone who cares to face the facts will admit that they are disposed differently from one social situation to the next and that they have different "sides" to their "personalities," which could be just as easily articulated by saying that they had diverse and specialized personae. For postmodernists, in particular Michel Foucault, these specialized personae are simply "subject positions" in "discursive practices."[15] We cling to the notion that, despite our obvious self-differentiation and awareness that we spend much of our lives in performances, our official selves are somehow who we actually are. But what are these official selves but constructions of what the American critic Irving Babbitt called the "interior monologue"?[16]

Perhaps it is a matter of degree or even semantics to call this ubiquitous self-differentiation the sides of the same self or multiple personae. Holmes was clear that he judged the latter to be the more accurate way of stating the case. In *Over the Teacups*, the character called the "squinting

---

[15]See Michel Foucault, *The Archaeology of Knowledge* (New York: Harper and Row, 1976). Foucault (1926–1984) assigned two meanings to "subject" in his theory: (1) the idea that how we communicate is determined by a particular discourse and its meanings, and (2) that we interpret such a discourse in a way that makes the most sense to us (a process which Foucault called *subjectivization*).

[16]See Irving Babbitt, *Rousseau and Romanticism* (Boston: Houghton Mifflin, 1919). The "interior monologue," as used in literature, refers to a narrative technique whereby the character's inner self is revealed in a way that appears to be uncontrolled by the author.

brain" challenges the Dictator, remaining a skeptic with his own enthusiasms. The "squinting brain," now familiar as the alter-ego, is a frequent co-tenant of many people's conscious experience. As Holmes put it in the *Autocrat of the Breakfast Table*, only God knows who a person really is.

A phenomenological interpretation and reconstruction of Holmes's depth psychology that confines itself to pervasive experiences of conscious life thus yields a description that begins with the heterogeneous flow of thinking that in itself is not reconciled; passes through a multifarious process of development, disciplinization, and circumstantial contingency that issues in the construction of an official self that both represents and occludes the substrate of mental Bedlam; and ends by displacing the official self by making it the most prominent persona in a "company," which to use another meaning of that word than Holmes intended, constitutes a repertory troop only imperfectly guided by the ego.

DISORDERED VOLITION

How strong the ego is or can become is dependent on the balance of power among the different personae—the more harmonious they are, the more consistent is the individual's proceptive direction and the more capable the ego is in exercising guidance, because, to use Holmes's image, when the ego leaps on the saddle of one thought, it will not collide with another and be psychologically unhorsed. The will, for Holmes, does not stand over and above the whirl of thoughts, because there are no "interspaces" between them, but can only attempt to take a ride on one of them for a time, until it is exhausted and/or other voices break through into focal attention, clamoring to be heard. For most people most of the time (although that might be too generous a judgment, because how much does one know about what goes on behind another's social mask?), there is enough harmony to maintain and adjust one's proceptive direction, if only by the expedient of holding fast to a fixed idea of one's destiny, which would be a form of predestination that was alien to Holmes after he rebelled against his minister father's orthodox Calvinism. Affirming Holmes's account of psychodynamics excludes taking the unity of personality as either the terminus *a quo* or terminus *ad quem*. Holmes is arguably the first in a line of American naturalists who eschewed perfectionism in favor of a possible movement towards integration of the personality that is never fully realized.

If most people make do and some are fortunate and/or gifted enough to achieve a preponderant harmony among the personifications of their motives, others are beset by conflicts between and among their co-tenants.

Such conflict deranges—unhorses—the ego and makes it impossible for the person to maintain a proceptive direction, leaving them prey to the solicitations of the members of their "company," who struggle against one another to take the position of "me," until the person becomes exhausted and falls into depression or plunges ahead on a path of self-destruction.

The name that Holmes gives to conflict within the company is "disordered volition,"[17] which has a contemporary ring as psychopathologies are increasingly being called "disorders" rather than "diseases" or "illnesses." In all three of Holmes's "medicated novels," disordered volition is at the root of the victims' discontents. In *Elsie Venner*, the title character is worn down to death in the struggle between her vital and loving self, and her sociopathic ophidian self, which, according to Holmes's conceit, could be traced to a snake bite contracted by her mother during pregnancy. In *The Guardian Angel*, the most achieved of Holmes's case studies of disordered volition, Myrtle Hazard, with the help of guardian angels (people who look out for her welfare), fights a successful struggle to achieve a coherent personality when faced with a conflict among four of her mental co-tenants (representing her ancestors)—a man-taming woman of the world, a Puritan martyr, a wild half-Native American, and a seeress accused of witchery. In the same novel, Murray Bradshaw, a fortune-hunting possessive individualist, who has been taken over by self-delusion and has hollowed out his wider self, descends into nihilism when he fails to win Myrtle's hand and confronts his emptiness. In *A Mortal Antipathy*, Lurida Vincent is racked by an imbalance between her over-developed intellect and under-developed body, until she is brought to admit to herself her limitations. In the same novel, Maurice Kirkwood struggles to overcome a traumatic neurosis that involves a conflict between his desire to love and his fear of traumatic repetition. Although Holmes adopts a different etiology for each of these cases—he never developed a fixed theory of the genesis of disordered volition—the phenomenological description remains constant in its general outlines.

Along with the lack of an explanatory theory of mental disorders, Holmes's depth psychology also fails to provide a systematic therapeutic program. Dr. Butts, who takes on Lurida's and Maurice's cases at a distance, intervenes strategically and judiciously, using proxies for the most part as he observes events unfold. The same is true for Byles Gridley, who is Myrtle's main guardian angel, although he plays a more active role than Dr. Butts does in facilitating successful overcoming. Elsie Venner is failed

[17]Oliver Wendell Holmes, *Elsie Venner* [The Works of Oliver Wendell Holmes, Standard Library Edition, Volume V] (Boston: Houghton, Mifflin and Company, 1892 [1861]), ix.

by those who might have helped her, and Murray Bradshaw does not even have anyone who would give him aid and is probably too far gone to accept it were it offered. Without an explanatory theory, there can be no systematic therapeutic program. In its stead, Holmes suggests the possibility of benevolent and discreet friendship offered by the older and wiser, which probably functions in everyday life to forestall the need that many people might have to seek professional help.

CONCLUSION

This phenomenological reconstruction of Holmes's depth psychology suggests that he should be appropriately placed among meta-psychologists or philosophers of psychology even more so than among psychoanalytical theorists or clinicians. Holmes was too concerned and fascinated with the strata and complexities of conscious experience to devise a second-order theory, such as Freud's account of unconscious psychodynamics, to explain it. That is not so much a criticism as a suggestion that Holmes's depth psychology belongs in the line of American naturalistic and pragmatist philosophy, which has left a definitive stamp on American culture. When one looks for Holmes's kindred spirits, one finds them in philosopher-sociologist George Herbert Mead, philosopher-educationist John Dewey, and philosopher-psychologist William James. That is not to say that Holmes anticipated his successors, but, rather, that he stood squarely as the first in their line. Reading back from them to Holmes, as has been done here allusively, allows him to stand out more clearly than he does when considered as an anticipator of psychoanalysis.

Nonetheless, Holmes's depth psychology of conscious experience does have a genuine kinship with Freud's psycho-analysis in the sphere of meta-psychological discourse; discontents proceed from conflicts within the psyche that are personified in imagined characters, and the ego is constitutively precarious with only a slim margin of executive control or, as Holmes would have it, "self-determination." We forget that judgment at our own risk.

Albumen print of Holmes, circa 1860. Holmes began to offer instruction in microscopic anatomy at the Tremont Street Medical School in the late 1840s and was offering practical instruction in the use of the microscope to medical students at Harvard by 1855. He was one of the first Americans to introduce microscopy into a medical curriculum. From the collection of the Boston Medical Library in the Francis A. Countway Library of Medicine

Part II
The Quotable Holmes

Holmes in his study, 1890. Note the two chambered nautilus shells on the posterior bookshelf. From the collection of the Boston Medical Library in the Francis A. Countway Library of Medicine.

Holmes the Physician

EDUCATION

The Science of Teaching

A medical school is not a scientific school, except just so far as medicine itself is a science. On the natural history side, medicine is a science; on the curative side, chiefly an art. This is implied in Hufeland's[1] aphorism: "the physician must generalize the disease and individualize the patient."

—*Scholastic and Bedside Teaching*, 275

---

[1]Christoph Wilhelm Friedrich Hufeland (1762–1836): the most eminent German practicing physician of his time, whose works included a widely-translated *System of Practical Medicine*.

The object of this school is to teach the Art of Healing with so much of science as is needed for its intelligent practice. Other schools are devoted to science as such, but the business of this institution is to fit young men for the difficult and laborious practical duties of the Medical Profession in all its branches.

—Introductory–September 26, 1879, 185

You can very often carry two facts fastened together more easily than one by itself, as a housemaid can carry two pails of water with a hoop more easily than one without it. You can remember a man's face better than you can his nose or his mouth or his eye-brow. . . . Systematic, or scientific study is invaluable as supplying a natural kind of mnemonics, if for nothing else.

—Scholastic and Bedside Teaching, 287–8

To the student I would say, that however plain and simple may be our teaching, he must expect to forget much which he follows intelligently in the lecture-room. But it is not the same as if he had never learned it. A man must *get* a thing before he can *for*get it. There is a great world of ideas we cannot voluntarily recall—they are outside the limits of the will. But they sway our conscious thought as the unseen planets influence the movements of those within the sphere of vision. No man knows how much he knows—how many ideas he has—any more than he knows how many blood-globules roll in his veins.[2]

—Scholastic and Bedside Teaching, 300

There are many things which we can afford to forget, which yet it was well to learn. Your mental condition is not the same as if you had never known what you now try in vain to recall. There is a perpetual metempsychosis of thought, and the knowledge of to-day finds a soil in the forgotten facts of yesterday. You cannot see anything in the new season of the guano you placed last year about the roots of your climbing plants, but it is blushing and breathing fragrance in your trellised roses; it has scaled your porch in the bee-haunted honey-suckle; it has found its way where the ivy is green; it is gone where the woodbine expands its luxuriant foliage.

—The Young Practitioner, 372–3

---

[2]For this quote, and the subsequent two, see also section on "Holmesian Psychology," pages 190–3.

It is perfectly true that you will forget or at least seem to have forgotten many things that you have learned in the three branches of the first year. I say *seem to have forgotten*, because no man knows how much is stored away in his memory. . . . We must not think our intellectual world is made up of the thoughts we can command at will. The unseen planet betrays itself by its action on the visible ones, and so the knowledge which we have lost sight of for the time is constantly acting on the thoughts which revolve in full view through our consciousness. As it is "better to have loved and lost than never to have lived at all," so it is better to have known and forgotten—if anything *can* be forgotten—than never to have known at all.

—*Introductory–September 26, 1879, 227*

When you come to handle life and death as your daily business, your memory will of itself bid good-by to such inmates as the well-known foramina of the sphenoid bone and the familiar oxides of methyl-ethyl-amyl-phenyl-ammonium. Be thankful that you have once known them, and remember that even the learned ignorance of a nomenclature is something to have mastered, and may furnish pegs to hang facts upon which would otherwise have strewed the floor of memory in loose disorder.

—*The Young Practitioner, 373*

The Art of Teaching

My advice to every teacher less experienced than myself would be, therefore: Do not fret over the details you have to omit; you probably teach altogether too many as it is.

—*Scholastic and Bedside Teaching, 299*

I hope we shall make everything as plain and as simple to you [students] as we can. I would never use a long word, even, where a short one would answer the purpose. I know there are professors in this country who "ligate" arteries. Other surgeons only tie them and it stops the bleeding just as well.

—*Scholastic and Bedside Teaching, 302*

In the earliest and embryonic stage of professional development, any violent impression on the instructor's mind is apt to be followed by some lasting effect on that of the pupil. No mother's mark is more permanent than the mental nævi and moles, and excrescences, and mutilations, that students carry with them out of the lecture-room, if once the teeming intellect which nourishes theirs has been scared from its propriety by any misshapen fantasy.

—*The Contagiousness of Puerperal Fever*, 108

The most essential part of a student's instruction is obtained, as I believe, not in the lecture-room, but at the bedside. Nothing seen there is lost; the rhythms of disease are learned by frequent repetition; its unforeseen occurrences stamp themselves indelibly in the memory.

—*Scholastic and Bedside Teaching*, 273

The student's eye must be trained, that his tact and sagacity—whatever they are naturally—must be developed by patiently following an expert—a first-rate medical practitioner—from bedside to bedside.

—*Introductory–September 26, 1879*, 199

I myself have nothing to do with clinical teaching. Yet I do not hesitate to say it is more essential than all the rest put together.

—*Scholastic and Bedside Teaching*, 291

A long course of lectures ties all the weaknesses of teachers and pupils. There is no little trick of the one and no impatient habit of the other which will not shew itself before they part company.

—*An Introductory Lecture Delivered at the Massachusetts Medical College*, 31

All the objects of anatomical research are visible ones, and many of the facts of physiology are capable of visible representation. I believe that the teacher who merely talks about that which he might show to the eye or make palpable to the touch, fails to give that particular subject the clearness and permanency in the student's mind of which it is susceptible.

—*An Introductory Lecture Delivered at the Massachusetts Medical College*, 32–3

All lecturers, all professors, all schoolmasters, have ruts and grooves in their minds into which their conversation is perpetually sliding.

—*The Autocrat of the Breakfast-Table*, 65

A new lecture always has a certain excitement connected with its delivery. One thinks well of it, as of most things fresh from his mind. After a few deliveries of it, one gets tired and then disgusted with its repetition.

Go on delivering it, and the disgust passes off, until, after one has repeated it a hundred or a hundred and fifty times, he rather enjoys the hundred and first or hundred and fifty-first time, before a new audience. But this is on one condition,—that he never lays the lecture down and lets it cool. If he does, there comes on a loathing for it which is intense, so that the sight of the old battered manuscript is as bad as sea-sickness.

A new lecture is just like any other new tool. We use it for a while with pleasure. Then it blisters our hands, and we hate to touch it. By and by our hands get callous, and then we have no longer any sensitiveness about it. But if we give it up, the calluses disappear; and if we meddle with it again, we miss the novelty and get the blisters . . . . A lecture doesn't begin to be old until it has passed its hundredth delivery; and some, I think, have doubled, if not quadrupled, that number. These old lectures are a man's best, commonly; they improve with age. . . .

—*The Autocrat of the Breakfast-Table*, 138–9

I am afraid that it is a good plan to get rid of old Professors.[3]

—*Some of My Early Teachers*, 423

MEDICAL SCIENCE

Holmes in Paris[4]

The whole walls round the Ecole de Médecine are covered with notices of lectures, the greater part of them gratuitous; the dissecting-rooms, which accommodate six hundred students, are open; lessons are ringing aloud through all the great hospitals. The students from all lands are gathered together, and the great harvest of the year is open to all of us. The consequence is that I am occupied from morning to night, and as everyone is happy when he is occupied, I enjoy myself as much as I could wish.

—*Life and Letters of Oliver Wendell Holmes*, 89

---

[3]Along similar lines, William Osler would write: "The teacher's life should have three periods, study until twenty-five, investigation until forty, profession until sixty, at which age I would have him retired on a double allowance." In William Osler, "The Fixed Period," in *Aequanimitas, with Other Addresses to Medical Students, Nurses, and Practitioners*, second edition (London: H.K. Lewis, 1906), 400.

[4]As noted in the prefatory essays, Holmes studied medicine in Paris from 1833 through 1835.

I have more fully learned at least three principles since I have been in Paris: not to take authority when I can have facts; not to guess when I can know; not to think a man must take physic because he is sick.

—*Life and Letters of Oliver Wendell Holmes*, 103

General Observations

I may remark, in the first place, that the striking character of the disease [intermittent fever, or malaria] renders it a favorable subject for the medical historian. . . . It does not call for ingenious speculations, which may at any time be annihilated by some unforeseen discovery, or thrown by some more captivating novelty. It does not ask for a few notions relating to some disease which future observation may contradict, or explain or extend, until they lose their meaning. It calls on some quiet student, who has a little time, a little patience, a little opportunity, to rescue from forgetfulness a series of facts, which but for him may perish from the memory of men. Many of the lips from which he is to learn, will soon be closed for ever.[5]

—*Boylston Prize Essay on Intermittent Fever*, 1–3

Where facts are numerous, and unquestionable, and unequivocal in their significance, theory must follow them as it best may, keeping time with their step, and not go before them, marching to the sound of its own drum and trumpet.

—*The Contagiousness of Puerperal Fever*, 107

Causes, causes, and again causes,—more and more we fall back on these as the chief objects of our attention.

—*Currents and Counter-Currents in Medical Science*, 195

Disease, being always an effect, is always in exact proportion to the sum of its causes, as much in the case of Spigelius,[6] who dies of a scratch, as in that of the man who recovers after an iron bar has been shot through his

---

[5]Holmes would repeat such a methodology several years later in conducting his research on puerperal fever.

[6]Adriaan van den Spieghel (1578–1625; commonly known as Spigelius, Spiegelius, or Spiegel): Flemish-born anatomist and botanist who is commonly regarded as the last of a great line of anatomists in Renaissance Padua, Italy, following Vesalius, Fallopius, Fabricius, and Casserius.

brain.[7] The one prevalent failing of the medical art is to neglect the causes and quarrel with the effect.

—*Currents and Counter-Currents in Medical Science*, 198

If it is true that we understand ourselves but imperfectly in health, the truth is more signally manifested in disease, where natural actions imperfectly understood, disturbed in an obscure way by half-seen causes, are creeping and winding along in the dark toward their destined issue, sometimes using our remedies as safe stepping-stones, occasionally, it may be, stumbling over them as obstacles.

—*Borderlines of Knowledge in Some Provinces of Medical Science*, 211–12

Medicine, sometimes impertinently, often ignorantly, often carelessly called "allopathy,"[8] appropriates everything from every source that can be of the slightest use to anybody who is ailing in any way, or like to be ailing from any cause.

—*Scholastic and Bedside Teaching*, 289

Your acquaintance with some of the accessory branches is probably greater now than it will be in a year from now,—much greater than it will be ten years from now. The progress of knowledge, it may be feared, or hoped, will have outrun the text-books in which you studied these branches. . . . Science is a great traveller, and wears her shoes out pretty fast, as might be expected.

—*The Young Practitioner*, 371–72

And Science, of all things, should be freest from servile adherence to territorial limits; Science, which, like the atmosphere, cannot exist in one place, without diffusing itself gently and gradually over others; which passes the custom-house untaxed, and the fortress unchallenged, making friends of the remotest strangers, and brothers of those whom war has arrayed against each other.

—*An Introductory Lecture Delivered at the Massachusetts Medical College*, 17

---

[7]The "iron bar" in question almost certainly refers to that which went through the skull of Phineas Gage (1823–1860), which today resides at the Warren Anatomical Museum at the Francis A. Countway Library of Medicine.

[8]"Allopathy" was the term coined and derisively applied by Samuel Hahnemann (1755–1833) to refer to orthodox medical practice, in contrast to homeopathy.

Pathology

We are poised midway between two material infinites, the infinitely great and the infinitely little. The confines of the first, strange as it may seem, were thoroughly explored before we had reached the inner borders of the second. Uranus and the asteroids were led in by Science like wild colts from the outskirts of creation, before the acarus and the cheesemite[9] had settled the duel concerning their identity. But when at length the microscope was taken with its sudden convulsion of improvement, a new world of wonders opened upon the eye of the observer of nature.

—*The Position and Prospects of the Medical Student*, 284

The self-styled practical men of provincial celebrity sometimes sneer at the labors of the pathologist, as ignorant sailors laugh at the landlubber who computes their captain's logarithms; alike unconscious that their path through doubt and danger is traced by the hand which is the object of their stupid laughter. At this very time, during this very day which passes over our heads, a hundred thousand leeches would have been draining the lifeblood from that noble army of martyrs whom the physicians of America call their patients, in the vain hope of subduing an imaginary inflammation, had not the great French pathologist wilted down his youth upon the stone floor of the amphitheatre of La Charité, and sent out his new truths upon the winds that turn the weather-cocks of medical Christendom!

—*The Position and Prospects of the Medical Student*, 292

Descriptive anatomy, as known from an early date, is to the body what geography is to the planet. . . . What geology has done for our knowledge of the earth, has been done for our knowledge of the body by that method of study to which is given the name of *General Anatomy*. It studies, not the organs as such, but the elements out of which the organs are constructed.

—*Borderlines of Knowledge in Some Provinces of Medical Science*, 222

The *strictum* and *laxum*, the increased and diminished action of the vessels, out of which medical theories and methods of treatment have grown

---

[9]"Acarus" is sometimes used as a general term for mites, especially if belonging to the genus *Acarus*, but Holmes possibly refers here to disputes pertaining to the identities of various food mites, such as the grain mite (*Acarus siro*) and the cheese mite (*Tyrolichus casei* and others).

up, have yielded to the doctrine of local cell-communities, belonging to this or that vascular district, from which they help themselves, as contractors are wont to do from the national treasury.

—*Borderlines of Knowledge in Some Provinces of Medical Science*, 236–7

The Numerical Method and Therapeutic Rationality[10]

"Experience" had been, from time immemorial, pouring its flowing treasures into buckets full of holes. At the existing rate of supply and leakage they would never be filled; nothing would ever be settled in medicine. But cases thoroughly recorded and mathematically analyzed would always be available for future use, and when accumulated in sufficient number would lead to results which would be trustworthy, and belong to science.

—*Some of My Early Teachers*, 432

It should be remembered what the numerical system professes and what it does not profess to do. It professes to furnish us the means of extracting the collective results of a mass of individual facts too long to be analyzed by the unaided memory. It *does not* profess to be answerable for all the conclusions we may see fit to draw from these results.

—*The Position and Prospects of the Medical Student*, 300–1

The numerical system can teach a wise and honest and diligent man a great deal, and . . . it can make a foolish, dishonest, careless man a greater fool, imposter, blunderer, than nature ever intended him to be.

—*Medical Highways and Byways*, 509

The true question for the jury is not, "Do hospital or other physicians try experiments?" for strictly speaking, every administration of a remedy is an experiment,—but, "Do they study diligently the claims of all new and old methods, and do they know how to select those which offer the best chance of proving useful?" . . . Why have a medical profession, except to know, first, what remedies are always certain, and ten times oftener, what are most deserving of trial where certainty does not exist?

—*The Position and Prospects of the Medical Student*, 308–9

---

[10]Regarding the advent of the "numerical method," or the means of quantitatively comparing outcomes of groups of patients receiving contrasting forms of care, under Pierre-Charles-Alexandre Louis in Paris in the 1820s and 1830s, see J. Rosser Matthews, *Quantification and the Quest for Medical Certainty* (Princeton: Princeton University Press, 1995).

Part of the blame of over-medication must, I fear, rest with the profession, for yielding to the tendency to self-delusion, which seems inseparable from the practice of the art of healing. . . . The inveterate logical errors to which physicians have always been subject are chiefly these:— The mode of inference per *enumerationem simplicem*, in scholastic phrase; that is, counting only their favorable cases. . . . The *post hoc ergo proper hoc* error: he got well after taking my medicine; therefore in consequence of taking it.

—*Currents and Counter-Currents in Medical Science*, 185–6

I have a known a practitioner,—perhaps more than one,—who was as much under the influence of the last article he had read in his favorite medical journal as a milliner under the sway of the last fashion-plate. The difference between green and seasoned knowledge is very great, and such practitioners never hold long enough to any of their knowledge to have it get seasoned.

—*Medical Libraries*, 408

Systems of Medical Knowledge[11]

A glance at the prevalent modes of treatment of any two successive generations will show that there is a changeable as well as a permanent element in the art of healing; not merely changeable as diseases vary, or as new remedies are introduced, but changeable by the going out of fashion of special remedies, by the decadence of a popular theory from which their fitness was deduced, or other cause not more significant.

—*Currents and Counter-Currents in Medical Science*, 175

There are, of course, in every calling, those who go about the work of the day before them, doing it according to the rules of their craft, and asking no questions of the past or of the future, or of the aim and end to which their special labor is contributing. These often consider and call themselves *practical men*. They pull the oars of society, and have no leisure to watch the currents running this or that way; let theorists and philosophers attend to them. In the mean time, however, these currents are carrying the practical men, too, and all their work may be thrown away, and worse than thrown away, if they do not take knowledge of them and get out of the wrong ones and into the right ones as soon as they may.

—*Currents and Counter-Currents in Medical Science*, 175–6

---

[11]See John Harley Warner, *Against the Spirit of System: The French Impulse in Nineteenth-Century American Medicine* (Princeton: Princeton University Press, 1998).

What is the meaning of these perpetual changes and conflicts of medical opinion and practice, from an early antiquity to our own time? Simply this: all "methods" of treatment end in disappointment of those extravagant expectations which men are wont to entertain of medical art. . . . In the course of a generation, more or less, physicians themselves are likely to get tired of a practice which has so little effect upon the average movement of vital decomposition. Then they are ready for a change, even if it were back again to a method which has already been tried, and found wanting.

—Borderlines of Knowledge in Some Provinces of Medical Science, 259–60

Then will come the usual talk about a change in the character of disease, which has about as much meaning, as that concerning "old-fashioned snow-storms." . . . That the whole type of diseases undergoes such changes that the practice must be reversed from depleting to stimulating, and *vice versa*, is much less likely than that methods of treatment go out of fashion and come in again.[12]

—Borderlines of Knowledge in Some Provinces of Medical Science, 260

Old theories, and old men who cling to them, must take themselves out of the way as the new generation with its fresh thoughts and altered habits of mind comes forward to take the place of that which is dying out.

—Some of My Early Teachers, 430

Constitution, Hygiene, and the Determinants of Disease

Even within the borders of our own State, the very interesting researches of Dr. Bowditch[13] show that there is a great variation in the amount of tuberculous disease in different towns, apparently connected with local conditions. The hygienic map of a State is quite as valuable as its geo-

---

[12]Holmes refers here to the "Change of Type Theory," which was often invoked by mid-nineteenth century physicians (roughly, between 1830 and 1870) to explain why they no longer relied on the older "heroic" therapies such as bleeding and purging. The argument went that "heroic" therapies were no longer indicated because diseases, people, or both had changed from a "sthenic" to an "asthenic" type. See John Harley Warner, *The Therapeutic Perspective: Medical Practice, Knowledge, and Identity in America, 1820–1885* (Cambridge: Harvard University Press, 1986), 166–8.

[13]Henry Ingersoll Bowditch (1808–1892): Holmes's friend and contemporary who is often considered the first American specialist in pulmonary disease. See John H. Felts, "Henry Ingersoll Bowditch and Oliver Wendell Holmes: Stethoscopists and Reformers," *Perspectives in Biology and Medicine* 45 (2002): 539–48.

logic map, and it is the business of every practicing physician to know it thoroughly.

—*Scholastic and Bedside Teaching*, 296

Is not the question why our young men and women so often break down, and how they can be kept from breaking down, far more important for physicians to settle than whether there is one cranial vertebra, or whether there are four, or none?

—*Scholastic and Bedside Teaching*, 297

There are many memorable events in recent medical history. Yet there is one gain so vast that we can hardly compare any curative measure with it for importance; I mean the knowledge which has been gained in the art of *preventing disease*; the hygiene of cities, the construction of hospitals, the better study of all those conditions, including climatic influences, which favor health in the two sexes and at different ages.

—*Medical Highways and Byways*, 508

Like all sensible men from the days of Hippocrates to the present, he [Dr. James Jackson] knew that diet and regimen were more important than any drug or than all drugs put together.[14]

—*Scholastic and Bedside Teaching*, 306

One would say that the regulation of the conditions of the body should be as simple as the ordering of the conditions which enable a skilful agri-culturist to raise healthy vegetables and fruits. There are only two difficulties,—we cannot always choose our constitutions, and we cannot always command many of the circumstances which have most influence on health. What do we mean by constitution? We mean the inherited sum of living force, with all its manifestations in form, in structure, in tendency. In the elements of which we are composed, and the processes by which our life is maintained, we are all alike. But in constitution there are differences so great between individuals that they hardly seem to inherit the same nature.

—*Talk Concerning the Human Body and its Management*, 203

---

[14]James Jackson (1777–1867), the second Hersey Professor of the Theory and Practice of Physic at Harvard Medical School, had a critical early influence upon Holmes, to whom he became a "second father." See Eleanor M. Tilton, *Amiable Autocrat: A Biography of Oliver Wendell Holmes* (New York: Henry Schuman, 1947), 76.

Most assuredly I do believe that body and mind are much influenced by the kind of food habitually depended upon.

—Over the Teacups, 185

The body is a soil capable of being improved by adding the elements in which it is deficient, as much as farming or garden land. Fresh vegetables are the fertilizers of human clay or dust that has grown scorbutic on a long course of salted food. Out of a proper study of the material wants of the system, and of the best nutritive substances for supplying these wants, we may expect a great improvement in the physical conditions of the race. The cook makes our bodies; the apothecary only cobbles them.

—Talk Concerning the Human Body and its Management, 216–7

It is probably pretty much like other inland New England towns in point of "salubrity,"—that is, gives people their choice of dysentery or fever every autumn, with a season-ticket for consumption, good all the year round.

—Elsie Venner, 23

Anesthesia

My dear Sir: Every body wants to have a hand in a great discovery. All I will do is to give you a hint or two as to names—or the name—to be applied to the state produced and the agent.

The state should, I think, be called "Anaesthesia." This signifies insensibility—more particularly (as used by Linnaeus and Cullen) to objects of touch. (See Good—Nosology, p. 259.[15])

The adjective will be "Anaesthetic." Thus we might say the state of Anaesthesia, or the anaesthetic state. The means employed would be properly called the anti-aesthetic agent. Perhaps it might be allowable to say anaesthetic agent, this admits of question.

The words anti-neuric, aneuric, neuron-leptic, neuro-lepsia, neuro-stasis, etc., seem too anatomical; whereas the change is a physiological one. I throw them out for consideration.

---

[15]Holmes refers here to John Mason Good, *A Physiological System of Nosology: with a Corrected and Simplified Nomenclature* (Boston: Wells and Lilly, 1823), 259.

I would have a name pretty soon, and consult some accomplished scholar, such as President Everett or Dr Bigelow, senior, before fixing upon the terms, which *will be repeated by the tongues of every civilized race of mankind*. You could mention these words which I suggest, for their consideration; but there may be others more appropriate and agreeable.[16]

—Holmes to William T. Morton, in
Some Account of the Letheon, or Who is the Discoverer?

To Ether—or Either

—Holmes's purported reply, in the context of the priority dispute between William T. Morton and Charles Jackson, concerning to whom the statue in Boston Common commemorating the first use of ether as anesthetic agent should be dedicated

Nature was before man with her anaesthetics: the cat's first shake stupefies the mouse; the lion's first shake deadens the man's fear and feeling; and the *crotalus*[17] paralyzes before he strikes.

—*Elsie Venner*, 191

Holmesian Neurology

The bold language of certain speculative men of science has frightened some more cautious persons away from a subject as much belonging to natural history as the study of any other function in connection with its special organ.

—*Mechanism in Thought and Morals*, 262

The brain being a double organ, like the eye, we naturally ask whether we can think with one side of it, as we can with one eye; whether the two sides commonly work together; whether one side may be stronger than the other; whether one side may not be healthy, and the other diseased; and what consequences may follow from these various conditions.

—*Mechanism in Thought and Morals*, 267

---

[16]This was Holmes's response to a query from William T. Morton regarding what to name "Morton's" discovery. See Edward Warren, *Some Account of the Letheon: or, Who is the Discoverer?*, third edition (Boston: Dutton and Wentworth, 1847), 84–5.

[17]*Crotalus*: The genus of venomous pit vipers commonly known as rattlesnakes.

The connection between thought and the structure and condition of the brain is evidently so close that all we have to do is to study it. It is not in this direction that materialism is to be feared: we do not find Hamlet and Faust, right and wrong, the valor of men and the purity of women, by testing for albumen, or examining fibres in microscopes.

—*Mechanism in Thought and Morals*, 301

All at once a conviction flashes through us that we have been in the same precise circumstances as at the present instance, once or many times before.[18]

—*Autocrat of the Breakfast Table*, 73

Memory, imagination, old sentiments and associations, are more readily reached through the sense of SMELL *than by almost any other channel.*

—*Autocrat of the Breakfast Table*, 75

To speak more truly, the olfactory "nerve" is not at a nerve at all, he says, but a part of the brain, in intimate connection with its anterior lobes.

—*Autocrat of the Breakfast Table*, 77

Holmesian Psychiatry

No doubt there are people born with impulses at every possible angle to the parallels of Nature, as you call them. If they happen to cut at right angles, of course they are beyond the reach of common influences. Slight obliquities are what we have most to do with in education. Penitentiaries and insane asylums take care of most of the right-angle cases.

—*Elsie Venner*, 74

When the nervous energy is depressed by any bodily cause, or exhausted by overworking, there follow effects which have often been misinterpreted by moralists, and especially by theologians. The conscience itself becomes neuralgic, sometimes actually inflamed.

—*Elsie Venner*, 169

---

[18]This passage is one of the first recordings of the phenomenon of *déjà vu* in the nineteenth century, though it followed by eight years Charles Dickens' own observation, in *David Copperfield*, that "we have all some experience of a feeling, that comes over us occasionally, of what we are saying and doing having been said and done before, in a remote time—of our having been surrounded, dim ages ago, by the same faces, objects, and circumstances—of our knowing perfectly what will be said next, as if we suddenly remember it!" See Dickens, *David Copperfield* (London: Thomas Nelson and Sons, 1906 [originally published in 1850]), 594. The actual term *déjà vu* was coined decades later by the French philosopher and psychic, Émile Boirac (1851–1917).

Conscience itself requires a conscience, or nothing can be more unscrupulous.

—*Elsie Venner*, 170

Our libraries are crammed with books written by spiritual hypochondriacs, who inspected all their moral secretions a dozen times a day. They are full of interest, but they should be transferred from the shelf of the theologian to that of the medical man who makes a study of insanity.

—*Elsie Venner*, 170

How long will it be before we shall learn that for every wound which betrays itself to the sight by a scar, there are a thousand unseen mutilations that cripple, each of them, some one or more of our highest faculties?

—*Elsie Venner*, 246

There are griefs men *never* put into words,—that there are fears which must not be spoken,—intimate matters of consciousness which must be carried, as bullets which have been driven deep into the living tissues are sometimes carried, for a whole lifetime,—*encysted* griefs, if we may borrow the chirurgeon's term, never to be reached, never to be seen, never to be thrown out, but to go into the dust with the frame that bore them about with it, during long years of anguish, known only to the sufferer and his Maker.

—*Elsie Venner*, 249

I believe that there are unexplained facts in the region of sympathies and antipathies which will repay study with a deeper insight into the mysteries of life than we have dreamed of hitherto. I often wonder there are not heart-waves and soul-waves as well as "brain-waves," which some have already recognized.[19]

—*A Mortal Antipathy*, 148

---

[19]Of this passage, the psychiatrist Clarence P. Oberndorf wrote: "So far as I know this is the first plea by any physician for the investigation of the mystifying paradoxes of normal human conduct through the study of the neuroses. Later the essential structure of the extensive psychoanalytic theory was built up by Freud through the clinical observation of neurotic conditions in patients whose infantile impressions and reactions he carefully studied." In Clarence P. Oberndorf, *The Psychiatric Novels of Oliver Wendell Holmes* (New York: Columbia University Press, 1943), 217.

MEDICAL ART

Physical Examination

At the present day it is well known that some practitioners of a certain merit, and particularly some who pride themselves on strong sense and intuitive sagacity, habitually neglect and depreciate the value of the physical signs, even of thoracic disease. . . . If with the most startling novelty, and with extravagant promises, an invention come forward which demands the laborious training of a sense hitherto uncultivated in its more delicate capacities, bearing in one hand an instrument which is to be the practitioner's inseparable companion, and in the other a treatise full of new terms and peculiar doctrines, is it to be supposed that the schools of Sydenham and Cullen[20] would consent, without a struggle, to recommence their education and remodel their nosology?

—Boylston Prize on Direct Exploration, 251

A physical exploration of a patient by a skillful person is an autopsy performed before death.

—The Position and Prospects of the Medical Student, 297

Remember that your instrument of examination is a probe, feeling among your patient's vitals, with more or less suffering to him, however it may be interesting to yourself. Do not indulge your curiosity at his expense, any more than you would thrust the exploring instrument of surgery to the bottom of every sinus in a wound beyond the reach of art.

—The Position and Prospects of the Medical Student, 298

Surgery is the branch of the healing art which is practiced in the daylight. Medicine is the branch which is practiced in the darkness. . . . Surgical diseases, speaking broadly, reveal themselves, as it were, in articulate confessions. The language of visceral disease is a kind of ventriloquy. . . . Our method with the first if we talked metaphysics, would be objective-subjective, and with the second subjective-objective.

—Introductory–September 26, 1879, 189

---

[20]Thomas Sydenham (1624–1689): English physician often called "The English Hippocrates" on account of his mastery of seventeenth-century medicine; William Cullen (1710–1790): Scottish physician and chemist and a prominent medical figure in Edinburgh during the Scottish Enlightenment.

Once in a while you will have a patient of sense, born with the gift of observation, from whom you may learn something.

—The Young Practitioner, 382–3

One can tell a man's business, if it is a handicraft, very often by just taking a look at his open hand.—Ah! Four calluses at the end of the fingers of the right hand. None on those of the left. Ah, ha! What do those mean?[21]

—The Professor at the Breakfast-Table, 260

Remember that the errors of stethoscopists spring much oftener from the faults of their brains than of their ears. Mistaking a single sound will rarely lead a man into important error who duly reflects upon the accompanying signs and symptoms. Observation may trip now and then without throwing you, for her gait is a walk; but inference always gallops, and if she stumbles, you are gone.[22]

—The Position and Prospects of the Medical Student, 299

Finally, if you are ever called, as I was a few years ago, to visit a patient in consultation with a physician much older than yourself, and your respected friend, as in that case, insists repeatedly, inveterately, and in every instance, on applying the *wrong end* of the stethoscope to his ear, while he gravely rests the ivory ear-piece upon the patient's thorax, remember the scene between Gil Blas and the archbishop,[23] and do not trifle with the wisdom of experience in attempting to teach your scientific grandfather.

—The Position and Prospects of the Medical Student, 299–300

If you are ever so accurate in your physical explorations, do not rely too much upon your results. Given fifty men with a certain fixed amount of organic disease, twenty may die, twenty may linger indefinitely, and ten

---

[21]"It is generally agreed that [Sherlock] Holmes was based on Oliver Wendell Holmes, a writer [Arthur] Conan Doyle greatly admired. . . . 'Never,' [Conan Doyle] would write later, 'have I so known and loved a man whom I had never seen.'" In Russell Miller, *The Adventures of Arthur Conan Doyle* (London: Harvill Secker, 2008), 54, 110.
[22]See also "The Stethoscope Song," pages 166–9.
[23]Holmes probably refers here to the scene in the picaresque novel *L'Historie de Gil Blas de Santillane* (commonly known as *Gil Blas*), by Alain-René Lesage (1668–1747), in which the main character secures the archbishop's favor by not disclosing his true opinion about the latter's sermon.

may never know they have anything the matter with them. . . . I will say that a diagnosis which maps out the physical condition ever so accurately, is, in a large proportion of cases, of less consequence than the opinion of a sensible man of experience, founded upon the history of the disease, though he has never seen the patient.

—Valedictory Address delivered to the Medical Graduates of Harvard University, 401

The Art of Patient Care

He [James Jackson] used to insist on one small point with a certain philological precision, namely, the true meaning of the word 'cure.' He would have it that to *cure* a patient was simply to *care* for him.[24]

—Scholastic and Bedside Teaching, 307–8

We have to educate ourselves through the pretentious claims of intellect, into the humble accuracy of instinct, and we end at last by acquiring the dexterity, the perfection, the certainty, which those masters of arts, the bee and the spider, inherit from Nature.

—The Young Practitioner, 376

Book-knowledge, lecture-knowledge, examination-knowledge, are all in the brain. But work-knowledge is not only in the brain, it is in the senses, in the muscles, in the ganglia of the sympathetic nerves, all over the man, as one may say, as instinct seems diffused through every part of those lower animals that have no such distinct organ as a brain. See a skilful surgeon handle a broken limb; see a wise old physician smile away a case that looks to a novice as if the sexton would soon be sent for; mark what a large experience has done for those who were fitted to profit by it, and you will feel convinced that, much as you know, something is still left for you to learn.

—The Young Practitioner, 377

---

[24]This passage evokes the famous advice by Francis Weld Peabody (1881–1927) that "the secret of the care of the patient is in caring for the patient." In Francis Weld Peabody, "The Care of the Patient," *Journal of the American Medical Association* 88 (1927): 877–82; See also Oglesby Paul, *The Caring Physician: The Life of Dr. Francis W. Peabody* (Boston: Francis A. Countway Library of Medicine, 1991).

The young man knows the rules but the old man knows the exceptions. The young man knows his patient, but the old man knows also his patient's family, dead and alive, up and down for generations.

—The Young Practitioner, 377

These young doctors are particularly strong, as I understand, on what they call *diagnosis*,—an excellent branch of the healing art, full of satisfaction to the curious practitioner, who likes to give the right Latin name to one's complaint; not quite so satisfactory to the patient, as it is not so very much pleasanter to be bitten by a dog with a collar round his neck telling you that he is called *Snap* or *Teaser*, than by a dog without a collar. Sometimes, in fact, one would a little rather not know the exact name of his complaint, as if he does he is pretty sure to look it out in a medical dictionary, and then if he reads, *This terrible disease is attended with vast suffering and is inevitably mortal*, or any such statement, it is apt to affect him unpleasantly!

—The Poet at the Breakfast-Table, 65

Science is a first-rate piece of furniture for a man's upper chamber, if he has common sense on the ground-floor. But if a man hasn't got plenty of good common sense, the more science he has the worse for his patient. . . . When a person is sick, there is always something to be done for him, and done at once. If it is only to open or shut a window, if it is only to tell him to keep on doing just what he is doing already, it wants a man to bring his mind right down to the fact of the present case and its immediate needs. . . . If a doctor has science without common sense, he treats a fever, but not this man's fever. If he has common sense without science, he treats this man's fever without knowing the general laws that govern all fevers and all vital movements. . . . The men that have science only, begin too far back, and before they get as far as the case in hand, the patient has very likely gone to visit his deceased relatives.

—The Poet at the Breakfast-Table, 120–1

I'll tell you, though, Mr. Langdon, when a man that's once started right lives among sick folks for five-and-thirty years, as I've done, if he hasn't got a library of five-and-thirty volumes bound up in his head at the end of that time, he'd better stop driving round and sell his horse and sulky. I know the bigger part of the families within a dozen miles' ride. I know the families that have a way of living through everything, and I know the other set that have the trick of dying without any kind of reason for it. I know the years when the fevers and dysenteries are in earnest, and when they're only make believe. I know the folks that think they're dying as soon as they're sick, and the folks that never find out they're sick till they're dead. I don't want to undervalue your science, Mr. Langdon. There are things I never learned, because they came in after my day, and I am very glad to send my patients to those that do know them, when I am at fault; but I know these people about here, fathers and mothers, and children and grandchildren, so as all the science in the world can't know them, without it takes time about it, and sees them grow up and grow old, and how the wear and tear of life comes to them. You can't tell a horse by driving him once, Mr. Langdon, nor a patient by talking half an hour with him.

—Dr. Kittredge, in *Elsie Venner*, 210–11

The old Doctor knew by sad experience that dreadful mistake against which all medical practitioners should be warned. His experience may well be a guide for others. Do not overlook the desire for spiritual advice and consolation which patients sometimes feel, and with the frightful *mauvaise honte*[25] peculiar to Protestantism, alone among all human beliefs, are ashamed to tell. As a part of medical treatment, it is the physician's business to detect the hidden longing for the food of the soul, as much as for any form of bodily nourishment.

—*Elsie Venner*, 449–50

I will venture to say this, that if every specific were to fail utterly, if the cinchona trees all died out, and the arsenic mines were exhausted, and the sulphur regions were burned up, if every drug from the vegetable, animal, and mineral kingdom were to disappear from the market, a body of enlightened men, organized as a distinct profession, would be required just as much as now, and respected and trusted as now, whose province should be to guard against the causes of disease, to eliminate them if possible when still present, to order all the conditions of the patient so as to favor the efforts of the system to right itself, and to give those predictions of the course of disease which only experience can warrant, and which in so many cases relieve the exaggerated fears of sufferers and their friends, or warn them in season of impending danger.

—*Currents and Counter-Currents in Medical Science*, 184

---

[25]*Mauvaise honte*: bad shame; bashfulness.

Therapeutic Skepticism

Here, look at medicine. Big wigs, gold-headed canes, Latin prescriptions, shops full of abominations, recipes a yard long, "curing" patients by drugging as sailors bring a wind by whistling, selling lies at a guinea apiece,—a routine, in short, of giving unfortunate sick people a mess of things either too odious to swallow or too acrid to hold, or, if that were possible both at once.

—*The Professor at the Breakfast-Table*, 11

The three learned professions [i.e., theology, medicine, and law] have but recently emerged from a state of *quasi* barbarism. None of them like too well to be told of it, but it must be sounded in their ears whenever they put on airs. . . . So we must keep the doctors awake by telling them that they have not yet shaken off astrology and the doctrine of signatures, as is shown by the form of their prescriptions, and their use of nitrate of silver, which turns epileptics into Ethiopians. If that is not enough, they must be given over to the scourgers, who like their task and get good fees for it. A few score years ago, sick people were made to swallow burnt toads and powdered earthworms and the expressed juice of wood-lice. The physician of Charles I. and II. prescribed abominations not to be named. Barbarism, as bad as that of Congo or Ashantee. Traces of this barbarism linger even in the greatly improved medical science of our century.

—*The Professor at the Breakfast-Table*, 105

No families take so little medicine as those of doctors, except those of apothecaries.

—*Currents and Counter-Currents in Medical Science*, 184

The popular belief is all but universal that sick persons should feed on noxious substances.

—*Currents and Counter-Currents in Medical Science*, 186

If all medicine were very costly, and the expense of it always came out of the physician's fee, it would really be a less objectionable arrangement than this other most pernicious one. He would naturally think twice before he gave an emetic or cathartic which evacuated his own pocket, and be sparing of the cholagogues that emptied the biliary ducts of his own wallet, unless he were *sure* they were needed.

—*Currents and Counter-Currents in Medical Science*, 191

If I wished him [a student] to understand the tendencies of the American medical mind, its sanguine enterprise, its self-confidence, its audacious handling of Nature, its impatience with her old-fashioned ways of taking time to get a sick man well, I would make him read the life and writings of Benjamin Rush.[26]

—*Currents and Counter-Currents in Medical Science*, 192

How could a people which has a revolution once in four years, which has contrived the Bowie-knife and the revolver, which has chewed the juice out of all the superlatives in the language of Fourth of July orations, and so used up its epithets in the rhetoric of abuse that it takes two great quarto dictionaries to supply the demand; which insists in sending out yachts and horses and boys to out-sail, out-run, out-fight, and checkmate all the rest of creation; how could such a people be content with any but 'heroic' practice?[27]

—*Currents and Counter-Currents in Medical Science*, 193

Presumptions are of vast importance in medicine, as in law. A man is presumed innocent until he is proved guilty. A medicine—that is, a noxious agent, like a blister, a seton, an emetic, or a cathartic—should always be presumed to be hurtful. It always is *directly* hurtful; it may sometimes be indirectly beneficial.

—*Currents and Counter-Currents in Medical Science*, 202

Throw out opium, which the Creator himself seems to prescribe, for we often see the scarlet poppy growing in the cornfields, as if it were foreseen that wherever there is hunger to be fed there must also be pain to be soothed; throw out a few specifics which our art did not discover, and is hardly needed to apply; throw out wine, which is a food, and the vapors which produce the miracle of anæsthesia, and I firmly believe that if the whole materia medica, *as now used*, could be sunk to the bottom of

---

[26]Benjamin Rush (1745–1813), famous in his own time as physician, educator, political figure, and writer, popularized bloodletting and other heroic therapies in the wake of the 1793 Philadelphia yellow fever epidemic.

[27]The term "heroic practice" is most commonly used by medical historians as Holmes uses the term here: to describe the aggressive use of such measures as bloodletting (and, more specifically, venesection), intestinal purging with calomel [mercury chloride], induced vomiting with tartar emetic, profuse sweating (diaphoretics), and blistering. For context, see Robert B. Sullivan, "Sanguine Practices: A Historical and Historiographic Reconsideration of Heroic Therapy in the Age of Rush," *Bulletin of the History of Medicine* 68 (1994): 211–34.

the sea, it would be all the better for mankind,—and all the worse for the fishes.[28]

—*Currents and Counter-Currents in Medical Science*, 202–3

If the materia medica were lost overboard, how much more pains would be taken in ordering all the circumstances surrounding the patient (as can be done everywhere out of the crowded pauper districts), than are taken now by too many who think they do their duty and earn their money when they write a recipe for a patient.

—*Currents and Counter-Currents in Medical Science*, 203

The disgrace of medicine has been that colossal system of self-deception, in obedience to which mines have been emptied of their cankering minerals, the vegetable kingdom robbed of all its noxious growths, the entrails of animals taxed for their impurities, the poison-bags of reptiles drained of their venom, and all the inconceivable abominations thus obtained thrust down the throats of human beings suffering from some fault of organization, nourishment, or vital stimulation.

—*Borderlines of Knowledge in Some Provinces of Medical Science*, 265

I cannot help believing that medical *curative* treatment will by and by resolve itself in great measure into modifications of the food, swallowed and breathed, and of the natural stimuli, and that less will be expected from specifics and noxious disturbing agents, either alien or assimilable.

—*Borderlines of Knowledge in Some Provinces of Medical Science*, 267

The very moment that disease passes into the category of vital processes, and is recognized as an occurrence absolutely necessary, inevitable, and as one may say, normal under certain given conditions of constitution

---

[28]"This sentence was misquoted, quoted without its qualifying conditions, and frightened some of my worthy professional brethren as much as if I had told them to throw all physic to the dogs. But for the epigrammatic sting the sentiment would have been unnoticed as a harmless overstatement at the very worst." (In "Preface to the New Edition," *Medical Essays*, xv.) "I have never seen good reason to change my opinion about over-medication especially over-drugging. A drug of any real power does harm if it does not do good. It may do both, good and harm, and the question is which is predominant in the joint result. I say I have not changed my opinion, but there has been a great change in medical practice since some twenty years ago I stated my opinion too epigrammatically for a few of my professional brethren."(In "Introductory Lecture, October 1881," 269.) For further commentary on this passage, see the essay by Charles E. Rosenberg, pages 59–60.

and circumstance, the medicine-man loses his half-miraculous endowments. The mythical serpent is untwined from the staff of Esculapius,[29] which thenceforth becomes a useful walking-stick, and does not pretend to be anything more.

—The Poet at the Breakfast-Table, 305–6

Many things are uncertain in this world, and among them the effect of a large proportion of the remedies prescribed by physicians.

—The Guardian Angel, 130

Evolving disease out of sin, he [Cotton Mather[30]] hates it, one would say, as he hates its cause, and would drive it out of the body with all noisome appliances.

—The Medical Profession in Massachusetts, 359

The lancet was the magician's wand of the dark ages of medicine.

—Some of My Early Teachers, 432

No remedy is useful unless employed at the right moment is an ancient axiom. Now "the right moment" is just what one man decides, and another, perhaps a much better pathologist, overlooks.

—Introductory–September 26, 1879, 197

I am afraid our barbarous method of writing prescriptions in what is sometimes fancifully called Latin, and with the old astrological sign of Jupiter at the head of them to bring good luck, may have helped to swell the list of casualties. We understand why plants and minerals should have technical names, but I am much disposed to think that good plain English, written out at full length, is good enough for the practical physician's use. Why should I employ the language of Celsus?[31] He commonly used none but his own.

—Valedictory Address delivered to the Medical Graduates of Harvard University, 404

---

[29]Staff of Esculapius (more commonly spelled Aesculapius or Asklepios today): The traditional symbol of the medical profession consisting of a rod or stick around which is coiled a single snake.

[30]Cotton Mather (1663–1728): New England Puritan minister perhaps best known in general history for his controversial role in the Salem witch trials and in medical history for encouraging smallpox inoculation.

[31]Celsus: Aulus Cornelius Celsus (ca. 25 B.C.–ca. 50): Roman encyclopedist, whose *De Medicina* affords an important source of our knowledge of Roman medicine and surgery.

Although remedies may often be combined advantageously, the difficulty of estimating the effects of a prescription is as the square of the number of its ingredients. The deeper you wade in polypharmacy, the less you see of the ground on which you stand.

—Valedictory Address delivered to the Medical Graduates of Harvard University, 405–6

The Healing Power of Nature (Vis Medicatrix Naturae)

We who are on the side of "Nature" please ourselves with the idea that we are in the great current in which the true intelligence of the time is moving.

—Currents and Counter-Currents in Medical Science, 183

If there is any State or city which might claim to be the American head-quarters of the nature-trusting heresy, provided it be one, that State is Massachusetts, and that city is its capital.[32]

—Currents and Counter-Currents in Medical Science, 183

The effect which these doctrines have upon the confidence reposed in the profession is a matter of opinion. For myself, I do not believe this confidence can be impaired by any investigations which tend to limit the application of troublesome, painful, uncertain, or dangerous remedies.

—Currents and Counter-Currents in Medical Science, 183

Medication without insuring favorable hygienic condition is like amputation without ligatures.

—Currents and Counter-Currents in Medical Science, 203

The healing process is a work of Nature—of the creative power—as much beyond our resources as the shaping of an embryo in the ovum. . . . We may find fault with the ancient expression *vis medicatrix* if we want to, but it is a convenient phrase for a manifestation of vital power which does in point of fact work towards the definitive end of eliminating sources of disturbance and healing the injuries they have affected.

—Introductory Lecture, October 1881, 251–3

---

[32]For a discussion of Holmes and the "nature-trusting heresy," see John Harley Warner, "'The Nature-Trusting Heresy': American Physicians and the Concept of the Healing Power of Nature in the 1850s and 1860s," *Perspectives in American History* 11 (1977–1978): 291–324.

What is the honest truth about the medical art? That by far the largest number of diseases which physicians are called to treat will get well at any rate, even in spite of reasonably bad treatment. That of the other fraction, a certain number will inevitably die, whatever is done. That there remains a small margin of cases where the life of the patient depends on the skill of the physician. That drugs now and then save life; that they shorten disease and remove symptoms; but that they are second in importance to food, air, temperature, and the other hygienic influences. That was a shrewd trick of Alexander's physician . . . of his [Alexander's] attack after bathing.[33] He asked three days to prepare his medicine. Time is the great physician as well as the great consoler.

—*Talk Concerning the Human Body and its Management*, 233

A man no sooner gets a cut, than the Great Physician, whose agency we often call *Nature*, goes to work, first to stop the blood, and then to heal the wound, and then to make the scar as small as possible.

—*Elsie Venner*, 320

Truth in Medicine

Truth is the breath of life to human society. It is the food of the immortal spirit. Yet a single word of it may kill a man as suddenly as a drop of prussic acid. I think the physician may, in extreme cases, deal with truth as he does with food, for the sake of his patient's welfare or existence. He may partly or wholly withhold it, or, under certain circumstances, medicate it with the deadly poison of honest fraud.

—*Valedictory Address delivered to the Medical Graduates of Harvard University*, 391–2

Always remember that words used before patients or their friends are like coppers given to children; you think little of them, but the children count them over and over, make all conceivable imaginary uses of them, and very likely change them into something or other which makes them sick, and causes you to be sent for to clean out the stomach you have so unwittingly filled with trash; a task not so easy as it was to give them the means of filling it.

—*Valedictory Address delivered to the Medical Graduates of Harvard University*, 400

---

[33]Alexander the Great (ca. 356 B.C.–ca. 323 B.C.) seems to have been an odd choice for Holmes, given the apparent inefficacies of the baths and time in Alexander's last days.

I think I am not the first to utter the following caution: Beware how you take away *hope* from any human being. Nothing is clearer than that the merciful Creator intends to blind most people as they pass down into the dark valley. Without very good reasons, temporal or spiritual, we should not interfere with his kind arrangements.

—*Valedictory Address delivered to the Medical Graduates of Harvard University*, 403

Your patient has no more right to all the truth you know than he has to all the medicine in your saddle-bags.

—*The Young Practitioner*, 388

What is the great secret of the success of every form of quackery? *Hope kept alive.* What is the too frequent fatal gift of science? *A prognosis of despair.*

—*Medical Highways and Byways*, 507

A physician is not—at last, ought not to be—an executioner; and a sentence of death on his face is as bad as a warrant for execution signed by the Governor. As a general rule, no man has a right to tell another by word or look that he is going to die. It may be necessary in some extreme cases; but as a rule, it is the last extreme of impertinence which one human being can offer to another.

—*The Professor at the Breakfast-Table*, 143

If we will only let Nature and the God of Nature alone, persons will commonly learn their condition as early as they ought to know it, and not be cheated out of their natural birthright of hope of recovery, which is intended to accompany sick people as long as life is comfortable, and is graciously replaced by the hope of heaven, or at least of rest, when life has become a burden which the bearer is ready to let fall.

—*The Professor at the Breakfast-Table*, 143–4

Euthanasia

After this, we visited the school-house hospital [a Civil War field hospital]. A fine young fellow, whose arm had been shattered, was just falling into the spasms of lock-jaw. The beads of sweat stood large and round on his flushed and contracted features. He was under the effect of opiates,— why not (if his case was desperate, as it seemed to be considered) stop his sufferings with chloroform? It was suggested that it might *shorten life*. "What then?" I said. "Are a dozen additional spasms worth living for?"

—*My Hunt after the Captain*, 66

The medical art has performed its duty in the face of traditional prejudices, in smoothing the bed of anguish to which maternity had been hopelessly condemned. It owes the same assertion of its prerogative to the sufferings sometimes attending the last period of life. That *euthanasia* often accorded by nature, sometimes prevented by want of harmony in the hesitating and awkwardly delaying functions, not rarely disturbed by intrusive influences, is a right of civilized humanity. The anæsthetics mercifully granted to a world grown sensitive in proportion to its culture will never have fulfilled their beneficent purpose until they have done for the scythe of death what they have done for the knife of the surgeon and the sharper trial hour of a woman.

—*Talk Concerning the Human Body and its Management*, 238

MEDICAL PRACTICE

The Ideal Practitioner

The best a physician can give is never too good for the patient.

—*Scholastic and Bedside Teaching*, 298

A man of very moderate ability may be a good physician, if he devotes himself faithfully to the work. More than this, a positively dull man, in the ordinary acceptation of the term, sometimes makes a safer practitioner than one who has, we will say, five per cent. more brains than his average neighbor, but who think it fifty per cent. more.

—*Scholastic and Bedside Teaching*, 300

You must take the community just as it is, and make the best of it. You wish to obtain its confidence; there is a short rule for doing this which you will find useful,—*deserve it*.

—*The Young Practitioner*, 383

As the basis of all the rest, you must have all those traits of character which fit you to enter into the most intimate and confidential relations with the families of which you are the privileged friend and counsellor. Medical Christianity, if I may use such a term, is of very early date. By the oath of Hippocrates, the practitioner of ancient times bound himself to enter his patient's house with the sole purpose of doing him good, and so to conduct himself as to avoid the very appearance of evil. Let the physician of to-day begin by coming up to this standard, and add to it all the more recently discovered virtues and graces.

—*The Young Practitioner*, 383

I warn you against all ambitious aspirations outside of your profession. Medicine is the most difficult of sciences and the most laborious of arts. It will ask all your powers of body and mind if you are faithful to it. Do not dabble in the muddy sewer of politics, nor linger by the enchanted streams of literature, nor dig in far-off fields for the hidden waters of alien sciences. The great practitioners are generally those who concentrate all their powers on their business. If there are here and there brilliant exceptions, it is only in virtue of extraordinary gifts, and industry to which very few are equal.[34]

—*The Young Practitioner*, 384

To get business a man must really want it. . . . I think I have known more than one young man whose doctor's sign proclaimed his readiness to serve mankind in that capacity, but who hated the sound of a patient's knock. . . . The community soon finds out whether you are in earnest, and really mean business, or whether you are one of those diplomaed dilettanti who likes the amusement of *quasi* medical studies, but have no idea of wasting their precious time in putting their knowledge in practice for the benefit of their suffering fellow-creatures.

—*The Young Practitioner*, 385

If you cannot acquire and keep the confidence of your patient, it is time for you to give place to some other practitioner who can. If you are wise and diligent, you can establish relations with the best of them which they will find it very hard to break. But, if they wish to employ another person, who, as they think, knows more than you do, do not take it as a personal wrong. . . . No matter whether the patient is right or wrong, it is a great impertinence to think you have any property in him. Your estimate of your own ability is not the question, it is what the patient thinks of it.

—*The Young Practitioner*, 389–90

---

[34]Any reader of Holmes's biography cannot fail to smile—or wince—at this passage.

To us of the medical profession, the great calamities of life present themselves under a strangely modified aspect. Disease is our playmate, and
Death is our familiar acquaintance. . . . By such a discipline even a tender
nature loses much of its ready impressibility, but not therefore of its sincere love and sympathy for its fellow-creatures in their anguish and trials. By such training a coarse nature may become brutalized, and forfeit
its heavenly birthright.

—*The Position and Prospects of the Medical Student*, 306, 307

I have heard it said that the art of healing makes men hard-hearted and
indifferent to human suffering. I am willing to own that there is often a
professional hardness in surgeons, just as there is in theologians,—only
much less in degree than in these last. It does not commonly improve the
sympathies of a man to be in the habit of thrusting knives into his fellow-
creatures. . . . A delicate nature will not commonly choose a pursuit
which implies the habitual infliction of suffering, so readily as some gen-
tler office. . . . You may be sure that some men, even among those who
have chosen the task of pruning their fellow-creatures, grow more and
more thoughtful and truly compassionate in the midst of their cruel
experience. They become less nervous, but more sympathetic. They have
a truer sensibility for others' pain, the more they study pain and disease
in the light of science. I have said this without claiming any special
growth in humanity for myself, though I do hope I grow tenderer in my
feelings as I grow older.

—*The Professor at the Breakfast-Table*, 263–4

The Country Doctor

Oh, yes! country doctor,—half a dollar a visit,—drive, drive, drive all
day,—get up at night and harness your own horse,—drive again ten miles
in a snow-storm,—shake powders out of two phials, (*pulv. glycyrrhiz.,
pulv. gum. acac. āā partes equales,*).—drive back again, if you don't happen
to get stuck in a drift,—no home, no peace, no continuous meals, no
unbroken sleep, no Sunday, no holiday, no social intercourse, but one
eternal jog, jog, jog, in a sulky, until you feel like the mummy of an
Indian who had been buried in the sitting posture, and was dug up a
hundred years afterwards!

—*Elsie Venner*, 20–1

If that primitive physician, CHIRON, M.D.,[35] appears as a Centaur, as we look at him through the lapse of thirty centuries, the modern country-doctor, if he could be seen about thirty miles off, could not be distinguished from a wheel-animalcule. He *inhabits* a wheel-carriage. He thinks of stationary dwellings as Long Tom Coffin did of land in general; a house may be well enough for incidental purposes, but for a "stiddy" residence give him a "kerridge." If he is to be classified in the Linnæan scale, he must be set down thus: Genus *Homo;* Species *Rotifer infusorius*,—the wheel-animal of infusions.

—*Elsie Venner*, 139

Oh, that narrow sulky! What hopes, what fears, what comfort, what anguish, what despair, in the roll of its coming or its parting wheels! In the spring, when the old people get the coughs which give them a few shakes and their lives drop in pieces like the ashes of a burned thread which have kept the thread-like shape until they were stirred,—in the hot summer noons, when the strong man comes in from the fields, like the son of the Shunamite,[36] crying, "My head, my head,"—in the dying autumn days, when youth and maiden lie fever-stricken in many a household, still-faced, dull-eyed, dark-flushed, dry-lipped, low-muttering in their daylight dreams, their fingers moving singly like those of slumbering harpers,—in the dead winter, when the white plague of the North has caged its wasted victims, shuddering as they think of the frozen soil which must be quarried like rock to receive them, if their perpetual convalescence should happen to be interfered with by any untoward accident,—at every season, the narrow sulky rolled round freighted with unmeasured burdens of joy and woe.[37]

—*Elsie Venner*, 140–1

---

[35]Chiron: In Greek mythology, a virtuous centaur who was, among other things, a master of the healing arts.

[36]Son of the Shunamite: For the story of the unexpected birth and unexpected death of the son of a Shunamite woman, see 2 Kings 4.

[37]In 1995, Allan Weisse had heroically traced the origins of the term "white plague" to Holmes's "The Medical Profession in Massachusetts [p. 352]," stating that "this hopefully final source of the term will probably put the question of the origin to rest once and for all." See Weisse, "Tuberculosis: Why the 'White Plague'?" *Perspectives in Biology and Medicine* 39 (1995): 132–8. However, Holmes appears to have introduced the term into the literature (and to a much wider audience) eight years earlier, in *Elsie Venner*. Its association here with winter perhaps also sheds light upon why Holmes used the term "white plague." However, his association, in "The Stethoscope Song," of the apparently consumptive "six young damsels" with symptoms of pica (itself now known to be associated with iron deficiency) would possibly support Holmes's use of "white plague" to refer to the signs of anemia. See also page 168.

Dr. Butts [fictional character] was the leading medical practitioner, not only of Arrowhead Village, but of all the surrounding region. He was an excellent specimen of the country doctor, self-reliant, self-sacrificing, working a great deal harder for his living than most of those who call themselves the laboring classes,—as if none but those whose hands were hardened by the use of farming or mechanical implements had any work to do. He had that sagacity without which learning is a mere incumbrance, and he had also a fair share of that learning without which sagacity is like a traveler with a good horse, but who cannot read the directions on the guideboards. He was not a man to be taken in by names. He well knew that oftentimes very innocent-sounding words mean very grave disorders; that all degrees of disease and disorder are frequently confounded under the same term; that "run down" may stand for a fatigue of mind or body from which a week or a month will completely restore the overworked patient, or an advanced stage of a moral illness. . . . He knew too well that what is spoken lightly of as a "nervous disturbance" may imply that the whole machinery of life is in a deranged condition, and that every individual organ would groan aloud if it had any other language than the terrible inarticulate one of pain by which to communicate with the consciousness.

—*A Mortal Antipathy*, 82–3

Only those who have lived the kindly, mutually dependent life of the country, can tell how near the physician who is the main reliance in sickness of all the families throughout a thinly settled region comes to the hearts of the people among whom he labors, how they value him while living, how they cherish his memory when dead.

—*Currents and Counter-Currents in Medical Science*, 173

The shrewd self-reliant "country doctor" who, having only himself to keep his wits about him, and who has just enough of the nurse in him to think of all those little appliances which have so much to do with the comfort and sometimes with the recovery of a patient.

—*Introductory–September 26, 1879*, 193

I suppose I should agree with many sensible persons if I should say that the best physician is the one who knows best how to manage the constitution and to palliate symptoms. *Curing* diseases that would not get well if the constitution was well managed is a comparatively rare occurrence, except in the case of immediately or mediately tangible affections. That is the reason why a sagacious country practitioner is often more to be trusted than the learned pathologist of a city hospital who can map out one's gall-bladder while he is living and give a name to every morbid change in one's body when he is dead. The hospital doctor must not be mistaken in his diagnosis or his students will laugh at him. If his palliative does not answer his purpose the house physician is at hand to try another. So in his city-practice. If things go wrong, he is at hand and can be called in. But the country practitioner is miles off before his anodyne has gone into effect and fifteen miles away while his cathartic is still muttering its yet unfulfilled promise in rumbling borborygmi.

—*On Physicians*

Patients, Allegiance of

The public will give every honest and reasonably competent worker in the healing art a hearty welcome. It is on the whole very loyal to the Medical Profession.

—*Scholastic and Bedside Teaching*, 301

In the first place, the persons who seek the aid of the physician are very honest and sincere in their wish to get rid of their complaints and, generally speaking, to live as long as they can. However attractively the future is painted to them, they are attached to the planet with which they are already acquainted.

—*The Young Practitioner*, 378

There is nothing men will not do, there is nothing they have not done, to recover their health and save their lives. They have submitted to be half-drowned in water, and half-choked with gases, to be buried up to their chins in earth, to be seared with hot irons like galley-slaves, to be crimped with knives, like cod-fish, to have needles thrust into their flesh, and bonfires kindled on their skin, to swallow all sorts of abominations, and to pay for all this, as if to be singed and scalded were a costly privilege, as if blisters were a blessing, and leeches were a luxury. What more can be asked to prove their honesty and sincerity?

—*The Young Practitioner*, 378–9

Every year gives you a more reasoning and reasonable people to deal with.[38]

—Scholastic and Bedside Teaching, 302

Theirs [physicians'] is the least learned of the professions, in this country at least. They have not half the general culture of the lawyers, nor a quarter of that of the ministers. I rather think, though, they are more agreeable to the common run of people than the men with black coats or the men with green bags. People can swear before 'em if they want to, and they can't very well before ministers. . . . Besides, everybody doesn't like to talk about the next world; people are modest in their desires, and find this world as good as they deserve; but everybody loves to talk physic. Everybody loves to hear of strange cases; people are eager to tell the doctor of the wonderful cures they have heard of; they want to know what is the matter with somebody or other who is said to be suffering from "a complication of diseases," and above all, to get a hard name, Greek or Latin, for some complaint which sounds altogether too commonplace in plain English. If you will only call a headache a *Cephalgia*, it acquires dignity at once, and a patient becomes rather proud of it. So I think doctors are generally welcome in most companies.

—The Poet at the Breakfast-Table, 126–7

For these [physician] friends of ours who have gone before, there is now no more toil; they start from their slumber no more at the cry of pain; they sally forth no more into the storms; they ride no longer over the lonely roads that knew them so well; their wheels are rusting on their axles or rolling with other burdens; their watchful eyes are closed to all the sorrows they lived to soothe. Not one of these was famous in the great world; some were almost unknown beyond their own immediate circle. But they have left behind them that loving remembrance which is better than fame, and if their epitaphs are chiseled briefly in stone, they are written at full length on living tablets in a thousand homes to which they carried their ever-welcome aid and sympathy.

—Currents and Counter-Currents in Medical Science, 173–4

---

[38]Stated with respect to the public's apparent opinion of homeopathy. Compare this with Holmes's complaint four years later in "The Young Practitioner," as depicted in section on "Patients, Difficulties Concerning."

Patients, Difficulties concerning

You are to enter upon your professional duties at a time which offers some peculiarities affecting your interests and comfort. . . . No authority is allowed to pass current, no opinion to remain unassailed, no profession to be the best judge of its own men and doctrines. . . . The dogmas of the learned have lost their usurped authority, but the dogmas of the ignorant rise in luxuriant and ever-renewing growths to take their place.

—*The Position and Prospects of the Medical Student*, 316–7

This same community is very intelligent with respect to a great many subjects—commerce, mechanics, manufactures, politics. But with regard to medicine it is hopelessly ignorant and never finds it out. . . . If the community could only be aware of its utter ignorance, and incompetence to form opinions on medical subjects, difficult enough to those who give their lives to the study of them, the practitioner would have an easier task.

—*The Young Practitioner*, 379

You cannot and need not expect to disturb the public in the possession of its medical superstitions. A man's ignorance is as much his private property, and as precious in his own eyes, as his family Bible.

—*The Young Practitioner*, 380

What I call a good patient is one who, having found a good physician, sticks to him till he dies. But there are many very good people who are not what I call good patients.

—*The Young Practitioner*, 390

Another portion of the blame [for therapeutic excess] rests with the public itself, which insists on being poisoned. Somebody buys all the quack medicines that build palaces for the mushroom, say rather, the toadstool millionaires.

—*Currents and Counter-Currents in Medical Science*, 186

In the natural course of things some thousands of persons must be getting well or better of slight attacks of colds, of rheumatic pains, every week, in this city alone. Hundreds of them do something or other in the way of remedy, by medical or other advice, or of their own motion, and the last thing they do gets the credit of the recovery. Think what a crop of remedies this must furnish, if it were all harvested!

—The Young Practitioner, 382

Invalidism is a function to which certain persons are born, as others are born to poetry or art as their calling.

—Talk Concerning the Human Body and its Management, 204

They [physicians] are called every day to patients with internal organs in ruin who expect to have their viscera made over again. I remember being told when I was a boy of a Doctor in Charlestown who took a man's liver out of his body, washed it in wine, and replaced it, thus restoring the patient to health. The story may have been invented by a jester, but I believed it, and why should not others believe it?

—Introductory Lecture, October 1881, 243

Patients, Advice to

If you mean to keep as well as possible, the less you think about your health the better. You know enough not to eat or drink what you have found does not agree with you. You ought to know enough not to expose yourself needlessly to draughts. . . . But except a few simple rules such as I have just given, let your health take care of itself so long as it behaves decently. . . . When one watches for symptoms, every organ in the body is ready to put in its claim.

—Over the Teacups, 186–7

If there happened to be among my audience, any person who wished to know on what principles the patient should choose his physician, I should give him these few precepts to think over:—Choose a man who is personally agreeable, for a daily visit from an intelligent, amiable, pleasant, sympathetic person will cost you no more than one from a sloven or a boor, and his presence will do more for you than any prescription the other will order.[39] Let him be a man of recognized good sense in other matters, and the chance is that he will be sensible as a practitioner. . . . Let him be one whose patients are willing to die in his hands, not one

---

[39]For parallel musings regarding the clergy, see pages 211–12.

whom they go to for trifles, and leave as soon as they are in danger, and who can say, therefore, that he never loses a patient.

—The Young Practitioner, 391

Do what you will to keep well, the time will probably come when you will want the advice of a PHYSICIAN. If you will trust a lecturer, who does not practise, and has not practised for a good many years, he will give you some rules in which he believes you may put confidence. Choose a sensible man, personally agreeable to yourself, if possible, whom you know to have had a good education, to stand well with the members of his own profession, and of whom other scientific men, as well as physicians, speak respectfully. Do not select your medical adviser on the strength of any vague stories of his "success." The best physician in a city loses the largest number of patients. You stare, no doubt, but reflect a moment. His patients trust him to the last, whereas people are apt to drop the charlatan as soon as they are in real danger. Once having chosen your medical adviser, be slow to leave him, except for good cause. He has served an apprenticeship to your constitution.

—Talk Concerning the Human Body and its Management, 232

But as your life and health are your own, you have a perfect right to invest them in patent medicines and fantastic systems to your heart's content. The same right that you have to invest your money in tickets to the different gift enterprises, or (if a bachelor) to answer the advertisements of the refined and accomplished ladies, twenty-nine years old and under, who wish to open a correspondence with middle-aged gentlemen of means, with a view to matrimony.

—Talk Concerning the Human Body and its Management, 236

On the whole, you will act wisely to adopt the principle that it is better to die in the hands of a regular physician than to get well under those of a charlatan or fancy practitioner. Wait one moment. I do not say that it is better to die of any one disease in good hands than to get well of that same disease in bad ones. *That* would be a rather robust assertion. But most people must get well of many complaints in the course of their lives, and it will be probably rather sooner and more comfortably in good than in bad hands. Besides, it is a bad thing that an ignorant or incompetent person should get the credit for curing them. Somebody will have to suffer for it sooner or later. On the other hand, as all must die at one time or another, it is a good thing that the last function of mortality, taking off its garments, should be tenderly watched by faithful, intelligent, and instructed professional friends.

—Talk Concerning the Human Body and its Management, 237

The Medical Profession

Professionalism

You are enrolled hereafter on that long list of the Healers of men, which stretches back unbroken to the days of Heroes and Demigods, until its earliest traditions blend with the story of the brightest of the ancient Divinities.

—Valedictory Address delivered to the Medical Graduates of Harvard University, 385

A physician's first duty is to his patient; his second only, to himself. All quackery reverses this principle as its fundamental axiom. Every practitioner who reverses it is a quack. A man who follows it may be ignorant, but his ignorance will often be safer than a selfish man's knowledge.

—Valedictory Address delivered to the Medical Graduates of Harvard University, 389

Respect your profession, and you will not chatter about your 'patrons,' thinking to gild yourselves by rubbing against wealth and splendor. Be a little proud,—it will not hurt you; and remember that it depends on how the profession bears itself whether its members are the peers of the highest, or the barely tolerated operatives of society.

—Valedictory Address delivered to the Medical Graduates of Harvard University, 396

Your relations to your professional brethren may be a source of lifelong happiness and growth in knowledge and character, or they may make you wretched and end by leaving you isolated from those who should be your friends and counselors. . . . There are common barrators among doctors as there are among lawyers,—stirrers up of strife under one pretext and another, but in reality because they like it. They are their own worst enemies.

—The Young Practitioner, 392

Doctors are the best-natured people in the world, except when they get fighting with each other.

—Elsie Venner, 325

Women in Medicine

These women who are hammering at the gates on which it is written, "No admittance for the mothers of mankind," will by and by organize an institution, which starting from that skilful kind of nursing which Florence Nightingale taught so well, will work backwards through anodynes, palliatives, curatives, preventives, until with little show of science it imparts most of what is most valuable in those branches of the healing art it professes to teach. When that time comes, the fitness of women for certain medical duties, which Hecquet advocated in 1708, which Douglas maintained in 1736, which John Ware, long the honored Professor of Theory and Practice in this Institution, upheld within our own recollection in the face of his own recorded opinion to the contrary, will very possibly be recognized.[40]

—*Scholastic and Bedside Teaching*, 299

One female practitioner, employed by her own sex,—Ann Moore,—was the precursor of that intrepid sisterhood whose cause it has long been my pleasure and privilege to advocate on all fitting occasions.[41]

—*The Medical Profession in Massachusetts*, 317

One has natural tact, swift apprehension, feminine delicacy of perception. I say *feminine* delicacy. I myself, all things considered, very much prefer a male practitioner, but a woman's eye, a woman's instinct, a woman's divining power are special gifts which ought in some way to be made useful. If there were only a well-organized and well-trained hermaphrodite physician I am not sure I would not send for him—her—it—them—as likely to combine more excellences than any unisexual individual. Mainly, however, I think the ovarian sex finds its most congenial employment in the office of nurse; and I would give more for a good nurse to take care of me while I was alive than for the best pathologist that ever lived to cut me up after I was dead.[42]

—*Introductory–September 26, 1879*, 197–9

---

[40]Philippe Hecquet (1661–1737), John Douglas (1675–1743), and John Ware (1796–1864) were specifically concerned with obstetrics and midwifery.
[41]Ann Moore appears to have been a midwife who practiced in Salem in the seventeenth century.
[42]Note minor changes from quotation in Tilton, *Amiable Autocrat*, 332–3.

You will often spoil a good nurse to make a poor doctor. . . . I am for giving women every chance for a medical education, and if they think medicine is one of their proper callings let them try it. I think they will find that they had better at least limit themselves to certain specialties, and always have an expert of the other sex to fall back upon. The trouble is that they are so impressible and imaginative that they are at the mercy of all sorts of fancy systems.

—Dr. Butts, in *A Mortal Antipathy*, 164

Lecture to students of your sex? Why not, I should like to know? I don't think it is the calling for which the average woman is especially adapted, but my teacher got a part of his medical education from a lady, Madame Lachapelle;[43] and I don't see why, if one can learn from a woman, he may not teach a woman, if he knows enough.

—*Over the Teacups*, 131

Now it is just in these little unimportant, all-important matters that a good nurse is of incalculable aid to the physician. And the growing conviction of the importance of thorough training of young women as nurses, is one of the most hopeful signs of medical advancement. . . . What is there in the hour of anguish like the gentle presence, the quiet voice, the thoroughly trained and skilful hand of the woman who was meant by nature, and has been taught by careful discipline, to render those services which money tries to reward, but only gratitude can repay? I have always felt that this was rather the vocation of women than general medical and especially surgical practice. Yet I myself followed a course of lectures given by the younger Madame Lachapelle in Paris, and if here and there an intrepid woman insists on taking by storm the fortress of medical education, I would have the gate flung open to her as if it were that of the citadel of Orleans and she were Joan of Arc returning from the field of victory.

—*Address [on the 100th Anniversary of the Foundation of the Medical School of Harvard University]*, 18–19

I have often wished that disease could be hunted by its professional antagonists in couples,—a doctor and a doctor's quick-witted wife making a joint visit and attacking the patient,—I mean the patient's malady,

---

[43]Marie Louise LaChapelle (1769–1821): French obstetrician who learned midwifery from her mother and went on to make many innovations in the management of labor.

of course,—with their united capacities. For I am quite sure that there is a natural clairvoyance in a woman which would make her as much the superior of man in some particulars of diagnosis as she certainly is in distinguishing shades of color. Many a suicide would have been prevented, if the doctor's wife had visited the victim the day before it happened. She would have seen in the merchant's face his impending bankruptcy, while her stupid husband was prescribing for his dyspepsia and indorsing his note; . . . She will find the right end of a case to get hold of, and take the snarls out as she would out of a skein of thread or a ball of worsted which he would have speedily have reduced to a hopeless tangle. I trust I have not dwelt too long on this point, which grew out of my consideration of the great change that has so largely substituted the careful regulation of all the conditions surrounding the patient, for the drugging system derived from the practice of the English "Apothecaries."

—*Address [on the 100th Anniversary of the Foundation of the Medical School of Harvard University], 19–20*

Specialists

We have Dermatologists, Gynaecologists, Oculists, Aurists, Dentists, and may expect to hear before long of Laryngologists, Pneumologists, Cardiologists, Urethrologists, Urinologists, Syphilologists, and for aught I know Rectologists.

—*Introductory-September 26, 1879, 209*

You can't get any talk out of these specialists away from their own subjects, any more than you can get help from a policeman outside of his own beat.

—*The Poet at the Breakfast-Table, 82*

It must not be supposed that we can return to the methods of the old Egyptians—who, if my memory serves me correctly, had a special physician for every part of the body—without falling into certain errors and incurring certain liabilities.

—*Over the Teacups, 128–9*

The specialist is much like other people engaged in lucrative business. He is apt to magnify his calling, to make much of any symptom which will bring a patient within range of his battery of remedies. . . . The

specialist has but one fang with which to seize and hold his prey, but that
fang is a fearfully long and sharp canine.

—Over the Teacups, 129

The "old-fogy" doctor, who knows the family tendencies of his patient,
who "understands his constitution," will often treat him better than the
famous specialist, who sees him for the first time, and has to guess at
many things "the old doctor" knows from his previous experience with
the same patient and the family to which he belongs.

—Over the Teacups, 130

It is a great luxury to practise as a specialist in almost any class of diseases. The special practitioner has his own hours, hardly needs a night-
bell, can have his residence out of town in which he exercises his
calling,—in short, lives like a gentleman; while the hard-worked general
practitioner submits to a servitude more exacting than that of the man
who is employed in his stable or in his kitchen.

—Over the Teacups, 130

The man who knows *too much* about one particular subject is liable to
become a terrible social infliction. Some of the worst bores (to use plain
language) we ever meet with are recognized as experts of high grade in
their respective departments. Beware of making so much as a pinhole in
the dam that holds back their knowledge. They ride their hobbies without bit or bridle. A poet on Pegasus, reciting his own verses, is hardly
more to be dreaded than a mounted specialist.

—Over the Teacups, 156

To be the supreme authority on anything is a satisfaction to self-love
next door to the precious delusions of dementia.

—The Poet at the Breakfast-Table, viii

Hospitals

The mortality of a hospital depends not merely on the treatment of the
patients, but on the class of diseases it is in the habit of receiving, on the
place where it is, on the season, and many other circumstances. For
instance, there are many hospitals in the great cities of Europe that
receive few diseases of a nature to endanger life, and, on the other hand,

there are others where dangerous diseases are accumulated out of the common proportion.

—Homœopathy and its Kindred Delusions, 73

Other things being equal, it must always be expected that those institutions and individuals enjoying to the highest degree the confidence of the community will lose the largest proportion of their patients; for the simple reason that they will naturally be looked to by those suffering from the gravest class of diseases; that many, who know that they are affected with mortal disease, will choose to die under their care of shelter, while the subjects of trifling maladies, and merely troublesome symptoms, amuse themselves to any extent among the fancy practitioners.

—Homœopathy and its Kindred Delusions, 73–4

The present century has seen the establishment of all those great charitable institutions for the cure of diseases of the body and of the mind, which our State and our city have a right to consider as among the chief ornaments of their civilization.

—The Medical Profession in Massachusetts, 350

It is the special advantage of large cities that they afford the opportunity of seeing a great deal of disease in a short space of time, and of seeing many cases of the same kind of disease brought together.

—The Young Practitioner, 373

Medical Information and Medical Libraries

Add to this the great number of Medical Journals, all useful, we hope, most of them necessary, we trust, many of them excellently well conducted, but which must find something to fill their columns, and so print all the new plans of treatment and new remedies they can get hold of, as the newspapers, from a similar necessity, print the shocking catastrophes and terrible murders.

—Currents and Counter-Currents in Medical Science, 193–4

I forbear to dilate upon the character of too many of our medical periodicals. Let us hope the time will come when their pages will be refused to all anonymous flippancies and unmanly gossip, and above all to those worrying paragraphs, which keep up a kind of fretfulness in their occasional readers.

—An Introductory Lecture Delivered at the Massachusetts Medical College, 12–13

The medical profession of our city, and, let us add, of all those neighboring places which it can ready with its iron arms, is united as never before by the *commune vinculum*, the common bond of a large, enduring, ennobling, unselfish interest. It breathes a new air of awakened intelligence. It marches abreast of the other learned professions, which have long had their extensive and valuable centralized libraries; abreast of them, but not promising to be content with that position. What glorifies a town like a cathedral? What dignifies a province like a university? What illuminates a country like its scholarship, and what is the nest that hatches scholars but a library?

—Medical Libraries, 399

There is a dead medical literature, and there is a live one. The dead is not all ancient, the live is not all modern. There is none, modern or ancient, which if it has no living value for the student, will not teach him something by its autopsy.

—Medical Libraries, 400

[Journals] will be also one of our chief expenses, for these journals must be bound in volumes and they require a great amount of shelf-room; all this, in addition to the cost of subscription for those which are not furnished us gratuitously.

—Medical Libraries, 401

Libraries are the standing armies of civilization, and an army is but a mob without a general who can organize and marshal it so as to make it effective.

—Medical Libraries, 406

Men talk of the nerve that runs to the pocket, but one who loves his books, and has lived long with them, has a nervous filament which runs from his sensorium to every one of them.

—Medical Libraries, 409

There comes a time for every book in the library when it is wanted by somebody.

—Medical Libraries, 413

Medical History

To you, young men, it belongs to judge all that has gone before you. You come nearer to the great fathers of modern medicine than some of you imagine.

—*Borderlines of Knowledge in Some Provinces of Medical Science*, 266

Do not look with contempt, then, on your old books as seem to be mere treatises of unwisdom. The debris of broken systems and exploded dogmas form a great mound—a *Monte Testaccio* of the shards and remnants of old vessels which once held human beliefs. If you take the trouble to climb to the top of it you will widen your horizon; and in these days of specialized knowledge, your horizon is not likely to be any too wide.

—*Address before the Boston Medical Library Association*, 129

MEDICINE AND SOCIETY

Medicine as Embedded in Society

The state of medicine is an index of the civilization of an age and country,—one of the best, perhaps, by which it can be judged.

—*The Medical Profession in Massachusetts*, 313

Nothing sheds such light on the superstitions of an age as the prevailing interpretation and treatment of disease.

—*The Medical Profession in Massachusetts*, 314

The truth is, that medicine, professedly founded on observation, is as sensitive to outside influences, political, religious, philosophical, imaginative, as is the barometer to the changes of atmospheric density.

—*Currents and Counter-Currents in Medical Science*, 177

Observe the coincidences between certain great political and intellectual periods and the appearance of illustrious medical reformers and teachers.

—*Currents and Counter-Currents in Medical Science*, 177

The freedom with which each of us speaks his thought in this presence, belongs in part to the assured position of the Profession in our Commonwealth, to the attitude of Science, which is always fearless, and to the genius of the soil on which we stand, from which Nature withheld the fatal gift of malaria only to fill it with exhalations that breed the fever of inquiry in our blood and in our brain.

—*Currents and Counter-Currents in Medical Science*, 206

Medicine and Religion

We reach the Creator chiefly through his creatures. . . . If performed in the right spirit, there is no higher worship than the unpurchased service of the medical profession. The sick man's faltered blessing reaches heaven through the battered roof of his hovel before the Te Deum[44] that reverberates in vast cathedrals.

—*Valedictory Address delivered to the Medical Graduates of Harvard University*, 387

The profession of medicine never could reach its full development until it became entirely separated from that of divinity. The spiritual guide, the consoler in affliction, the confessor who is admitted into the secrets of our souls, has his own noble sphere of duties; but the healer of men must confine himself solely to the revelations of God in nature, as he sees their miracles with his own eyes. No doctrine of prayer or special providence is to be his excuse for not looking straight at secondary causes, and acting, exactly so far as experience justifies him, as if he were himself the divine agent which antiquity fabled him to be.

—*The Medical Profession in Massachusetts*, 363–4

Thus, then, our library is a temple as truly as the dome-crowned cathedral hallowed by the breath of prayer and praise, where the dead repose and the living worship. May it, with all its treasures, be consecrated like that to the glory of God, through the contributions it shall make to the advancement of sound knowledge, to the relief of human suffering, to the promotion of the harmonious relations between the members of the two noble professions which deal with the diseases of the soul and with those of the body, and to the common cause in which all good men are working, the furtherance of the well-being of their fellow-creatures!

—*Medical Libraries*, 418

---

[44]*Te Deum* (also known as *Te Deum Laudamus*, Ambrosian Hymn or A Song of the Church): An early Christian hymn of praise that remains in use in Roman Catholicism and certain other denominations. On account of its length it is sometimes pronounced "tedium," which is perhaps what Holmes (tongue-in-cheek) implied here.

Perhaps no laymen have given the clergy more trouble than the doctors. The old reproach against physicians, that where there were three of them together there were two atheists, had a real significance, but not that which was intended by the sharp-tongued ecclesiastic who first uttered it. Undoubtedly there is a strong tendency in the pursuits of the medical profession to produce disbelief in that figment of tradition and diseased human imagination which has been installed in the seat of divinity by the priesthood of cruel and ignorant ages. It is impossible, or at least very difficult, for a physician who has seen the perpetual efforts of Nature— whose diary is the book he reads oftenest—to heal wounds, to expel poisons, to do the best that can be done under the given conditions,—it is very difficult for him to believe in a world where wounds cannot heal, where opiates cannot give a respite from pain, where sleep never comes with its sweet oblivion of suffering, where the art of torture is the only science cultivated, and the capacity for being tormented is the only faculty which remains to the children of that same Father who cares for the falling sparrow. The Deity has often been pictured as Moloch,[45] and the physician has, no doubt, frequently repudiated him as a monstrosity.

—*The Pulpit and the Pew*, 414–5

On the other hand, the physician has often been renowned for piety as well as for his peculiarly professional virtue of charity,—led upward by what he sees to the source of all the daily marvels wrought before his own eyes. So it was that Galen gave utterance to that psalm of praise which the sweet singer of Israel need not have been ashamed of; and if this "heathen" could be lifted into such a strain of devotion, we need not be surprised to find so many devout Christian worshippers among the crowd of medical "atheists."

—*The Pulpit and the Pew*, 415

HOMEOPATHY AND ITS KINDRED DELUSIONS

Enough of this long history of miscalled Science [i.e., astrology and alchemy]. We might even question how far it is profitable to search the records of so much folly long displaced by better knowledge. Cunning and

---

[45]*Moloch*: In modern usage, a person or object that demands or requires costly sacrifices. Historically, either the name of a god or the name of a sacrificial ritual associated with fire. Molochs were associated with numerous cultures throughout the Middle East and went by various names including "Ba'al," "Golden Calf," and "Apis Bull."

arrogance and credulity will never again tread this deserted path in company, and as old folios drop to pieces and the eating bookworm destroys that which the writing bookworm does not replace, the once precious legends of antiquity will pass out of the memory of men. Every age must have its own growth of errors and the scholar may guard himself against those of his own time by calmly reviewing those of the past. The dead weeds that have been mown down look very differently it is true from the tall growing ones that hang out their gaudy flowers in his path.

—*Astrology and Alchemy*,[46] 124

Let us all endeavor according to our capacities to keep back every noxious thing that would intrude into the fair fields of knowledge. Astrology and alchemy are dead—so far as the mere outward shape is concerned—but do not suppose that the nineteenth or twentieth or the hundredth century will witness the extinction of the thirst which lived under their deceitful features and now lurks under a mask as fair and as false as they were.

—*Astrology and Alchemy*, 124–5

Whatever the names of the demon who plays his fantastic tricks upon successive generations—whether it be Mephistopheles or Maurmon, let us be warned against the new deceptions by old stories. As one phantom after another passes by on the shades of his magic lantern, let it be our province to persuade all agitated children and their nurses that the show is but painted glass, and will come out of the blaze in a little while to be laid in the same heap with so many others.

—*Astrology and Alchemy*, 125

Berkeley[47] died at the age of about seventy; he might have lived longer, but his fatal illness was so sudden that there was not time enough to stir up a quart of the panacea. He was an illustrious man, but he held two very odd opinions; that tar water was everything, and that the whole material universe was nothing.

—*Homœopathy and its Kindred Delusions*, 15

---

[46] This was the first of three lectures which Holmes would relate before The Society for the Diffusion of Useful Knowledge in February of 1842. The latter two lectures would be printed together as "Homœopathy and its Kindred Delusions," while "Alchemy and Astrology" would remain unpublished. See also Tilton, *Amiable Autocrat*, 165–6.

[47] George Berkeley (1685–1753): Irish philosopher and polymath.

There is every reason to suppose that the existing folly will follow in the footsteps of the past, and after displaying a given amount of cunning and credulity in those deceiving and deceived, will drop from the public view like a fruit which has ripened into spontaneous rottenness, and be succeeded by the fresh bloom of some other delusion required by the same excitable portion of the community.

—Homœopathy and its Kindred Delusions, 17

Of course a large number of apparent cures were due solely to nature; which is true under every form of treatment, orthodox or empirical. Of course many persons experienced at least temporary relief from the strong impression made upon their minds by this novel and marvellous method of treatment.

—Homœopathy and its Kindred Delusions, 37

Many, again, influenced by the sanguine hopes of those about them, like dying people, who often say sincerely, from day to day, that they are getting better, cheated themselves into a false and short-lived belief that they were cured; and as happens in such cases, the public never knew more than the first half of the story.

—Homœopathy and its Kindred Delusions, 37

Swallowers of globules, one of your little pellets, moistened in the mingled waves of one million lakes of alcohol, each two miles in circumference, with which had been blended that one drop of Tincture of Camomile, would be of precisely the strength recommended for that medicine in your favorite Jahr's Manual,[48] against the most sudden, frightful, and fatal diseases!

—Homœopathy and its Kindred Delusions, 53–4

Medical accuracy is not to be looked for in the florid reports of benevolent associations, the assertions of illustrious patrons, the lax effusions of daily journals, or the effervescent gossip of the tea-table.

—Homœopathy and its Kindred Delusions, 71

---

[48] Jahr refers to Gottlieb Heinrich Georg Jahr (1800–1875), whose *Manual of Homoeopathic Medicine* was first translated into English by Constantine Hering.

Probably all are willing to allow that a large majority, for instance, ninety in a hundred, of such cases as a physician is called to in daily practice, would recover, sooner or later, with more or less difficulty, provided nothing were done to interfere seriously with the efforts of nature.

Suppose, then, a physician who has a hundred patients prescribes to each of them pills made of some entirely inert substance, as starch, for instance. Ninety of them get well, or if he chooses to use such language, he cures ninety of them. It is evident, according to the doctrine of chances, that there must be a considerable number of coincidences between the relief of the patient and the administration of the remedy. It is altogether probable that there will happen two or three *very striking* coincidences out of the whole ninety cases, in which it would seem evident that the medicine produced the relief, though it had, as we assumed, nothing to do with it. Now suppose that the physician publishes these cases, will they not have a plausible appearance of proving that which, as we granted at the outset, was entirely false? Suppose that instead of pills of starch he employs microscopic sugar-plums, with the five million billion trillionth part of a suspicion of aconite or pulsatilla, and then publishes his successful cases, through the leaden lips of the press, or the living ones of his female acquaintances—does that make the impression a less erroneous one?

—Homœopathy and its Kindred Delusions, 75–6

Now to suppose that any [therapeutic] trial can absolutely *silence* people would be to forget the whole experience of the past.

—Homœopathy and its Kindred Delusions, 77

It takes time for truth to operate as well as Homœopathic globules.

—Homœopathy and its Kindred Delusions, 78

Such is the pretended science of Homœopathy, to which you are asked to trust your lives and the lives of those dearest to you. A mingled mass of perverse ingenuity, of tinsel erudition, or imbecile credulity, and of artful misrepresentation.

—Homœopathy and its Kindred Delusions, 101

As one humble member of a profession which for more than two thousand years has devoted itself to the pursuit of the best earthly interests of mankind, always assailed and insulted from without by such as are igno-

rant of its infinite perplexities and labors, always striving in unequal con-
test with the hundred-armed giant who walks in the noonday, and sleeps
not in the midnight, yet still toiling, not merely for itself and the present
moment, but for the race and the future, I have lifted my voice against
this lifeless delusion, rolling its shapeless bulk into the path of a noble
science it is too weak to strike, or to injure.

—*Homœopathy and its Kindred Delusions*, 101–2

A scheming drug-vender, (inventive genius,) an utterly untrustworthy
and incompetent observer, (profound searcher of Nature,) a shallow
dabbler in erudition, (sagacious scholar,) started the monstrous fiction
(founded the immortal system) of Homoeopathy. I am very fair, you
see,—you can help yourself to either of these sets of phrases. All the
reason in the world would not have had so rapid and general an effect on
the public mind to disabuse it of the idea that a drug is a good thing in
itself, instead of being, as it is, a bad thing, as was produced by the trick
(system) of this German charlatan (theorist).[49]

—*The Professor at the Breakfast-Table*, 12

While the solemn farce of over-drugging is going on, the world over, the
harlequin pseudo-science jumps on to the stage, whip in hand, with half-
a-dozen somersets, and begins laying about him.

—*The Professor at the Breakfast-Table*, 105

There are those whose minds are satisfied with the decillionth dilution
of a scientific proof. No wonder they believe in the efficacy of a similar
attenuation of bryony or pulsatilla.[50]

—*The Young Practitioner*, 392

There is a *pica* or false appetite in many intelligences; they take to odd
fancies in place of wholesome truth, as girls gnaw at chalk and charcoal.

—*Borderlines of Knowledge in Some Provinces of Medical Science*, 245

---

[49] The "German charlatan" in question was Samuel Hahnemann (1755–1843), founder of
homeopathy.
[50] Bryony: A member of the plant genus *Bryonia* which, like *Pulsatilla*, is used in herbal
medicine.

On some occasions, and before some audiences, it may be justifiable, and perhaps useful, to show up some extreme and insupportable extravagance as an example, not for the sake of the sharpers who live by it, or the simpletons whom they live upon, but for that of a few sensible listeners who are disturbed by their clamor, and wish to know its meaning. Even then you must expect a shoal of pamphlets to spring upon you with the eagerness of sharks, and the ability of barnacles.

—*The Position and Prospects of the Medical Student*, 319

You may depend upon it that half the success of Homœopathy is due to the sweet peace it has brought into the nursery. Between the gurgling down of loathsome mixtures and the saccharine deliquescence of a minute globule, what tender mother could for a moment hesitate?

—*Valedictory Address delivered to the Medical Graduates of Harvard University*, 405

I hope, therefore, that our library will admit the works of the so-called Eclectics, the Thomsonians, if any are in existence, of the Clairvoyants, if they have a literature, and especially of the Homœopathists. This country seems to be the place for such a collection, which will by and by be curious and of more value than at present, for Homœopathy seems to be following the pathological law of erysipelas, fading out where it originated as it spreads to new regions.

—*Medical Libraries*, 415

I will try to speak of homœopathy, not exactly as Isaac Walton[51] says the angler should treat his frog, "as if he loved him," but at least as kindly as frogs are treated in our physiological laboratory.

—*Medical Highways and Byways*, 509

So far as I can take account of the stock, the present assets of homœopathy consist of a pleasing and sonorous designation, a nomenclature of symptoms, with sets of little phials, containing globules, which are the prettiest and most fascinating of amulets, arranged to correspond with the nomenclature, a collection of 'provings' which prove more about the prover than about the questions to be proved, and a doctrine which slips on or off like a kid glove, according to the company in which the practitioner finds himself.

—*Medical Highways and Byways*, 510

---

[51] Izaak Walton (1593–1683): English writer and author of *The Compleat Angler*.

Again, we must not deny that there is such a thing as the *faith-cure*, quite independent of any special divine intervention. Every form of medical imposture can shew [sic] such cures, for the imagination is a very powerful physiological agent.

—*Medical Highways and Byways*, 512

I shall begin, my friends, with the definition of a *Pseudo-science*. A Pseudo-science consists of a *nomenclature*, with a self-adjusting arrangement, by which all positive evidence, or such as favors its doctrines, is admitted, and all negative evidence, or such as tells against it, is excluded. It is invariably connected with some lucrative practical application. Its professors and practitioners are usually shrewd people; they are very serious with the public, but wink and laugh a good deal among themselves. The believing multitude consists of women of both sexes, feeble-minded inquirers, poetical optimists, people who always get cheated in buying horses, philanthropists who insist on hurrying up the millennium, and others of this class, with here and there a clergyman, less frequently a lawyer, very rarely a physician, and almost never a horse-jockey or a member of the detective police. . . .

A Pseudo-science does not necessarily consist wholly of lies. It may contain many truths, and even valuable ones. The rottenest bank starts with a little specie . . . . The practitioners of the Pseudo-sciences know that common minds, after they have been bated with a real fact or two, will jump at the merest rag of a lie, or even at the bare hook. When we have one fact found us, we are very apt to supply the next out of our own imagination. . . .

It is so hard to prove a negative, that, if a man should assert the moon was in truth a green cheese, formed by the coagulable substance of the Milky Way, and challenge me to prove the contrary, I might be puzzled. But if he offer to sell me a ton of this lunar cheese, I call on him to prove the truth of the caseous nature of our satellite, before I purchase.

—*The Professor at the Breakfast-Table*, 197–9

Homœopathy has proved lucrative, and so long as it continues to be so will surely exist,—as surely as astrology, palmistry, and other methods of getting a living out of the weakness and credulity of mankind and womankind.

—Preface to *Medical Essays*, New Edition, xiii

Two opposite inferences may be drawn from [homeopathy's] doctrines and practices. The first is that which is accepted by its disciples. This is that all diseases are "cured" by drugs. The opposite conclusion is drawn by a much larger number of persons. As they see that patients are very commonly getting well under treatment by infinitesimal drugging, which they consider equivalent to no medication at all, they come to disbelieve in every form of drugging and put their whole trust in "nature." Thus experience, "from seeming evil still educing good," has shown that the dealers in this preposterous system of pseudo-therapeutics have cooperated with the wiser class of practitioners in breaking up the system of over-dosing and over-drugging which has been one of the standard reproaches of medical practice.

—Preface to *Medical Essays*, New Edition, xiii–xiv

Similia similibus[52] may prove fatally true for once, if Homœopathy is killed out by its new-born rivals.

—Preface to *Medical Essays*, New Edition, xiv

Quackery and idolatry are all but immortal.

—*The Medical Profession in Massachusetts*, 367

The Contagiousness of Puerperal Fever

These results of observation, being admitted, may, we will suppose, be *interpreted* in different methods. Thus the coincidences may be considered the effect of *chance*. I have had the chances calculated by a competent person, that a given practitioner, A., shall have sixteen fatal cases in a month, on the following data: A. to average attendance upon two hundred and fifty births in a year; three deaths in one thousand births to be assumed as the average from puerperal fever; no epidemic to be at the time prevailing. It follows, from the answer given me, that if we suppose every one of the five hundred thousand annual births of England to have been recorded during the last half-century, there would not be one chance in a million million million millions that one such series should be noted. No possible fractional error in this calculation can render the chance a working probability. Applied to dozens of series of various

---

[52] *Similia similibus* (or, more completely, *similia similibus curantur*): The doctrine in homeopathy that a drug that causes undesirable symptoms in healthy persons will relieve similar symptoms in diseased persons.

lengths, it is obviously an absurdity. Chance, therefore, is out of the question as an explanation of the admitted coincidences.

—The Contagiousness of Puerperal Fever, 114

Until it is proved to what *removable condition* attaching to the attendant the disease is owing, he is bound to stay away from his patients so soon as he finds himself singled out to be tracked by the disease.

—The Contagiousness of Puerperal Fever, 115

A physician who talks about *ceremony* and *gratitude*, and *services rendered*, and the *treatment he got*, surely forgets himself; it is impossible that he should seriously think of these small matters where there is even a question whether he may not carry disease, and death, and bereavement into any one of "his families," as they are sometimes called.

—The Contagiousness of Puerperal Fever, 115

It is by notes of cases, rather than notes of admiration, that we must be guided, when we study the Revised Statutes of Nature, as laid down from the curule chairs of Medicine.

—The Contagiousness of Puerperal Fever, 119

If all the hideous catalogues of cases now accumulated were fully brought to the knowledge of the public, nothing, since the days of Burke and Hare,[53] has raised such a cry of horror as would be shrieked in the ears of the Profession.

—The Contagiousness of Puerperal Fever, 125

Let it be remembered that *persons* are nothing in this matter; better that twenty pamphleteers should be silenced, or as many professors unseated, than that one mother's life should be taken. There is no quarrel here between men, but there is deadly incompatibility and exterminating warfare between doctrines.

—The Contagiousness of Puerperal Fever, 128

---

[53] William Burke and William Hare: Irish immigrants to Edinburgh, Scotland, who in 1827 and 1828 murdered at least 17 persons and sold the corpses to Edinburgh Medical College for dissection. Public outcry prompted the Anatomy Act of 1832, which expanded the legal supply of cadavers in order to discourage body snatching and even murder.

No tongue can tell the heart-breaking calamity they have caused; they have closed the eyes just opened upon a new world of love and happiness; they have bowed the strength of manhood into the dust; they have cast the helplessness of infancy into the stranger's arms, or bequeathed it, with less cruelty, the death of its dying parent. There is no tone deep enough for regret, and no voice loud enough for warning.

—*The Contagiousness of Puerperal Fever*, 167

The woman about to become a mother, or with her new-born infant upon her bosom, should be the object of trembling care and sympathy wherever she bears her tender burden, or stretches her aching limbs. The very outcast of the streets has pity upon her sister in degradation, when the seal of promised maternity is impressed upon her. The remorseless vengeance of the law, brought down upon its victim by a machinery as sure as destiny, is arrested in its fall at a word which reveals her transient claim for mercy. The solemn prayer of the liturgy singles out her sorrows from the multiplied trials of life, to plead for her in the hour of peril. God forbid that any member of the profession to which she trusts her life, doubly precious at that eventful period, should hazard it negligently, unadvisedly, or selfishly!

—*The Contagiousness of Puerperal Fever*, 167

If a question should ever arise between your private advantage and a score or two of innocent lives, remember that you have been warned against adding your names to the list of those who, with a smile upon their faces, have carried death from bedside to bedside, sometimes ignorantly and innocently, and sometimes negligently, if not criminally; but compared to whom Toffana[54] was a public benefactress, and the Marchioness of Brinvilliers[55] a nursing mother!

—*The Position and Prospects of the Medical Student*, 306

---

[54] Giulia Toffana: a woman of Palermo, Italy, who with her daughter (Girolama Spera) perfected a colorless and tasteless liquid commonly known as "Acqua Toffana" containing arsenic and lead and, possibly, belladonna. Most of the victims of this poison, of whom there were more than 600 during the seventeenth century, were men to whose unhappy wives the compound was sold along with instructions for its use (generally, admixture with water or wine, to be served during meals).

[55] The Marchioness of Brinvilliers: Marie-Madeleine-Marguerite d'Aubray (1630–1676), who attempted unsuccessfully to murder her father, brother, and two sisters in order to inherit their property, and who probably used Toffana water for this purpose.

Of course the whole matter has been looked at in a new point of view since the *microbe* as a vehicle of contagion has been brought into light, and explained the mechanism of that which was plain enough as a fact to all who were not blind or who did not shut their eyes.

—Preface to *Medical Essays*, New Edition, xvii

MEDICAL CRITICS

Should you become authors, express your opinions freely; defend them rarely. It is not often that an opinion is worth expressing, which cannot take care of itself. Opposition is the best *mordant* to fix the color of your thought in the general belief.

—*Borderlines of Knowledge in Some Provinces of Medical Science*, 271–2

The character of the opposition which some of these papers have met with suggests the inference that they contain really important, but unwelcome truths. Negatives multiplied into each other change their sign and become positive. Hostile criticisms meeting together are often equivalent to praise, and the square of fault-finding turns out to be the same thing as eulogy.

—Preface to *Currents and Counter-Currents in Medical Science*, iii

The only important inference the writer has been able to draw from the greater number of the refutations of his opinions which have been kindly sent him, is that the preliminary education of the Medical Profession is not always what it ought to be.

—Preface to *Currents and Counter-Currents in Medical Science*, iv

One thing is certain. A loud outcry on a slight touch reveals the weak spot in a profession, as well as in a patient.

—Preface to *Currents and Counter-Currents in Medical Science*, vi

SELECTED POEMS

The Stethoscope Song (1848)[56]

A PROFESSIONAL BALLAD

There was a young man in Boston town,
He bought him a stethoscope nice and new,
All mounted and finished and polished down,
With an ivory cap and a stopper too.

It happened a spider within did crawl,
And spun him a web of ample size,
Wherein there chanced one day to fall
A couple of very imprudent flies.

The first was a bottle-fly, big and blue,
The second was smaller, and thin and long;
So there was a concert between the two,
Like an octave flute and a tavern gong.

Now being from Paris but recently,
This fine young man would show his skill;
And so they gave him, his hand to try,
A hospital patient extremely ill.

Some said that his *liver* was short of *bile*,
And some that his *heart* was over size,
While some kept arguing, all the while,
He was crammed with *tubercles* up to his eyes.

This fine young man then up stepped he,
And all the doctors made a pause;
Said he, The man must die, you see,
By the fifty-seventh of Louis's laws.[57]

---

[56] On Holmes's depiction of the "overzealous auscultator" and the proliferating realm of terms used to describe various pulmonary, cardiac, and vascular sounds, see Stanley Joel Reiser, *Medicine and the Reign of Technology* (Cambridge: Cambridge University Press, 1978), 23–44.

[57] On the devotion of a generation of American medical students to Pierre-Charles-Alexandre Louis, see William Osler, "The Influence of Louis on American Medicine," in *An Alabama Student and other Biographical Essays* (New York: Oxford University Press, 1908), 189–210; Warner, *Against the Spirit of System*, 127–131.

But since the case is a desperate one,
To explore his chest it may be well;
For if he should die and it were not done,
You know the *autopsy* would not tell.

Then out his stethoscope he took,
And on it placed his curious ear;
Mon Dieu! said he, with a knowing look,
Why, here is a sound that's mighty queer!

The *bourdonnement* is very clear,—
Amphoric buzzing, as I'm alive!
Five doctors took their turn to hear;
Amphoric buzzing, said all the five.

There's *empyema* beyond a doubt;
We'll plunge a *trocar* in his side.
The diagnosis was made out,—
They tapped the patient; so he died.

Now such as hate new-fashioned toys
Began to look extremely glum;
They said that *rattles* were made for boys,
And vowed that his *buzzing* was all a hum.

There was an old lady had long been sick,
And what was the matter none did know:
Her pulse was slow, though her tongue was quick;
To her this knowing youth must go.

So there the nice old lady sat,
With phials and boxes all in a row;
She asked the young doctor what he was at,
To thump her and tumble her ruffles so.

Now, when the stethoscope came out,
The flies began to buzz and whiz:
Oh ho! the matter is clear, no doubt;
An *aneurism* there plainly is.

The *bruit de râpe* and the *bruit de scie*
And the *bruit de diable* are all combined;

How happy Bouillaud would be,
If he a case like this could find![58]

Now, when the neighboring doctors found
A case so rare had been descried,
They every day her ribs did pound
In squads of twenty; so she died.

Then six young damsels, slight and frail,
Received this kind young doctor's cares;
They all were getting slim and pale,
And short of breath on mounting stairs.

They all made rhymes with "sighs" and "skies,"
And loathed their puddings and buttered rolls,
And dieted, much to their friends' surprise,
On pickles and pencils and chalk and coals.[59]

So fast their little hearts did bound,
The frightened insects buzzed the more;
So over all their chests he found
The *râle sifflant* and the *râle sonore*.

He shook his head. There's grave disease,—
I greatly fear you all must die;
A slight *post-mortem*, if you please,
Surviving friends would gratify.

The six young damsels wept aloud,
Which so prevailed on six young men
That each his honest love avowed,
Whereat they all got well again.

---

[58] Of Jean-Baptiste Bouillaud (1796–1881) and his tendency to bleed patients, Holmes would write, nearly forty years later: "Where now is the fame of Bouillaud, Professor and Deputy, the Sangrado of his time?" In "Some of My Early Teachers," 437.

[59] These would appear to the modern reader to constitute the symptoms of pica, likely signifying iron-deficiency anemia. Holmes apparently associates anemia with consumption here; for its possible contribution to his coinage of the term "white plague," see note 37, page 139.

This poor young man was all aghast;
The price of stethoscopes came down;
And so he was reduced at last
To practise in a country town.

The doctors being very sore,
A stethoscope they did devise
That had a rammer to clear the bore,
With a knob at the end to kill the flies.

Now use your ears, all you that can,
But don't forget to mind your eyes,
Or you may be cheated, like this young man,
By a couple of silly, abnormal flies.

The Morning Visit (1849)

A sick man's chamber, though it often boast
The grateful presence of a literal toast,
Can hardly claim, amidst its various wealth,
The right unchallenged to propose a health;
Yet though its tenant is denied the feast,
Friendship must launch his sentiment at least,
As prisoned damsels, locked from lovers' lips,
Toss them a kiss from off their fingers' tips.

The morning visit,—not till sickness falls
In the charmed circles of your own safe walls;
Till fever's throb and pain's relentless rack
Stretch you all helpless on your aching back;
Not till you play the patient in your turn,
The morning visit's mystery shall you learn.

'T is a small matter in your neighbor's case,
To charge your fee for showing him your face;
You skip up-stairs, inquire, inspect, and touch,
Prescribe, take leave, and off to twenty such.

But when at length, by fate's transferred decree,
The visitor becomes the visitee,
Oh, then, indeed, it pulls another string;
Your ox is gored, and that's a different thing!

Your friend is sick: phlegmatic as a Turk,
You write your recipe and let it work;
Not yours to stand the shiver and the frown,
And sometimes worse, with which your draught goes down.
Calm as a clock your knowing hand directs,
Rhei, jalapæ ana grana sex,[60]
Or traces on some tender missive's back,
Scrupulos duos pulveris ipecac;[61]
And leaves your patient to his qualms and gripes,
Cool as a sportsman banging at his snipes.
But change the time, the person, and the place,
And be yourself "the interesting case,"
You'll gain some knowledge which it's well to learn;
In future practice it may serve your turn.
Leeches, for instance,—pleasing creatures quite;
Try them,—and bless you,—don't you find they bite?
You raise a blister for the smallest cause,
But be yourself the sitter whom it draws,
And trust my statement, you will not deny
The worst of draughtsmen is your Spanish fly!
It's mighty easy ordering when you please,
Infusi sennæ capiat uncias tres;[62]
It's mighty different when you quackle down
Your own three ounces of the liquid brown.
Pilula, pulvis,[63]—pleasant words enough,
When other throats receive the shocking stuff;
But oh, what flattery can disguise the groan
That meets the gulp which sends it through your own!
Be gentle, then, though Art's unsparing rules
Give you the handling of her sharpest tools;
Use them not rashly,—sickness is enough;
Be always "ready," but be never "rough."

Of all the ills that suffering man endures,
The largest fraction liberal Nature cures;

---

[60] Six grains of Jalap and Rhei. Both Jalap (powdered root of Exogonium purga) and Rhei (root of Chinese rhubarb) were used as cathartics. See J. Worth Estes, *Dictionary of Protopharmacology: Therapeutic Practices, 1700–1850* (Canton: Science History Publications, 1990).
[61] Two scruples (2.6 grams, or 40 grains) of powdered ipecap (emetic).
[62] Three ounces of infused senna (cathartic).
[63] Pills, powder.

Of those remaining, 't is the smallest part
Yields to the efforts of judicious Art;
But simple *Kindness*, kneeling by the bed
To shift the pillow for the sick man's head,
Give the fresh draught to cool the lips that burn,
Fan the hot brow, the weary frame to turn,—
Kindness, untutored by our grave M.D.'s,
But Nature's graduate, when she schools to please,
Wins back more sufferers with her voice and smile
Than all the trumpery in the druggist's pile.

Once more, be *quiet*: coming up the stair,
Don't be a plantigrade, a human bear,
But, stealing softly on the silent toe,
Reach the sick chamber ere you're heard below.
Whatever changes there may greet your eyes,
Let not your looks proclaim the least surprise;
It's not your business by your face to show
All that your patient does not want to know;
Nay, use your optics with considerate care,
And don't abuse your privilege to stare.
But if your eyes may probe him overmuch,
Beware still further how you rudely touch;
Don't clutch his carpus in your icy fist,
But warm your fingers ere you take the wrist.
If the poor victim needs must be percussed,
Don't make an anvil of his aching bust;
(Doctors exist within a hundred miles
Who thump a thorax as they'd hammer piles;)
If you must listen to his doubtful chest,
Catch the essentials, and ignore the rest.
Spare him; the sufferer wants of you and art
A track to steer by, not a finished chart.
So of your questions: don't in mercy try
To pump your patient absolutely dry;
He's not a mollusk squirming in a dish,
You're not Agassiz;[64] and he's not a fish.

---

[64] Louis Agassiz (1807–1873): fellow Saturday Club member, founder of Harvard's Museum of Comparative Zoology, and opponent of Darwinian theory, Agassiz originally gained fame through his *Recherches sur les poissons fossiles* ("Research on Fossil Fish").

And last, not least, in each perplexing case,
Learn the sweet magic of a *cheerful face*;
Not always smiling, but at least serene,
When grief and anguish cloud the anxious scene.
Each look, each movement, every word and tone,
Should tell your patient you are all his own;
Not the mere artist, purchased to attend,
But the warm, ready, self-forgetting friend,
Whose genial visit in itself combines
The best of cordials, tonics, anodynes.

Such is the *visit* that from day to day
Sheds o'er my chamber its benignant ray.
I give his health, who never cared to claim
Her babbling homage from the tongue of Fame;
Unmoved by praise, he stands by all confest,
The truest, noblest, wisest, kindest, best.

Holmes the Man of Letters

COMMUNICATION AND CREATIVITY
> *Conversation and its Dynamics*
> *Writing and Writers*
> *Poetry and Poets*
> *Wit and Humor*
> *Critics*
> *Talent and Genius*

SOCIETY AND THE BODY POLITIC
> *The Body Politic*
> *The Civil War*
> *Provincialism*
> *Boston*
> *Material Progress and the Future*

SELECTED NON-MEDICAL POEMS
> *"Old Ironsides"*
> *"The Last Leaf"*
> *"The Chambered Nautilus"*
> *"The Deacon's Masterpiece, or, the Wonderful 'One-Hoss Shay'"*

THE HUMAN CONDITION

Virtues

I find the great thing in the world is not so much where we stand, as in the direction we are moving: To reach the port of heaven, we must sail sometimes with the wind and sometimes against it,—but we must sail, and not drift, nor lie at the anchor.

> —*The Autocrat of the Breakfast-Table*, 93

It's faith in something and enthusiasm for something that makes a life worth looking at.

> —*The Poet at the Breakfast-Table*, 82

My life shall be a challenge, not a truce!

> —from "Wind-Clouds and Star-Drifts," in *The Poet at the Breakfast-Table*, 201

But what if I should lay down the rule, Be cheerful; take all the troubles and trials of life with perfect equanimity and a smiling countenance? Admirable directions! . . . The truth is that the persons of that buoyant disposition which comes always heralded by a smile, as a yacht driven by a favoring breeze carries a wreath of sparkling foam before her, are born with their happiness ready made. They cannot help being cheerful any more than their saturnine fellow-mortal can help seeing everything through the cloud he carries with him. I give you the precept, then, *Be cheerful*, for just what it is worth, as I would recommend to you to be six feet, or at least five feet ten, in stature. You cannot settle that matter for yourself, but you can stand up straight, and give your five feet five its full value. You can help along a little by wearing high-heeled shoes. So you can do something to encourage yourself in serenity of aspect and demeanor, keeping your infirmities and troubles in the background instead of making them the staple of your constitution. This piece of advice, if followed, may be worth from three to five years of the fourscore which you hope to attain.

—*Over the Teacups*, 182

How many people live on the reputation of the reputation they might have made!

—*The Autocrat of the Breakfast-Table*, 61

I advise aimless young men to choose some profession without needless delay, and so get into a good strong current of human affairs, and find themselves bound up in interests with a compact body of their fellow-men.

—*The Poet at the Breakfast-Table*, 157–8

—Beware of making your moral staple consist of the negative virtues. It is good to abstain, and teach others to abstain, from all that is sinful and hurtful. But making a business of it leads to emaciation of character, unless one feeds largely also on the more nutritious diet of active sympathetic benevolence.

—*The Autocrat of the Breakfast-Table*, 262

—I don't think I have a genuine hatred for anybody. I am well aware that I differ herein from the sturdy English moralist and the stout American tragedian. I don't deny that I hate *the sight* of certain people; but the qualities which make me tend to hate the man himself are such as I am

so much disposed to pity, that, except under immediate aggravation, I
feel kindly enough to the worst of them.

—*The Autocrat of the Breakfast-Table*, 219

Sɪɴ has many tools, but a lie is the handle which fits them all.

—*The Autocrat of the Breakfast-Table*, 124

Manners

Though books on ᴍᴀɴɴᴇʀꜱ are not out of print,
An honest tongue may drop a harmless hint.
Stop not, unthinking, every friend you meet,
To spin your wordy fabric in the street;
While you are emptying your colloquial pack,
The fiend *Lumbago* jumps upon his back.
Nor cloud his features with the unwelcome tale
Of how he looks, if haply thin and pale;
Health is a subject for his child, his wife,
And the rude office that insures his life.
Look in his face, to meet thy neighbor's soul,
Not on his garments, to detect a hole;
"How to observe," is what thy pages show,
Pride of thy sex, Miss Harriet Martineau![1]
O, what a precious book the one would be
That taught observers what they're *not* to see!

—from "A Rhymed Lesson" (Urania) (1846), in *Poetical Works I*, 107–33

. . . a very distinguished philosopher, whom several of our boarders and
myself go to hear . . . treated this matter of *manners* . . . . He told us it
was childish to lay down rules for deportment,—but he could not help
laying down a few.

Thus,—*Nothing so vulgar as to be in a hurry.* —True, but hard of application. . . . *Stillness* of person and steadiness of features are signal marks of
good-breeding. . . . *Talking of one's own ails and grievances.*—Bad enough,
but not so bad as insulting the person you talk with by remarking on his
ill-looks, or appearing to notice any of his personal peculiarities.

---

[1]Harriet Martineau (1802–1876): English writer, journalist, sociologist, and anti-slavery
crusader who described and interpreted North American society and customs in *Society in
America* (New York: Saunders and Otley, 1837).

Apologizing. —A very desperate habit,—and one that is rarely cured. Apology is only egotism wrong side out. . . . It is mighty presumptuous on your part to suppose your small failures of so much consequence that you must make a talk about them. . . .

Good dressing, quiet ways, low tones of voice, lips that can wait, and eyes that do not wander,—shyness of personalities, except in certain intimate communications,—to be *light in hand* in conversation, to have ideas, but to be able to make small talk, if necessary, without them,—to belong to the company you are in, and not to yourself,—to have nothing in your dress or furniture so fine that you cannot afford to spoil it and get another like it, yet to preserve the harmonies, throughout your person and dwelling: I should say that this was a fair capital of manners to begin with.

Under bad manners, as under graver faults, lies very commonly an over-estimate of our special individuality, as distinguished from our generic humanity.

—*The Professor at the Breakfast-Table*, 138–40

I think it is unpopular in this country to talk much about gentlemen and gentlewomen. People are touchy about social distinctions, which no doubt are often invidious and quite arbitrary and accidental, but which it is impossible to avoid recognizing as facts of natural history. Society stratifies itself everywhere, and the stratum which is generally recognized as the uppermost will be apt to have the advantage of easy grace of manner and in unassuming confidence, and consequently be more agreeable in the superficial relations of life. To compare these advantages with the virtues and utilities would be foolish. Much of the noblest work in life is done by ill-dressed, awkward, ungainly persons; but that is no more reason for undervaluing good manners and what we call high-breeding, than the fact that the best part of the sturdy labor of the world is done by men with exceptional hands is to be urged against the use of Brown Windsor[2] as a preliminary to appearance in cultivated society.

—*The Poet at the Breakfast-Table*, 57–8

---

[2]Presumably Brown Windsor soap, which was a favorite of Queen Victoria and Napoleon and has a spicy scent. There is also a Brown Windsor soup, which was popular during the Victorian and Edwardian eras.

Don't you know how hard it is for some people to get out of a room after their visit is really over? They want to be off, and you want to have them off, but they don't know how to manage it. One would think they had been built in your parlor or study, and were waiting to be launched. I have contrived a sort of ceremonial inclined plane for such visitors, which being lubricated with certain smooth phrases, I back them down, metaphorically speaking, stern-foremost, into their "native element," the great ocean of out-doors.

—*The Autocrat of the Breakfast-Table*, 17

Habits

There is one mark of age which strikes me more than any of the physical ones;—I mean the formation of *Habits*. An old man who shrinks into himself falls into ways which become as positive and as much beyond the reach of outside influences as if they were governed by clock work. . . . Every man's *heart* (this organ belongs, you know, to the organic system) has a regular mode of action; but I know a great many men whose *brains*, and all their voluntary existence flowing from their brains, have a *systole* and *diastole* as regular as that of the heart itself.

—*The Autocrat of the Breakfast-Table*, 154–5

Habit is the approximation of the animal system to the organic. It is a confession of failure in the highest function of being, which involves perpetual self-determination, in full view of all existing circumstances. But habit, you see, is an action in present circumstances from past motives. It is substituting a *vis a tergo*[3] for the evolution of living force.

—*The Autocrat of the Breakfast-Table*, 155

Among the gentlemen that I have known, few, if any, were ruined by drinking. My few drunken acquaintances were generally ruined before they became drunkards. The habit of drinking is often a vice, no doubt,—sometimes a misfortune,—as when an almost irresistible heredi-tary propensity exists to indulge in it,—but oftenest of all a *punishment*.

—*The Autocrat of the Breakfast-Table*, 190

---

[3]*vis a tergo*: a force acting from behind.

What do I say to smoking? I cannot grudge an old man his pipe, but I think tobacco often does a good deal of harm to the health. . . . I myself gave it up many years ago. Philosophically speaking, I think self-narcotization and self-alcoholization are rather ignoble substitutes for undisturbed self-consciousness and unfettered self-control.

—Over the Teacups, 184–5

The Chinese have a punishment which consists simply in keeping the subject of it awake, by the constant teasing of a succession of individuals employed for the purpose. The best of our social pleasures, if carried beyond the natural power of physical and mental endurance, begin to approach the character of such a penance.

—One Hundred Days in Europe, 89–90

Character—its Nature, Inheritance, and Development

Each of us is only the footing-up of a double column of figures that goes back to the first pair. Every unit tells,—and some of them are *plus*, and some *minus*. If the columns don't add up right, it is commonly because we can't make out all the figures.

—Elsie Venner, 74

To be a parent is almost to be a fatalist. This boy sits with legs crossed, just as his uncle used to whom he never saw; his grandfathers both died before he was born, but he has the movement of the eyebrows which we remember in one of them, and the gusty temper of the other.

—Elsie Venner, 271

—Two and two do not always make four, in this matter of hereditary descent of qualities. Sometimes they make three, and sometimes five. It seems as if the parental traits at one time showed separate, at another blended,—that occasionally the force of two natures is represented in the derivative one by a diagonal of greater value than either original line of living movement,—that sometimes there is a loss of vitality hardly to be accounted for, and again a forward impulse of variable intensity in some new and unforeseen direction.

—The Professor at the Breakfast-Table, 68

Phrenology juggles with nature. It is so adjusted as to soak up all evidence that helps it, and shed all that harms it. . . . It does not stand at the boundary of our ignorance . . . but is one of the will-o'-the-wisps of its undisputed central domain of bog and quicksand. Yet I should not have devoted so many words to it, did I not recognize the light it has thrown on human actions by its study of congenital organic tendencies.

—Borderlines of Knowledge in Some Provinces of Medical Science, 245

All these newer modes of thought are to a large extent outgrowths of what we may call physiological psychology. The foundations of this were laid in those studies of individual character made by the phrenologists, much in the same way that the foundations of chemistry were laid by the alchemists. In the pursuit of an unattainable end, and in the midst of great hallucinations, they made those observations and discoveries which, divorced from their fancies and theories, lent themselves to the building up of a true science.

—Crime and Automatism, 329

. . . just as the celestial movements are regulated by fixed laws, just as bodily monstrosities are produced according to rule, and with as good reason as normal shapes, so obliquities of character are to be accounted for on perfectly natural principles; they are just as capable of classification as the bodily ones, and they all diverge from a certain average or middle term which is the type of its kind.

—The Poet at the Breakfast-Table, 225

The more we study the will in the way of analysis, the more strictly does it appear to be determined by the infinitely varied conditions of the individual. At the bottom of all these lies the moral "personal equation" of each human being.

—Jonathan Edwards, 379

Nature is always applying her reagents to character, if you will take the pains to watch her. Our studies of character, to change the image, are very much like the surveyor's triangulation of a geographical province. We get a base-line in organization, always; then we get an angle by sighting some distant object to which the passions or aspirations of the subject of our observation are tending; then another;—and so we construct our first triangle. Once fix a man's ideals, and for the most part the rest is easy. *A* wants to die worth half a million. Good. *B* (female) wants to catch him,—and outlive him. All right. Minor details at our leisure.

—The Professor at the Breakfast-Table, 90

I think you will find that people who honestly mean to be true really contradict themselves much more rarely than those who try to be "consistent." But a great many things we say can be made to appear contradictory, simply because they are partial views of a truth, and may often look unlike at first, as a front view of a face and its profile often do.

—*The Professor at the Breakfast-Table*, 33–4

People, young or old, are wonderfully different, if we contrast extremes in pairs. They approach much nearer, if we take them in groups of twenty. Take two separate hundreds as they come, without choosing, and you get the gamut of human character in both so completely that you can strike many chords in each which shall be in perfect unison with corresponding ones in the other. If we go a step farther, and compare the population of two villages of the same race and region, there is such a regularly graduated distribution and parallelism of character, that it seems as if Nature must turn out human beings in sets like chessmen.

—*Elsie Venner*, 173

Here and there a sagacious person, old, or of middle age, who has *triangulated* a race, that is, taken three or more observations from the several standing-places of three different generations, can tell pretty nearly the range of possibilities and the limitations of a child, actual or potential, of a given stock,—errors excepted always, because children of the same stock are not bred just alike, because the traits of some less known ancestor are liable to break out at any time, and because each human being has, after all, a small fraction of individuality about him which gives him a flavor, so that he is distinguishable from others by his friends or in a court of justice, and which occasionally makes a genius or a saint or a criminal out of him. It is well that young persons cannot read these fatal oracles of Nature. Blind impulse is her highest wisdom, after all. We make our great jump, and then she takes the bandage off our eyes. That is the way the broad sea-level of average is maintained, and the physiological democracy is enabled to fight against the principle of selection which would disinherit all the weaker children. The magnificent constituency of mediocrities of which the world is made up,—the people without biographies, whose lives have made a clear solution in the fluid menstruum of time, instead of being precipitated in the opaque sediment of history.

—*Elsie Venner*, 271–2

The longer I live, the more I am satisfied of two things: first, that the truest lives are those that are cut rose-diamond-fashion, with many facets answering to the many-planed aspects of the world around them; secondly, that society is always trying hard in some way or other to grind us down to a single flat surface. It is hard work to resist this grinding-down action.

—*The Professor at the Breakfast-Table*, 33

Friendship

There is no friend like the old friend, who has shared our morning days,
    No greeting like his welcome, no homage like his praise:
Fame is the scentless sunflower, with gaudy crown of gold;
    But friendship is the breathing rose, with sweets in every fold.

—from "No Time Like the Old Time" (1865), in *Poems II*, 146–7

Put not your trust in money, but put your money in trust.[4]

—*The Autocrat of the Breakfast-Table*, 49

If one's intimate in love or friendship cannot or does not share all one's intellectual tastes or pursuits, that is a small matter. Intellectual companions can be found easily in men and books. After all, if we think of it, most of the world's loves and friendships have been between people that could not read nor spell.

—*The Autocrat of the Breakfast-Table*, 131

Every person's feelings have a front-door and a side-door by which they may be entered. The front-door is on the street. Some keep it always open; some keep it latched; some, locked, some bolted,—with a chain that will let you peep in, but not get in, and some nail it up, so that nothing can pass its threshold. This front-door leads into a passage which opens into an ante-room, and this into the interior apartments. The side-door opens at once into the sacred chambers.

---

[4]This advice was also intended as double entendre, specifically for young women before marriage. During the nineteenth century, women who failed to put their money in trust before marriage were required to hand over their assets to their husbands. Trust officers and wealth managers continue to quote Holmes in this respect.

There is almost always at least one key to this side-door. This is carried for years hidden in a mother's bosom. Fathers, brothers, sisters, and friends, often, but by no means so universally, have duplicates of it. The wedding-ring conveys a right to one; alas, if none is given with it!

If nature or accident has put one of these keys into the hands of a person who has the torturing instinct, I can only solemnly pronounce the words that Justice utters over its doomed victim, *The Lord have mercy on your soul!* You will probably go mad within a reasonable time, or, if you are a man, run off and die with your head on a curb-stone, in Melbourne or San Francisco,—or, if you are a woman, quarrel and break your heart, or, turn into a pale, jointed petrifaction that moves about as if it were alive, or play some real life-tragedy or other.

Be very careful to whom you trust one of these keys of the side-door.

—*The Autocrat of the Breakfast-Table*, 128–9

I hope I love good people, not for their sake, but for my own.

—*The Professor at the Breakfast-Table*, 104

—Don't flatter yourselves that friendship authorizes you to say disagreeable things to your intimates. On the contrary, the nearer you come into relation with a person, the more necessary do tact and courtesy become. Except in cases of necessity, which are rare, leave your friend to learn unpleasant truths from his enemies; they are ready enough to tell them.

—*The Autocrat of the Breakfast-Table*, 51

Love

Well, Time alone can lift the future's curtain,—
    Science may teach our children all she knows,
But Love will kindle fresh young hearts,'tis certain,
    And June will not forget her blushing rose.

—from "The Coming Era" (1880), *Poetical Works* II, 226–8

Of all things beautiful in this fair world, there is nothing so enchanting to look upon, to dream about, as the first opening of the flower of young love.

—*Over the Teacups*, 147

Nothing is older than the story of young love. Nothing is newer than that same old story.

—*Over the Teacups*, 308

The study of love is very much like that of meteorology. We know that just about so much rain will fall in a season; but on what particular day it will shower is more than we can tell. We know that just about so much love will be made every year in a given population; but who will rain his young affections upon the heart of whom is not known except to the astrologers and fortune-tellers. And why rain falls as it does and why love is made just as it is are equally puzzling questions.

—*Elsie Venner*, 282

The idea that in this world each young person is to wait until he or she finds that precise counterpart who alone of all creation was meant for him or her, and then fall instantly in love with it, is pretty enough, only it is not Nature's way.

—*The Professor at the Breakfast-Table*, 286

Love does not thrive without hope . . .

—*The Guardian Angel*, 262

Love has many languages, but the heart talks through all of them.

—*A Mortal Antipathy*, 233

The sound of a kiss is not so loud as that of a cannon, but its echo lasts a deal longer.

—*The Professor at the Breakfast-Table*, 269

One could never remember himself in eternity by the mere fact of having loved or hated any more than by that of having thirsted; love and hate have no more individuality in them than single waves in the ocean;—but the accidents or trivial marks which distinguished those whom we loved or hated make their memory our own forever, and with it that of our own personality also.

—*The Autocrat of the Breakfast-Table*, 201

Youth fades; love droops; the leaves of friendship fall:
A mother's secret hope outlives them all.

—"A Mother's Secret," in *The Professor at the Breakfast-Table*, 129

Youth

O for one hour of youthful joy!
Give me back my twentieth spring!
I'd rather laugh a bright-haired boy
Than reign a gray-beard king!

—from "The Old Man Dreams," in *The Autocrat of the Breakfast-Table*, 68

The voices of morning! How sweet is their thrill
When the shadows have turned, and the evening grows still!
The text of our lives may get wiser with age,
But the print was so fair on its twentieth page!

—from "Our Indian Summer" (1856), in *Poetical Works II*, 299–300

—I like children. . . . Pretty much all the honest truth-telling there is in the world is done by them. Do you know they play the part in the household which the king's jester, who very often had a mighty long head under his cap and bells, used to play for a monarch. There's no radical club like a nest of little folks in a nursery.

—*The Poet at the Breakfast-Table*, 50–1

It is very easy to criticise other people's modes of dealing with their children. Outside observers see results; parents see processes.

—*Elsie Venner*, 271

A good many young people think nothing about life as it presents itself in the far horizon, bounded by the snowy ridges of threescore and the dim peaks beyond that remote barrier.

—*Over the Teacups*, 173

Aging and Old Age

Every decade is a defence of the one next behind it. At thirty the youth has sobered into manhood, but the strong men of forty rise in almost unbroken rank between him and the approaches of old age as they show in the men of fifty. At forty he looks with a sense of security at the strong men of fifty, and sees behind them the row of sturdy sexagenarians. When fifty is reached, somehow sixty does not look so old as it once used to, and seventy is still afar off. After sixty the stern sentence of the burial services seems to have a meaning that one did not notice in former years. There begins to be something personal about it. But if one lives to seventy he soon gets used to the text with the threescore years and ten in it, and begins to count himself among those who by reason of strength are destined to reach fourscore, of whom he can see a number still in reasonably good condition. The octogenarian loves to read about people of ninety and over. He peers among the asterisks of the triennial catalogue of the University for the names of graduates who have been seventy years out of college and remain still unstarred. He is curious about the biographies of centenarians.

—*Over the Teacups*, 36–7

We have settled when old age begins. Like all Nature's processes, it is gentle and gradual in its approaches, strewed with illusions, and all its little griefs are soothed by natural sedatives. But the iron hand is not less irresistible because it wears the velvet glove. The button-wood throws off its barks in large flakes, which one may find lying at its foot, pushed out, and at last pushed off, by that tranquil movement from beneath, which is too slow to be seen, but too powerful to be arrested. One finds them always, but one rarely sees them fall. So it is our youth drops from us,—scales off, sapless and lifeless, and lays bare the tender and immature fresh growth of old age. Looked at collectively, the changes of old age appear as a series of personal insults and indignities, terminating at last in death, which Sir Thomas Browne has called "the very disgrace and ignominy of our natures."

—*The Autocrat of the Breakfast-Table*, 153

The great delusion of mankind is in supposing that to be individual and exceptional which is universal and according to law. A person is always startled when he hears himself seriously called an old man for the first time.

—*The Autocrat of the Breakfast-Table*, 154

OLD TIME, in whose bank we deposit our notes,
Is a miser who always wants guineas for groats;
He keeps all his customers still in arrears
By lending them minutes and charging them years.

—from "Our Banker" (1874), in *Poetical Works II*, 350–2

Nature is wiser than we give her credit for being; never wiser than in her dealings with the old. She has no idea of mortifying them by sudden and wholly unexpected failure of the chief servants of consciousness. The sight, for instance, begins to lose something of its perfection long before its deficiency calls the owner's special attention to it. . . . Nature is pitiless in carrying out the universal sentence, but very pitiful in her mode of dealing with the condemned on his way to the final scene.

—*Over the Teacups*, 294

It is not every kind of old age or of wine that grows sour with time.

—*The Autocrat of the Breakfast-Table*, 158–9

I have no doubt that we should die of shame and grief at the indignities offered us by age, if it were not that we see so many others as badly as or worse off than ourselves. We always compare ourselves with our contemporaries.

—*The Autocrat of the Breakfast-Table*, 160–1

. . . as the disease of old age is epidemic, endemic, and sporadic, and everybody who lives long enough is sure to catch it, I am going to say, for the encouragement of such as need it, how I treat the malady in my own case.

First. As I feel, that, when I have anything to do, there is less time for it than when I was younger, I find that I give my attention more thoroughly, and use my time more economically than ever before; so that I can learn anything twice as easily as in my earlier days. I am, not, therefore, afraid to attack a new study. . . .

Secondly. I have opened my eyes to a good many neglected privileges and pleasures within my reach, and requiring only a little courage to enjoy them. . . .

Thirdly, I have found that some of those active exercises, which are commonly thought to belong to young folks only, may be enjoyed at a much later period.

—*The Autocrat of the Breakfast-Table*, 163

If the time comes when you must lay down the fiddle and the bow, because your fingers are too stiff, and drop the ten-foot sculls, because your arms are too weak, and, after dallying a while with eye-glasses, come

at last to the undisguised reality of spectacles,—if the time comes when
that fire of life . . . has burned so low that where its flames reverberated
there is only the somber strain of regret, and where its coals glowed, only
the white ashes that cover the embers of memory,—don't let your heart
grow cold, and you may carry cheerfulness and love with you into the
teens of your second century, if you can last so long.

—*The Autocrat of the Breakfast-Table*, 173–4

Life is a fatal complaint, and an eminently contagious one. I took it early,
as we all do, and have treated it all along with the best palliatives I could
get hold of, inasmuch as I could find no radical cure for its evils, and
have so far managed to keep pretty comfortable under it.

—*The Poet at the Breakfast-Table*, 337

Habits are the crutches of old age; by the aid of these we manage to hob-
ble along after the mental joints are stiff and the muscles rheumatic, to
speak metaphorically,—that is to say, when every act of self-determination costs an effort and a pang. We become more and more automatic as
we grow older, and if we lived long enough we should come to pieces of
creaking machinery.

—*Over the Teacups*, 37–8

More and more the old man finds his pleasures in memory, as the present becomes unreal and dreamlike, and the vista of his earthly future
narrows and closes in upon him. At last, if he live long enough, life
comes to be little more than a gentle and peaceful delirium of pleasing
recollections.

—*Over the Teacups*, 46

A man who has passed his eighth decade feels as if he were already in the
antechamber of the apartments which he may be called to occupy in the
house of many mansions. His convictions regarding the future of our
race are likely to be serious, and his expressions not lightly uttered.

—*Over the Teacups*, 246

As to old persons, it seems as if we never know how much they have to
tell until we are old ourselves and they have been gone twenty or thirty
years. Once in a while we come upon some survivor of his or her generation that we have overlooked, and feel as if we had recovered one of the

lost books of Livy[5] or fished up the golden candlestick from the ooze of the Tiber.[6]

—The Poet at the Breakfast-Table, 169

The feeling must of necessity come to many aged persons that they have outlived their usefulness; that they are no longer wanted, but rather in the way, drags on the wheels rather than helping them forward. But let them remember the often-quoted line of Milton,

"They also serve who only stand and wait."[7]

This is peculiarly true of them. They are helping others without always being aware of it. They are the shields, the breakwaters, of those who come after them.

—Over the Teacups, 36

The first thing to be done is, some years before birth, to advertise for a couple of parents both belonging to long-lived families.

—Over the Teacups, 181

I have sometimes thought that I love so well the accidents of this temporary terrestrial residence, its endeared localities, its precious affections, its pleasing variety of occupation, its alternations of excited and gratified curiosity, and whatever else comes nearest to the longings of the natural man, that I might be wickedly homesick in a far-off spiritual realm where such toys are done with.

—One Hundred Days in Europe, 168

---

[5]Livy: Titus Livius (ca. 59 B.C.–17 A.D.): Roman historian whose masterpiece, *Ab Urbe Condita* ("From the City having been founded"), originally consisted of 142 books, of which only 35 are extant.

[6]*Golden candlestick from the Tiber*: This refers to the giant seven-branched candelabra made by Moses (Exodus 25:31–40), one of the great treasures of Jerusalem. In 70 A.D., Titus Flavius suppressed a revolt by the Jews against Rome and reportedly took Jerusalem's treasures, including the Ark of the Covenant and the great candlestick to Rome. According to one tradition, the candlestick fell or was thrown from the Milvian Bridge into the Tiber in 312 A.D. while in the possession of the emperor Maxentius, who, fleeing from the victorious Constantine, likewise fell into the Tiber and drowned. Maxentius's body was recovered, but the candlestick has never been found. Holmes wrote playfully: "I have often thought of going fishing for it some year when I wanted a vacation, as some of my friends used to go to Ireland to fish for salmon" (*The Poet at the Breakfast-Table*, 332). Another opinion holds that the candlestick was taken from Rome by the Visigoths in 410 A.D. or by the Vandals in 455 A.D.

[7]John Milton (1608–1674): English poet. The famous line is from "Sonnet XIX. When I Consider How my Light is Spent," and represents the first reference in Milton's poetry to his own blindness.

Epistemology, Wisdom, and Truth

Holmesian Psychology

Just as we find a mathematical rule at the bottom of many of the bodily movements, just so thought may be supposed to have its regular cycles.

—*Autocrat of the Breakfast Table*, 72–3

Any new formula which suddenly emerges in our consciousness has its roots in long trains of thought; it is virtually old when it first makes its appearance among the recognized growths of our intellect.

—*Autocrat of the Breakfast-Table*, 37

My thoughts flow in layers or strata, at least three deep. I follow a slow person's talk, and keep a perfectly clear under-current of my own beneath it. Under both runs obscurely a consciousness belonging to a third train of reflections, independent of the two others. I will try to write out a Mental movement in three parts.

A.—First voice, or Mental Soprano,—thought follows a woman talking.

B.—Second voice, or Mental Barytone,—my running accompaniment.

C.—Third voice, or Mental Basso,—low grumble of an importune self-repeating idea.

—*The Professor at the Breakfast-Table*, 37

. . . there are at least six personalities to be recognized as taking part in that dialogue between John and Thomas.[8]

Three Johns.

1. The real John; known only to his Maker.

2. John's ideal John; never the real one, and often very unlike him.

3. Thomas's ideal John, never the real John, nor John's John, but often very unlike either.

---

[8]For discussion of the three Johns and three Thomases, see chapter by Peter Gibian in this volume, pages 89–90.

Three Thomases.

1. The real Thomas.

2. Thomas's ideal Thomas.

3. John's ideal Thomas.

—The Autocrat of the Breakfast-Table, 53

My bucolic friends tell me that our horned cattle always keep a cud in their mouths: when they swallow one, another immediately replaces it. If the creature happens to lose its cud, it must have an artificial one given it, or, they assure me, it will pine, and perhaps die. Without committing myself to the exactness or the interpretation of the statement, I may use it as an illustration. Just in the same way, one thought replaces another; and in the same way the mental cud is sometimes lost while one is talking, and he must ask his companion to supply its place.

—Mechanism in Thought and Morals, 267

Unconscious activity is the rule with the actions most important to life. The lout who lies stretched on the tavern-bench, with just mental activity enough to keep his pipe from going out, is the unconscious tenant of a laboratory where such combinations are being constantly made as never Wöhler or Berthelot[9] could put together; where such fabrics are woven, such colors dyed, such problems of mechanism solved, such a commerce carried on with the elements and forces of the outer universe, that the industries of all the factories and trading establishments in the world are mere indolence and awkwardness and unproductiveness compared to the miraculous activities of which his lazy bulk is the unheeding centre.

— Mechanism in Thought and Morals, 277

We wish to remember something in the course of conversation. No effort of the will can reach it; but we say, 'Wait a minute, and it will come to me,' and go on talking. Presently, perhaps some minutes later, the idea we are in search of comes all at once into the mind, delivered like a prepaid bundle, laid at the door of consciousness like a foundling in a basket. How it came there we know not. The mind must have been

---

[9]Friedrich Wöhler (1800–1882): German chemist who pioneered organic chemistry, synthesized urea, and discovered several of the elements; Marcellin Berthelot (1827–1907): French chemist who synthesized numerous organic compounds and advanced thermochemistry and physical chemistry.

at work groping and feeling for it in the dark: it cannot have come of itself. Yet all the while, our consciousness, so far as we are conscious of our consciousness, was busy with other thoughts.

—*Mechanism in Thought and Morals*, 278–9

Our definite ideas are stepping-stones; how we get from one to the other, we do not know: something carries us; we do not take the step.

—*Mechanism in Thought and Morals*, 285

Persons who talk most do not always think most. I question whether persons who think most—that is, have most conscious thought pass through their minds—necessarily do most mental work. The tree you are sticking in "will be growing when you are sleeping." So with every new idea that is planted in a real thinker's mind: it will be growing when he is least conscious of it. An idea in the brain is not a legend carved on a marble slab: it is an impression made on a living tissue, which is the seat of active nutritive processes. Shall the initials I carved in bark increase from year to year with the tree? And shall not my recorded thought develop into new forms and relations with my growing brain?

—*Mechanism in Thought and Morals*, 289

The idea of a man's "interviewing" himself *is* rather odd, to be sure. But then that is what we are all of us doing every day. I talk half the time to find out my own thoughts as a school-boy turns his pockets out to see what is in them. One brings to light all sorts of personal property he had forgotten in his memory.

—*The Poet at the Breakfast-Table*, 1

It's a very queer place, that receptacle a man fetches his talk out of. The library comparison doesn't exactly hit it. You stow away some idea and don't want it, say for ten years. When it turns up at last it has got so jammed and crushed out of shape by the other ideas packed with it, that it is no more like what it was than a raisin is like a grape on the vine, or a fig from a drum like one hanging on the tree. Then, again, some kinds of thoughts breed in the dark of one's mind like the blind fishes in the Mammoth cave. We can't see them and they can't see us; but sooner or later the daylight gets in and we find that some cold, fishy little negative has been spawning all over our beliefs, and the brood of blind questions it has given birth to are burrowing round and under and butting their blunt noses against the pillars of faith we thought the whole world might lean on. And then, again, some of our old beliefs are dying out every year, and others feed on them and grow fat, or get poisoned as the case may be. And so, you see, you can't tell what the thoughts are that you have got salted down, as one may say, till you run a streak of talk through them, as the market people run a butter-scoop through a firkin.

—The Poet at the Breakfast-Table, 2

Undoubtedly every brain has its own set of moulds ready to shape all material of thought into its own individual set of patterns.

—Ralph Waldo Emerson, 304

There is a natural tendency in many persons to run their adjectives together in *triads*, as I have heard them called. . . . It is, I suspect, an instinctive and involuntary effort of the mind to present a thought or image with the three dimensions which belong to every solid,—an unconscious handling of an idea as if it had length, breadth, and thickness.

—The Autocrat of the Breakfast-Table, 85

Education and the Intellect

Education is only second to nature. Imagine all the infants born this year in Boston and Timbuctoo to change places!

—The Autocrat of the Breakfast-Table, 89

Many ideas grow better when transplanted into another mind than in the one where they sprang up. That which was a weed in one intelligence becomes a flower in the other. A flower, on the other hand, may dwindle down to a mere weed by the same change. Healthy growths may become poisonous by falling upon the wrong mental soil, and what seemed a night-shade in one mind unfold as a morning-glory in the other.

—The Poet at the Breakfast-Table, 146

There is a continual tendency in men to fence in themselves and a few of their neighbors who agree with them in their ideas, as if they were an exception to the race.

—The Poet at the Breakfast-Table, 306

. . . persons with a strong instinctive tendency to contradiction are apt to become unprofitable companions. Our thoughts are plants that never flourish in inhospitable soils or chilling atmospheres. They are all started under glass, so to speak; that is, sheltered and fostered in our own warm and sunny consciousness. They must expect some rough treatment when we lift the sash from the frame and let the outside elements in upon them. They can bear the rain and the breezes, and be all the better for them; but perpetual contradiction is a pelting hailstorm, which spoils their growth and tends to kill them out altogether.

—Over the Teacups, 281

The wider the intellect, the larger and simpler the expressions in which its knowledge is embodied.

—The Professor at the Breakfast-Table, 297

One-story intellects, two-story intellects, three-story intellects with sky-lights. All fact-collectors, who have no aim beyond their facts, are one-story men. Two-story men compare, reason, generalize, using the labors of the fact-collectors as well as their own. Three-story men idealize, imagine, predict; their best illumination comes from above, through the skylight. There are minds with large ground floors, that can store an infinite amount of knowledge; some librarians, for instance, who know enough of books to help other people, without being able to make much other use of their knowledge, have intellects of this class. Your great working lawyer has two spacious stories; his mind is clear, because his mental floors are large, and he has room to arrange his thoughts so that he can get at them,—facts below, principle above, and all in ordered series; poets are often narrow below, incapable of clear statement, and with small power of consecutive reasoning, but full of light, if sometimes rather bare of furniture, in the attics.

—The Poet at the Breakfast-Table, 43

Every man of reflection is vaguely conscious of an imperfectly-defined circle which is drawn around his intellect. He has a perfectly clear sense that the fragments of his intellectual circle include the curves of many other minds of which he is cognizant. He often recognizes these as manifestly concentric with his own, but of less radius. On the other hand, when we find a portion of an arc on the outside of our own, we say it *intersects* ours, but are very slow to confess or to see that it *circumscribes* it. Every now and then a man's mind is stretched by a new idea or sensation, and never shrinks back to its former dimensions.

—The Autocrat of the Breakfast-Table, 266

There is one disadvantage which the man of philosophical habits of mind suffers, as compared with the man of action. While he is taking an enlarged and rational view of the matter before him, he lets his chance slip between his fingers.

—The Professor at the Breakfast-Table, 269

Knowledge and Wisdom

I always believed in life rather than books. I suppose every day of earth, with its hundred thousand deaths and something more of births,—with its loves and hates, its triumphs and defeats, its pangs and blisses, has more of humanity in it than all the books that were ever written, put together. I believe the flowers growing at this moment send up more fragrance to heaven than was ever exhaled from all the essences ever distilled.

—The Autocrat of the Breakfast-Table, 134

. . . there are times in which every active mind feels itself above any and all human books.

—The Autocrat of the Breakfast-Table, 132

Nothing is clearer than that all things are in all things, and that just according to the intensity and extension of our mental being we shall see the many in the one and the one in the many.

—The Autocrat of the Breakfast-Table, 83–4

The simplest things turn out to be unfathomable mysteries; the most mysterious appearances prove to be the most commonplace objects in disguise.

—The Professor at the Breakfast-Table, 256

He who would bound the possibilities of human knowledge by the limitations of present acquirements would take the dimensions of the infant in ordering the habiliments of the adult.

—The Poet at the Breakfast-Table, 264

You can't keep gas in a bladder, and you can't keep knowledge tight in a profession. Hydrogen will leak out and air will leak in, through India-rubber; and special knowledge will leak out, and general knowledge will leak in, though a profession were covered with twenty thicknesses of sheepskin diploma. By Jove, Sir, till common sense is well mixed up with medicine, and common manhood with theology, and common honesty with law, *We the people*, Sir, some of us with nut-crackers, and some of us with trip-hammers,[10] and some of us with pile-drivers, and some of us coming with a whish! like air-stones out of a lunar volcano, will crash down on the lumps of nonsense in all of them till we have made powder of them like Aaron's calf![11]

—*The Professor at the Breakfast-Table*, 14–15

Keep any line of knowledge ten years and some other line will intersect it.

—*The Autocrat of the Breakfast-Table*, 285

Knowledge and timber shouldn't be much used till they are seasoned.

—*The Autocrat of the Breakfast-Table*, 134

Don't talk, thinking you are going to find out your neighbor, for you won't do it, but talk to find out yourself. There is more of you—and less of you, in spots, very likely—than you know.

—*The Poet at the Breakfast-Table*, 2

There are persons I meet occasionally who are too intelligent by half for my liking. They know my thoughts beforehand, and tell me what I was going to say. Of course they are masters of all my knowledge, and a good deal besides; have read all the books I have read, and in later editions; have had all the experiences I have been through, and more too. In my private opinion every mother's son of them will lie at any time rather than confess ignorance.

—*The Poet at the Breakfast-Table*, 333

Most lives, though their stream is loaded with sand and turbid with alluvial waste, drop a few golden grains of wisdom as they flow along. Often

---

[10]Trip-hammer: A large powered hammer used in blacksmithing, forging, mining, and agriculture.

[11]Aaron's calf: During the prolonged absence of Moses on Mount Sinai, the restless Israelites persuaded Aaron to make a Golden Calf in homage to the various deities who, they believed, had delivered them from Egypt (Exodus 32:1–6). Upon his return, the infuriated Moses burned the calf and ground it into powder, which he then mixed in water and forced the Israelites to drink.

times a single *cradling* gets them all, and after that the poor man's labor is only rewarded by mud and worn pebbles.

—*The Autocrat of the Breakfast-Table*, 60

But I maintain that I, the Professor, am a good listener. If a man can tell me a fact which subtends an appreciable angle in the horizon of thought, I am as receptive as the contribution-box in a congregation . . .

—*The Professor at the Breakfast-Table*, 17

It is the province of knowledge to speak and it is the privilege of wisdom to listen.

—*The Poet at the Breakfast-Table*, 264

Wisdom is the abstract of the past, but beauty is the promise of the future.

—*The Professor at the Breakfast-Table*, 31

Truth and Logic

—Truth is tough. It will not break, like a bubble, at a touch; nay, you may kick it about all day, like a football, and it will be round and full at evening. . . . I never heard that a mathematician was alarmed for the safety of a demonstrated proposition. I think, generally, that fear of open discussion implies feebleness of inward conviction, and great sensitiveness to the expression of individual opinion is a mark of weakness.

—*The Professor at the Breakfast-Table*, 109

You can hire logic, in the shape of a lawyer, to prove anything that you want to prove. You can buy treatises to show that Napoleon never lived, and that no battle of Bunker-hill was ever fought. The great minds are those with a wide span, which couple truths related to, but far removed from, each other. Logicians carry the surveyor's chain over the track of which these are the true explorers. I value a man mainly for his primary relations with truth, as I understand truth,—not for any secondary artifice in handling his ideas. Some of the sharpest men in argument are notoriously unsound in judgment. I should not trust the counsel of a clever debater, any more than that of a good chess-player. Either may of course advise wisely, but not necessarily because he wrangles or plays well.

—*The Autocrat of the Breakfast-Table*, 14

A man's logical and analytical adjustments are of little consequence, compared to his primary relations with Nature and truth; and people have sense enough to find it out in the long run; they know what "logic" is worth.

—*The Professor at the Breakfast-Table*, 114

A man's opinions . . . are generally of much more value than his arguments. These last are made by his brain, and perhaps he does not believe the proposition they tend to prove,—as is often the case with paid lawyers; but opinions are formed by our whole nature,—brain, heart, instinct, brute life, everything all our experience has shaped for us by contact with the whole circle of our being.

—*The Professor at the Breakfast-Table*, 116

METAPHYSICS, PSYCHOPATHOLOGY, AND RELIGION

Free Will and Responsibility

The moral universe includes nothing but the exercise of choice: all else is machinery. What we can help and what we cannot help are on two sides of a line which separates the sphere of human responsibility from that of the Being who has arranged and controls the order of things.

— *Mechanism in Thought and Morals*, 301–2

But mind this: the more we observe and study, the wider we find the range of the automatic and instinctive principles in body, mind, and morals, and the narrower the limits of the self-determining conscious movement.

—*The Autocrat of the Breakfast-Table*, 85

The will does not act in the interspaces of thought, for there are no such interspaces, but simply steps from the back of one moving thought upon that of another.

—*The Professor at the Breakfast-Table*, 39

Physiological psychology has taken up the problem of the will as coming under the general laws of life.

—*Jonathan Edwards*, 378

If a man has a genuine, sincere, hearty wish to get rid of his liberty, if he is really bent upon becoming a slave, nothing can stop him. And the temptation is to some natures a very great one. Liberty is often a heavy burden on a man. It involves that necessity for perpetual choice which is the kind of labor men have always dreaded. In common life we shirk it by forming *habits*, which take the place of self-determination. In politics party-organization saves us the pains of much thinking before deciding how to cast our vote. In religious matters there are great multitudes watching us perpetually, each propagandist ready with his bundle of finalities, which having accepted we may be at peace. . . .

So it is that in all the quiet bays which indent the shores of the great ocean of thought, at every sinking wharf, we see moored the hulks and the razees[12] of enslaved or half-enslaved intelligences. . . . They have escaped the dangers of the wave, and lie still henceforth, evermore. Happiest of souls, if lethargy is bliss, and palsy the chief beatitude!

—*Elsie Venner*, 252–3

Psychopathology and Sin

Do you think there may be predispositions, inherited or ingrafted, but at any rate constitutional, which shall take out certain apparently voluntary determinations from the control of the will, and leave them as free from moral responsibility as the instincts of lower animals? Do you not think there may be a *crime* which is not a *sin*?

—*Elsie Venner*, 220

Crime and sin, being the *preserves* of two great organized interests, have been guarded against all reforming poachers with as great jealousy as the Royal Forests. It is so easy to hang a troublesome fellow! It is so much simpler to consign a soul to perdition, or say masses, for money, to save it, than to take the blame on ourselves for letting it grow up in neglect and run to ruin for want of humanizing influences!

—*Elsie Venner*, 226

The limitations of human responsibility have never been properly studied, unless it be by the phrenologists. You know from my lectures that I

---

[12]Razees: A wooden warship whose upper deck has been cut away in such a way as to result in a smaller ship with fewer guns. The term refers to three 64-gun Third Rate British war ships that were thus cut down to 44-gun Fifth Rate frigates in 1794, in response to rumors that the French were building a series of very large frigates. Thus, by the Holmes's writing, these ships would have been obsolete or moored "at every sinking wharf."

consider phrenology, as taught, a pseudo-science, and not a branch of
positive knowledge; but for all that, we owe it an immense debt. . . . If it
has failed to demonstrate its system of special correspondences, it has
proved that there are fixed relations between organization and mind and
character. It has brought out that great doctrine of moral insanity, which
has done more to make men charitable and soften legal and theological
barbarism than any one doctrine that I can think of since the message of
peace and good-will to men.

—*Elsie Venner*, 226–7

Shut up the robber and the defaulter, we must. But what if your oldest
boy had been stolen from his cradle and bred in a North-Street cellar?

—*Elsie Venner*, 227

Treat bad men exactly as if they were insane. They are *in-sane*, out of health,
morally. . . . Restrain them from violence, promptly, completely, and
with the least possible injury, just as in the case of maniacs,—and when
you have got rid of them, or got them tied hand and foot so that they can
do no mischief, sit down and contemplate them charitably, remembering
that nine tenths of their perversity comes from outside influences,
drunken ancestors, abuse in childhood, bad company, from which you
have happily been preserved, and for some of which you, as a member of
society, may be fractionally responsible.

—*Elsie Venner*, 228

We have nothing but compassion for a large class of persons
condemned as sinners by theologians, but considered by us as invalids.
We have constant reasons for noticing the transmission of qualities
from parents to offspring, and we find it hard to hold a child account-
able in any moral point of view for inherited bad temper or tendency
to drunkenness,—as hard as we should to blame him for inheriting
gout or asthma.

—*Elsie Venner*, 322

We are constantly seeing weakness where you see depravity. . . . We used
to be as hard on sickness as you were on sin. We know better now.

—*Elsie Venner*, 323

I have heard of an old character, Colonel Jaques, I believe it was, a
famous cattle-breeder, who used to say he could breed to pretty much

any pattern he wanted to.[13] Well, we doctors see so much of families, how the tricks of the blood keep breaking out, just as much in character as they do in looks, that we can't help feeling as if a great many people hadn't a fair chance to be what is called "good," and that there isn't a text in the Bible worth keeping always in mind than that one, "Judge not, that ye be not judged."

—Elsie Venner, 324

We are getting to be predestinarians as much as Edwards[14] or Calvin[15] was, only instead of universal corruption of nature derived from Adam, we recognize inherited congenital tendencies,—some good, some bad,— for which the subject of them is in no sense responsible.

—Jonathan Edwards, 380

Sin, like disease, is a vital process. It is a function, and not an entity. It must be studied as a section of anthropology. No preconceived idea must be allowed to interfere with our investigation of the deranged spiritual function, any more than the old ideas of demoniacal possession must be allowed to interfere with our study of epilepsy. Spiritual pathology is a proper subject for direct observation and analysis, like any other subject involving a series of living actions.

—The Poet at the Breakfast-Table, 306

The scientific study of man is the most difficult of all branches of knowledge. It requires, in the first place, an entire new terminology to get rid of that enormous load of prejudices with which every term applied to the malformations, the functional disturbances, and the

---

[13]Colonel Samuel Jaques: An early nineteenth-century businessman and sportsman of Charlestown and Somerville, Massachusetts, whose innovations included the Cream-Pot breed of cattle. One of his Cream-Pot cows, fed only on grass, produced nine pounds of butter in three days.

[14]Jonathan Edwards (1703–1758): Congregational minister, theologian, and missionary who, while sometimes considered to be American's most original philosophical theologian, is perhaps best known for his defense of the metaphysics of theological determinism (Calvinism). In a sermon entitled "Sinners in the Hands of an Angry God," he contrasted a God justly wrathful against sin with a God of salvation. Edwards exemplified the "fire and brimstone" preaching of the Great Awakening, a religious revival movement that began in the 1740s. He eventually became unpopular in New England and spent much of his last years as a missionary to Native Americans. Edwards died from complications of inoculation against smallpox. His followers became known as "New Light Calvinists."

[15]John Calvin (1509–1564): French theologian and pastor of the Protestant Reformation whose systematic theology, now known as Calvinism, heavily influenced Presbyterian and other Reformed churches.

organic diseases of the moral nature is at present burdened. Take that one word, *Sin*, for instance: all those who have studied the subject from nature and not from books know perfectly well that a certain fraction of what is so called is nothing more than hysteria; that another fraction is the index of a limited degree of insanity; that still another is the result of a congenital tendency which removes the act we sit in judgment upon from the sphere of self-determination, if not entirely, at least to such an extent that the subject of the tendency cannot be judged with any normal standard.

—*The Poet at the Breakfast-Table*, 307

In place of the doctrine of predestination, in virtue of which certain individuals were to become or remain subjects of wrath, we are discussing organic tendencies, inborn idiosyncrasies, which, so far as they go, are purely mechanical, and are the best excuse that can be pleaded for a human being, exempting him from all moral responsibility when they reach a certain extreme degree, and exculpating him just so far as they are uncontrollable, or unenlightened by any moral sense.

—*Crime and Automatism*, 327

Science and Religion

Once giving in our complete adhesion to the doctrine of the "immanent Deity," we get rid of many difficulties in the way of speculative inquiry into the nature and origin of things. . . . We are ready, therefore, to examine the mystery of life with the same freedom that we should carry into the examination of any other problem; for it is only a question of what mechanism is employed in its evolution and sustenance.

—*Mechanism of Vital Actions*, 333–4

The problem of force meets us everywhere, and I prefer to encounter it in the world of physical phenomena before reaching that of living actions. It is only the name for the incomprehensible cause of certain changes known to our consciousness, and assumed to be outside of it. For me it is the Deity Himself in action.

—*Border Lines of Knowledge in Some Provinces of Medical Science*, 219

Science . . . in other words, knowledge,—is not the enemy of religion; for, if so, then religion would mean ignorance. But it is often the antagonist of school-divinity.

Thinking people are not going to be scared out of explaining or at least trying to explain things by the shrieks of persons whose beliefs are disturbed thereby.

—The Poet at the Breakfast-Table, 223–4

If the sovereign Artificer lets us into his own laboratories and workshops, we need not ask more than the privilege of looking on at his work. We do not know where we stand in the hierarchy of created intelligences. We were *made* a little lower than the angels. I speak it not irreverently; as the lower animals surpass man in some of their attributes, so it may be that not every angel's eye can see as broadly and as deeply into the material works of God as man himself, looking at the firmament through an equatorial of fifteen inches' aperture, and searching into the tissues with a twelfth of an inch objective.

—Borderlines of Knowledge in Some Provinces of Medical Science, 236

To fear science or knowledge, lest it disturb our old beliefs, is to fear the influx of the Divine wisdom into the souls of our fellow-men; for what is science but the piece-meal *revelation*,—uncovering,—of the plan of creation by the agency of those chosen prophets of nature whom God has illuminated from the central light of truth for that single purpose?

—Borderlines of Knowledge in Some Provinces of Medical Science, 251

The attitude of modern Science is erect, her aspect serene, her determination inexorable, her onward movement unflinching; because she believes herself, in the order of Providence, the true successor of the men of old who brought down the light of heaven to men. She has reclaimed astronomy and cosmogony, and is already laying a firm hand on anthropology, over which another battle must be fought, with the usual result, to come sooner or later.

—Mechanism in Thought and Morals, 310

This invisible Universe to which the art of the optician has given you the master-key has wonders, grandeurs, miracles, all its own, and you have only to enter and take possession of a realm of knowledge into which, it may be, the intelligence of some orders of archangels has never penetrated.

—An Address Delivered at the Annual Meeting of the Boston Microscopical Society, 612

I suppose the life of every century has more or less special resemblance to that of some particular Apostle. I cannot help thinking this century has Thomas for its model. How do you suppose the other Apostles felt when that experimental philosopher explored the wounds of the Being who to them was divine with his inquisitive forefinger? In our time that finger has multiplied itself into ten thousand thousand implements of research, challenging all mysteries, weighing the world as in a balance, and sifting through its prisms and spectroscopes the light that comes from the throne of the Eternal.

—*The Poet at the Breakfast-Table*, 194–5

It is not science alone that the old Christian pessimism has got to struggle with, but the instincts of childhood, the affections of maternity, the intuitions of poets, the contagious humanity of the philanthropist,—in short, human nature and the advance of civilization.

—*The Pulpit and the Pew*, 432–3

Nature and the Divine

. . . a tree is an underground creature, with its tail in the air. All its intelligence is in its roots. All the senses it has are in its roots. Think what sagacity it shows in its search after food and drink! . . . The next time you see a tree waving in the wind, recollect that it is the tail of a great underground, many-armed, polypus-like creature, which is as proud of its caudal appendage, especially in summer-time, as a peacock of his gorgeous expanse of plumage.

—*Over the Teacups*, 212–3

Nobody knows New England who is not on terms of intimacy with one of its elms. The elm comes nearer to having a soul than any other vegetable creature among us. It loves man as man loves it.

—*Elsie Venner*, 56

We do not say that it is not probable, but we cannot say it is not true, that new types may be intercalated every century or every year into the existing flora. If the Dix pear was created for the first time in a garden in Washington Street,[16] who shall say that the same power may not have just given us a new fungus in some corner of its vast nursery?

—*Mechanism of Vital Actions*, 374

---

[16]The Dix pear was cultivated by the family of Dr. Elijah Dix, grandfather of Dorothea Lynde Dix (1802–1887), who became famous for advocating for the indigent insane and also for serving as Superintendent of Union Army Nurses during the Civil War. Elijah Dix, after

What is the secret of the profound interest which "Darwinism" has excited in the minds and hearts of more persons than dare to confess their doubts and hopes? It is because it restores "Nature" to its place as a true divine manifestation. It is that it removes the traditional curse from that helpless infant lying in its mother's arms. It is that it lifts from the shoulders of man the responsibility for the fact of death. It is that, if it is true, woman can no longer be taunted with having brought down on herself the pangs which make her sex a martyrdom. If development upward is the general law of the race; if we have grown by natural evolution out of the cave-man, and even less human forms of life, we have everything to hope from the future. That the question can be discussed without offence shows that we are entering on a new era, a Revival greater than that of Letters, the Revival of Humanity.

—*The Poet at the Breakfast-Table*, 304–5

The doctrine of evolution, so far as it is accepted, changes the whole relations of man to the creative power. It substitutes infinite hope in the place of infinite despair for the vast majority of mankind. Instead of a shipwreck, from which a few cabin passengers and others are to be saved in the long-boat, it gives mankind a vessel built to endure the tempests, and at last to reach a port where at the worst the passengers can find rest, and where they may hope for a home better than any which they ever had in their old country.[17]

—*Over the Teacups*, 255–6

We must study man as we have studied stars and rocks. We need not go, we are told, to our sacred books for astronomy or geology or other scientific knowledge. Do not stop there! . . . Say now, bravely, as you will sooner or later have to say, that we need not go to any ancient records

---

becoming successful as a physician and merchant in Worcester, Massachusetts, moved to Boston in 1795, aspiring to wealth and social status similar to that of other prominent families who had moved to Boston, such as the Cabots, Appletons, and Lawrences. He therefore built a mansion with a large garden on Orange Street, which was later incorporated into Washington Street. Having a garden in the crowded city was considered not only a sign of wealth but also of morality; hence, the Dix's garden with its unique pear was the family's special pride.

[17]"There is grandeur in this view of life, with its several powers having been originally breathed into a few forms or into one; and that, whilst this planet has gone cycling on according to the fixed law of gravity, from so simple a beginning endless forms most beautiful and most wonderful have been, and are being, evolved."—Charles Darwin, *On the Origin of Species* (London: John Murray, 1859), 490.

for our anthropology. Do we not all *hope*, at least, that the doctrine of man's being a blighted abortion, a miserable disappointment to his Creator, and hostile and hateful to him from his birth, may give way to the belief that he is the latest terrestrial manifestation of an ever upward-striving movement of divine power? If there lives a man who does not *want* to disbelieve the popular notions about the condition and destiny of the bulk of his race, I should like to have him look me in the face and tell me so.

—The Poet at the Breakfast-Table, 268–9

What shall we say to the doctrine of the fall of man as the ground of inflicting endless misery on the human race? A man to be *punished* for what he could not help! He was expected to account for Adam's sin. . . .

How shall we characterize the doctrine of endless torture as the destiny of most of those who have lived, and are living, on this planet? . . .

All the reasoning of the world, all the proof-texts in old manuscripts, cannot reconcile this supposition of a world of sleepless and endless torment with the declaration that "God is love."

—Over the Teacups, 252–3

There is now to be seen in a tall glass jar, in the Museum of Comparative Anatomy at Cantabridge in the territory of the Massachusetts,[18] a huge *crotalus*,[19] of a species which grows to more frightful dimensions than our own, under the hotter skies of South America. Look at it, ye who would know what is the tolerance, the freedom from prejudice, which can suffer such an incarnation of all that is devilish to lie unharmed in the cradle of Nature! Learn, too, that there are many things in this world which we are warned to shun, and are even suffered to slay, if need be, but which we must not hate, unless we would hate what God loves and cares for.

—Elsie Venner, 208

---

[18]Holmes presumably uses literary puff to the locate the museum at Harvard College in Cambridge, Massachusetts, which took its name from Cambridge, England, the name for which evolved from "Camberitum" (under the Romans) to "Grantchester," then "Grantabric," then "Cantabridge," and finally "Cambridge" (under the Saxons).
[19]*Crotalus*: See page 121, note 17.

Yet a lump of puddingstone is a thing to look at, to think about, to study over, to dream upon, to go crazy with, to beat one's brains out against. Look at that pebble in it. From what cliff was it broken? On what beach rolled by the waves of what ocean? How and *when* imbedded in soft ooze, which itself became stone, and by-and-by was lifted into bald summits and steep cliffs, such as you may see on Meetinghouse-Hill any day—yes, and mark the scratches on their faces left when the boulder-carrying glaciers planed the surface of the continent with such rough tools that the storms have not worn the marks out of it with all the polishing of ever so many thousand years?

—The Professor at the Breakfast-Table, 256

A pebble and the spawn of a mollusk! Before you have solved their mysteries, this earth where you first saw them may be a vitrified slag, or a vapor diffused through the planetary spaces. Mysteries are common enough, at any rate, whatever the boys in Roxbury and Dorchester think of "brickbats" and the spawn of creatures that live in roadside pebbles.

—The Professor at the Breakfast-Table, 257

Every age has to shape the Divine image it worships over again.

—Over the Teacups, 40

The Absurd

Poor everybody that sighs for earthly remembrance in a planet with a core of fire and a crust of fossils!

—Elsie Venner, 145

I once inhaled a pretty full dose of ether, with the determination to put on record, at the earliest moment of regaining consciousness, the thought I should find uppermost in my mind. The mightiest music of the triumphal march into nothingness reverberated through my brain, and filled me with a sense of infinite possibilities which made me an archangel for the moment. The veil of eternity was lifted. The one great truth which underlies all human experience, and is the key to all the mysteries that philosophy has sought in vain to solve, flashed upon me in a sudden revelation. Henceforth all was clear: a few words had lifted my intelligence to the level of the knowledge of the cherubim. As my natural condition returned, I remembered my resolution; and, staggering to my desk, I wrote, in ill-shaped, straggling characters, the all-embracing truth still glimmering in my consciousness. The words were these (children may smile; the wise will ponder): *"A strong smell of turpentine prevails throughout."*

—*Mechanism in Thought and Morals*, 283–4

It was on the morning of my fiftieth birthday that the solution of the great problem I had sought so long came to me as a simple formula, with a few grand but obvious inferences. I will repeat the substance of this final intuition: *The one central fact in the Order of Things which solves all questions is*—At this moment we were interrupted by a knock at the Master's door [and the fact was never revealed].

—*The Poet at the Breakfast-Table*, 339

Religion

We know a good deal about the earth on which we live. But the study of man has been so completely subjected to our preconceived opinions, that we have got to begin all over again. We have studied anthropology through theology; we have now to begin the study of theology through anthropology. Until we have exhausted the human element in every form of belief, and that can only be done by what we may call comparative spiritual anatomy, we cannot begin to deal with the alleged extra-human elements without blundering into all imaginable puerilities. If you think for one moment that there is not a single religion in the world which does not come to us through the medium of a preexisting language; and if you remember that this language embodies absolutely nothing but human conceptions and human passions, you will see at once that every religion presupposes its own elements as already existing in those to whom it is addressed.

—*The Poet at the Breakfast-Table*, 183

We are all tattooed in our cradles with the beliefs of our tribe; the record may seem superficial, but it is indelible. You cannot educate a man wholly out of the superstitious fears which were early implanted in his imagination; no matter how utterly his reason may reject them, he will still feel as the famous woman did about ghosts, *Je n'y crois pas, mais je les crains,*—"I don't believe in them, but I am afraid of them, nevertheless."

—*The Poet at the Breakfast-Table*, 327–8

Do you know that every man has a religious belief peculiar to himself? Smith is always a Smithite. He takes in exactly Smith's worth of knowledge, Smith's-worth of truth, of beauty, of divinity. And Brown has from time immemorial been trying to burn him, to excommunicate him, to anonymous-article him, because he did not take in Brown's-worth of knowledge, truth, beauty, divinity.—Truth is invariable; but the *Smithate* of truth must always differ from the *Brownate* of truth.

—*The Professor at the Breakfast-Table*, 297

People are beginning to find out now that you can't study any religion by itself to any good purpose. You must have comparative theology as you have comparative anatomy. What would you make of a cat's foolish little good-for-nothing collar-bone, if you did not know how the same bone means a good deal in other creatures,—in yourself, for instance, as you'll find out if you break it? You can't know too much of your race and its beliefs, if you want to know anything about your Maker. I never found but one sect large enough to hold the whole of me.

—*The Poet at the Breakfast-Table*, 149

To grow up in a narrow creed and to grow out of it is a tremendous trial of one's nature. There is always a bond of fellowship between those who have been through such an ordeal.

—*Over the Teacups*, 247

—Can a man love his own soul too well? Who, on the whole, constitute the nobler class of human beings? those who have lived mainly to make sure of their own personal welfare in another and future condition of existence, or they who have worked with all their might for their race, for their country, for the advancement of the kingdom of God, and left all personal arrangements concerning themselves to the sole charge of Him who made them and is responsible to himself for their safe-keeping? Is an anchorite[20] who has worn the stone floor of his cell into basins with his knees bent in prayer, more acceptable than the soldier who gives his life for the maintenance of any sacred right or truth, without thinking what will specially become of him in a world where there are two or three million colonists a month, from this one planet, to be cared for? These are grave questions, which may suggest themselves to those who know that there are many profoundly selfish persons who are sincerely devout and perpetually occupied with their own future, while there are others who are perfectly ready to sacrifice themselves for any

---

[20]Anchorite: One who lives in seclusion, usually for religious reasons.

worthy object in this world, but are really too little occupied with their exclusive personality to think so much as many do about what is to become of them in another.

—*Elsie Venner*, 415–6

Perpetual self-inspection leads to spiritual hypochondriasis. If a man insists on counting his pulse twenty times a day, on looking at his tongue every hour or two, on taking his temperature with the thermometer morning and evening, on weighing himself three or four times a week, he will soon find himself in a doubtful state of bodily health. It is just so with those who are perpetually counting their spiritual pulse, taking the temperature of their feelings, weighing their human and necessarily imperfect characters against the infinite perfections placed in the other scale of the balance.

—*Jonathan Edwards*, 397

All men are born with conservative or aggressive tendencies: they belong naturally with the idol-worshippers or the idol-breakers. Some wear their father's old clothes, and some will have a new suit. One class of men must have their faith hammered in like a nail, by authority; another class must have it worked in like a screw, by argument.

—*The Pulpit and the Pew*, 419

Religious Tolerance

We must not allow any creed or religion whatsoever to confiscate to its own private use and benefit the virtues which belong to our common humanity.

—*The Poet at the Breakfast-Table*, 306

—If men would only open their eyes to the fact which stares them in the face from history, and is made clear enough by the slightest glance at the condition of mankind, that humanity is of immeasurably greater importance than their own or any other particular belief, they would no more attempt to make private property of the grace of God than to fence in the sunshine for their own special use and enjoyment.

—*The Poet at the Breakfast-Table*, 327

The golden rule should govern us in dealing with those whom we call unbelievers, with heathen, and with those who do not accept our religious views. The Jews are with us as a perpetual lesson to teach us modesty and civility. The religion we profess is not self-evident. It did not convince the people to whom it was sent. We have no claim to take it for granted that we are all right, and they are all wrong. And, therefore, in the midst of all the triumphs of Christianity, it is well that the stately synagogue should lift its walls by the side of the aspiring cathedral, a perpetual reminder that there are many mansions in the Father's early house as well as in the heavenly one; that civilized humanity, longer in time and broader in space than any historical form of belief, is mightier than any one institution or organization it includes.

—*Over the Teacups*, 197

The Clergy

The old minister . . . had read a great deal of hard theology, and had at last reached that curious state which is so common in good ministers,— that, namely, in which they contrive to switch off their logical faculties on the narrow sidetrack of their technical dogmas, while the great freight-train of their substantial human qualities keeps in the main highway of common-sense, in which kindly souls are always found by all who approach them by their human side.

—*Elsie Venner*, 233–4

To know whether a minister, young or still in flower, is in safe or dangerous paths, there are two psychometers, a comparison between which will give as infallible a return as the dry and wet bulbs of the ingenious "Hygrodeik."[21] The first is the black broadcloth forming the knees of his pantaloons; the second, the patch of carpet before his mirror. If the first is unworn and the second is frayed and threadbare, pray for him. If the first is worn and shiny, while the second keeps its pattern and texture, get him to pray for you.

—*The Guardian Angel*, 157

. . . in choosing your clergyman, other things being equal, prefer the one of a wholesome and cheerful habit of mind and body. If you can get along with people who carry a certificate in their faces that their goodness is so great as to make them very miserable, your children cannot.

---

[21]Hygrodeik [Hydrodeik]: a type of psychrometer or hydrometer (device for measuring humidity) containing wet- and dry-bulbed thermometers.

And whatever offends one of these little ones cannot be right in the eyes of Him who loved them so well.

—The Professor at the Breakfast-Table, 144

COMMUNICATION AND CREATIVITY

Conversation and its Dynamics

Language!—the blood of the soul, Sir! into which our thoughts run and out of which they grow!

—The Professor at the Breakfast-Table, 41

—Language is a solemn thing, —I said. —It grows out of life, —out of its agonies and ecstasies, its wants and its weariness. Every language is a temple, in which the soul of those who speak it is enshrined.

—The Professor at the Breakfast-Table, 43

This business of conversation is a very serious matter. There are men whom it weakens one to talk with an hour more than a day's fasting would do . . . .

There are men of *esprit* who are excessively exhausting to some people. They are the talkers who have what may be called *jerky* minds. Their thoughts do not run in the natural order of sequence. They say bright things on all possible subjects, and their zigzags rack you to death. After a jolting half-hour with one of these jerky companions, talking with a dull friend affords great relief. It is like taking the cat in your lap after holding a squirrel.

—The Autocrat of the Breakfast-Table, 5–6

—What are the great faults of conversation? Want of ideas, want of words, want of manners, are the principal ones, I suppose you think. I don't doubt it, but I will tell you what I have found spoil more good talks than anything else;—long arguments on special points between people who differ on the fundamental principles upon which these points depend. No men can have satisfactory relations with each other until they have agreed on certain *ultima* of belief not to be disturbed in ordinary conversation, and unless they have sense enough to trace the secondary questions depending upon these ultimate beliefs to their source. In short, just as a written constitution is essential to the best social order, so a code of finalities is a necessary condition of profitable talk between two persons.

—*The Autocrat of the Breakfast-Table*, 10–11

Some persons seem to think that absolute truth, in the form of rigidly stated propositions, is all that conversation admits. This is precisely as if a musician should insist on having nothing but perfect chords and simple melodies,—no diminished fifths, no flat sevenths, no flourishes, on any account. Now it is fair to say, that, just as music must have all these, so conversation must have its partial truths, its embellished truths, its exaggerated truths. It is in its highest forms an artistic product, and admits the ideal element as much as pictures or statues. One man who is a little too literal can spoil the talk of a whole tableful of men of *esprit*. . . . Remember that talking is one of the fine arts,—the noblest, the most important, and the most difficult,—and that its fluent harmonies may be spoiled by the intrusion of a single harsh note. Therefore conversation which is suggestive rather than argumentative, which lets out the most of each talker's results of thought, is commonly the pleasantest and the most profitable. It is not easy, at the best, for two persons talking together to make the most of each other's thoughts, there are so many of them.

—*The Autocrat of the Breakfast-Table*, 51–2

—It is a fine thing to be an oracle to which an appeal is always made in all discussions. The men of facts wait their turn in grim silence, with that slight tension about the nostrils which the consciousness of carrying a "settler" in the form of a fact or a revolver gives the individual thus armed. When a person is really full of information, and does not abuse it to crush conversation, his part is to that of the real talkers what the instrumental accompaniment is in a trio or quartette of vocalists.

—*The Autocrat of the Breakfast-Table*, 142

—What do I mean by the real talkers?—Why, the people with fresh ideas, of course, and plenty of good warm words to dress them in. Facts always yield the place of honor in conversation, to thoughts about facts, but if a false note is uttered, down comes the finger on the key and the man of facts asserts his true dignity.

—*The Autocrat of the Breakfast-Table*, 143

Better, I think, the hearty abandonment of one's self to the suggestions of the moment at the risk of an occasional slip of the tongue, perceived the instant it escapes, but just one syllable too late, than the royal reputation of never saying a foolish thing.

*—The Professor at the Breakfast-*Table, 18

Nobody talks much that doesn't say unwise things,—things he did not mean to say; as no person plays much without striking a false note sometimes. Talk, to me, is only spading up the ground for crops of thought.

—The Professor at the Breakfast-Table, 18

How much better this thorough interpenetration of ideas than a barren interchange of courtesies, or a bush-fighting argument, in which each man tries to cover as much of himself and expose as much of his opponent as the tangled thicket of the disputed ground will let him!

—The Professor at the Breakfast-Table, 36–7

Sir,—said he, —it isn't what a man thinks or says, but when and where and to whom he thinks and says it. A man with a flint and steel striking sparks over a wet blanket is one thing, and striking them over a tinder-box is another.

—The Professor at the Breakfast-Table, 81

Do you think I don't understand what my friend, the Professor, long ago called *the hydrostatic paradox of controversy*? Don't know what that means?— Well, I will tell you. You know, that, if you had a bent tube, one arm of which was of the size of a pipe-stem, and the other big enough to hold the ocean, water would stand at the same height in one as in the other. Controversy equalizes fools and wise men in the same way,—*and the fools know it.*

—The Autocrat of the Breakfast-Table, 114

There is a point of mental saturation, beyond which argument cannot be forced without breeding impatient, if not harsh, feeling toward those who refuse to be convinced.

—The Contagiousness of Puerperal Fever, 126

. . . it is a good thing once in a while to break in upon the monotony of a steady talker at a dinner-table, tea-table, or any other place of social converse. The best talker is liable to become the most formidable of bores. It is a peculiarity of the bore that he is the last person to find himself out.

Many a terebrant[22] I have known who, in that capacity, to borrow a line from Coleridge,[23]

"Was great, nor knew how great he was."

—*Over the Teacups*, 83

If you ever saw a crow with a king-bird after him, you will get an image of a dull speaker and a lively listener. The bird in sable plumage flaps heavily along his straightforward course, while the other sails round him, over him, under him, leaves him, comes back again, tweaks out a black feather, shoots away once more, never losing sight of him, and finally reaches the crow's perch at the same time the crow does, having cut a perfect labyrinth of hoops and knots and spirals while the slow fowl was painfully working from one end of his straight line to the other.

—*The Autocrat of the Breakfast-Table*, 29–30

—I have a kind of dread, rather than hatred, of persons with a large excess of vitality; great feeders, great laughers, great story-tellers, who come sweeping over their company with a huge tidal wave of animal spirits and boisterous merriment. I have pretty good spirits myself, and enjoy a little mild pleasantry, but I am oppressed and extinguished by these great lusty, noisy creatures, and feel as if I were a mute at a funeral when they get into full blast.

—I cannot get along much better with those drooping, languid people, whose vitality falls short as much as that of the others is in excess. I have not life enough for two; I wish I had.

—*The Poet at the Breakfast-Table*, 333–4

—Do you mean to say the pun-question is not clearly settled in your minds? Let me lay down the law upon the subject. Life and language are alike sacred. Homicide and *verbicide*—that is, violent treatment of a word with fatal results to its legitimate meaning, which is its life—are alike forbidden. Manslaughter, which is the meaning of the one, is the same as man's laughter, which is the end of the other. A pun is *primâ facie* an insult to the person you are talking with. It implies utter indifference to or sublime contempt for his remarks, no matter how serious.

The Autocrat of the Breakfast-Table, 11–12

---

[22]Terebrant: A boring *Hymenoptera* insect, such as sawflies; hence (humorous), a bore.
[23]Samuel Taylor Coleridge (1772–1834): English poet. The line is from "Tell's Birthplace."

People that make puns are like wanton boys that put coppers on the railroad tracks. They amuse themselves and other children, but their little trick may upset a freight train of conversation for the sake of a battered witticism.

—The Autocrat of the Breakfast-Table, 12

—I think there is one habit . . . worse than that of punning. It is the gradual substitution of cant or slang terms for words which truly characterize their objects. I have known several very genteel idiots whose whole vocabulary had deliquesced into some half dozen expressions. . . . As we hear slang phraseology, it is commonly the dish-water from the washings of English dandyism, schoolboy or full-grown, wrung out of a three-volume novel which had sopped it up . . . and diluted to suit the provincial climate.

—The Autocrat of the Breakfast-Table, 256–7

Writing and Writers

That every articulately-speaking human being has in him stuff for *one* novel in three volumes duodecimo has long been with me a cherished belief. It has been maintained, on the other hand, that many persons cannot write more than one novel,—that all after that are likely to be failures. . . . Now an author's first novel is naturally drawn, to a great extent, from his personal experiences; that is, is a literal copy of nature under various slight disguises. But the moment the author gets out of his personality, he must have the creative power, as well as the narrative art and the sentiment, in order to tell a living story, and this is rare.

—The Autocrat of the Breakfast-Table, 59–60

The foolishest book is a kind of leaky boat on a sea of wisdom; some of the wisdom will get in anyhow. . . . You must write a book or two to find out how much and how little you know and have to say.

—The Poet at the Breakfast-Table, 302–3

The creative action is not voluntary at all, but automatic; we can only put the mind into the proper attitude, and wait for the wind, that blows where it listeth, to breath over it. Thus the true state of creative genius is allied to *reverie*, or dreaming.

—The Autocrat of the Breakfast-Table, 191

Creation is always preceded by chaos.

—The Guardian Angel, 221

A chief pleasure which the author of novels and stories experiences is
that of becoming acquainted with the characters he draws. It is perfectly
true that his characters must, in the nature of things, have more or less of
himself in their composition.

—Over the Teacups, 299

I am a very particular person about having all I write printed as I write it.
I require to see a proof, a revise, a re-revise, and a double re-revise, or
fourth-proof rectified impression of all my productions, especially verse.
A misprint kills a sensitive author. An intentional change of his text murders him. No wonder so many poets die young![24]

—The Autocrat of the Breakfast-Table, 48–9

A sick man that gets talking about himself, a woman that gets talking
about her baby, and an author that begins reading out of his own book,
never know when to stop.

—The Poet at the Breakfast-Table, 309

—I should like to see any man's biography with corrections and emendations by his ghost. We don't know each other's secrets quite so well as we
flatter ourselves we do. We don't always know our own secrets as well as
we might.

—The Poet at the Breakfast-Table, 165

It takes a generation or two to find out what are the passages in a great
writer which are to become commonplaces in literature and conversation.

—Ralph Waldo Emerson, 244

---

[24]"Some twenty or thirty years ago, I said to Longfellow that certain statistical tables I had
seen went to show that poets were not a long-lived race. He doubted whether there was anything to prove they were particularly short-lived." Henry Wadsworth Longfellow
(1807–1882) lived to the age of seventy-five, and Holmes to the age of eighty-five. In *Over
the Teacups*, 40–1.

How small a matter literature is to the great seething, toiling, struggling, love-making, bread-winning, child-rearing, death-awaiting men and women who fill this huge, palpitating world of ours!

—*One Hundred Days in Europe*, 93

I find the great charm of writing consists in its surprises. When one is in the receptive attitude of mind, the thoughts which are sprung upon him, the images which flash through his consciousness are a delight and an excitement. I am impatient of every hindrance in setting down my thoughts,—of a pen that will not write, of ink that will not flow, of paper that will not receive the ink. And here let me pay the tribute which I owe to one of the humblest but most serviceable of my assistants, especially in poetical composition. Nothing seems more prosaic than the stylographic pen. It deprives the handwriting of its beauty, and to some extent of its individual character. The brutal communism of the letters it forms covers the page it fills with the most uniformly uninteresting characters. But, abuse it as much as you choose, there is nothing like it for the poet, or the imaginative writer. Many a fine flow of thought has been checked, perhaps arrested, by the ill behavior of a goose-quill. Many an idea has escaped while the author was dipping his pen in the inkstand. But with the stylographic pen, in the hands of one who knows how to care for it and how to use it, unbroken rhythms and harmonious cadences are the natural products of the unimpeded flow of the fluid which is the vehicle of the author's thoughts and fancies.[25]

—*Over the Teacups*, 298–9

An immortality of a whole generation is more than most writers are entitled to expect.

—*Over the Teacups*, 305

A few can touch the magic string,
And noisy Fame is proud to win them;—
Alas for those who never sing,
But die with all their music in them!

—from "The Voiceless," in *The Autocrat of the Breakfast-Table*, 306

---

[25]Most people who write with word processors will no doubt smile at Holmes's joy over the advent of the stylographic pen. What next?

An old author is constantly rediscovering himself in the more or less fossilized productions of his earlier years.

—*Over the Teacups*, 307–8

Poetry and Poets

Poets are never young, in one sense. Their delicate ear hears the far-off whispers of eternity, which coarser souls must travel towards for scores of years before their dull sense is touched by them. A moment's insight is sometimes worth a life's experience.

—*The Professor at the Breakfast-Table*, 239

The works of other men live, but their personality dies out of their labors; the poet, who reproduces himself in his creation, as no other artist does or can, goes down to posterity with all his personality blended with whatever is imperishable in his song.

—*The Poet at the Breakfast-Table*, 109–10

The scientific man connects objects in sequences and series, and in so doing is guided by their collective resemblances. His aim is to classify and index all that he sees and contemplates so as to show the relations which unite, and learn the laws that govern, the subjects of his study. The poet links the most remote objects together by the slender filament of wit, the flowery chain of fancy, or the living, pulsating cord of imagination, always guided by his instinct for the beautiful.

—*Ralph Waldo Emerson*, 249–50

—What do you think, Sir—said the divinity-student,—opens the souls of poets most fully?

Why, there must be the internal force and the external stimulus. Neither is enough by itself. A rose will not flower in the dark, and a fern will not flower anywhere.

—*The Autocrat of the Breakfast-Table*, 182

Shall a man who in his younger days has written poetry, or what passed for it, continue to attempt it in his later years? Certainly, if it amuses or interests him, no one would object to his writing in verse as much as he likes. Whether he should continue to write for the public is another question. Poetry is a good deal a matter of heart-beats, and the circulation is more languid in the later periods of life. The joints are less supple; the arteries are more or less "ossified." Something like these changes has taken place in the mind. It has lost the flexibility, the plastic docility, which it had in youth and early manhood, when the gristle had but just become hardened into bone. It is the nature of poetry to writhe itself along through the tangled growths of the vocabulary, as a snake winds through the grass, in sinuous, complex, and unexpected curves, which crack every joint that is not supple as india-rubber.

—*Over the Teacups*, 41–2

It is not every poet who is at once appreciated. Some will tell you that the best poets never are.

—*Over the Teacups*, 88

Certain things are good for nothing until they have been kept a long while; and some are good for nothing until they have been long kept and *used*. Of the first, wine is the illustrious and immortal example. Of those which must be kept and used I will name three,—meerschaum pipes, violins, and poems. . . .

Now I tell you a poem must be kept *and used*, like a meerschaum, or a violin. A poem is just as porous as the meerschaum;—the more porous it is, the better. I mean to say that a genuine poem is capable of absorbing an indefinite amount of the essence of our own humanity,—its tender-ness, its heroism, its regrets, its aspirations, so as to be gradually stained through with a divine secondary color derived from ourselves. So you see it must take time to bring the sentiment of a poem into harmony with our nature, by staining ourselves through every thought and image our being can penetrate. . . .

Then again, as to the mere music of a new poem, why, who can expect anything more than that from the music of a violin fresh from the maker's hands? Now, you know very well that there are no less than fifty-eight different pieces in a violin. These pieces are strangers to each other, and it takes a century, more or less, to make them thoroughly acquainted. At last they learn to vibrate in harmony and the instrument becomes an organic whole. . . .

Don't you see that all this is just as true of a poem? Counting each word as a piece, there are more pieces in an average copy of verses than in a violin. The poet has forced all these words together, and fastened them, and they don't understand it at first. But let the poem be repeated aloud and murmured over in the mind's muffled whisper often enough, and at length the parts become knit together in such absolute solidarity that you could not change a syllable without the whole world's crying out against you for meddling with the harmonious fabric.

—The Autocrat of the Breakfast-Table, 101–5

I am sorry that I did not ask Tennyson to read or repeat to me some lines of his own. Hardly any one perfectly understands a poem but the poet himself. One naturally loves his own poem as no one else can. It fits the mental mould in which it was cast, and it will not exactly fit any other. For this reason, I had rather listen to a poet reading his own verses than hear the best elocutionist that ever spouted recite them. He may not have a good voice or enunciation, but he puts his heart and his inter-penetrative intelligence into every line, word, and syllable.

—One Hundred Days in Europe, 70–1

Every poem that is worthy of the name, no matter how easily it seems to be written, represents a great amount of vital force expended at some time or other.

—The Poet at the Breakfast-Table, 97

The highways of literature are spread over with the shells of dead novels, each of which has been swallowed at a mouthful by the public, and is done with. But write a volume of poems. No matter if they are all bad but one, if that one is very good. It will carry your name down to posterity like the coin of Alexander.[26] I don't suppose one would care a great deal about it a hundred or a thousand years after he is dead, but I don't feel quite sure. It seems as if, even in heaven, King David might remember "The Lord is my Shepherd" with a certain twinge of earthly pleasure.

—The Poet at the Breakfast-Table, 112

---

[26]Coin of Alexander: Most commonly, a silver tetradrachm coin that was extremely common during and after the reign of Alexander the Great (356–323 B.C.). The obverse features a bust of the young (beardless) Hercules wearing a lion skin headdress and with lion's paws around his neck. The reverse features a seated image of Zeus holding an eagle in his right hand and a scepter in his left hand, with the inscription (in Greek) "Of Alexander."

Poetry is as contagious as measles, and if a single case of it break out in any social circle, or in a school, there are certain to be a number of similar cases, some slight, some serious, and now and then one so malignant that the subject of it should be put on a spare diet of stationery, say from two to three penfuls of ink and a half sheet of note-paper *per diem*.

—*Over the Teacups*, 50

I have sometimes thought I might consider it worth while to set up a course for instruction in the art. "*Poetry taught in twelve lessons.*" Congenital idiocy is no disqualification. Anybody can write "poetry." It is a most unenviable distinction to have published a thin volume of verse, which nobody wanted, nobody buys, nobody reads, nobody cares for except the author, who cries over its pathos, poor fellow, and revels in its beauties, which he has all to himself. Come! Who will be my pupils in a Course,— Poetry taught in twelve lessons?

—*Over the Teacups*, 78

Poetry is commonly thought to be the language of emotion. On the contrary, most of what is so called proves the absence of all passionate excitement. It is a cold-blooded, haggard, anxious, worrying hunt after rhymes which can be made serviceable, after images which will be effective, after phrases which are sonorous; all this under limitations which restrict the natural movements of fancy and imagination. There is a secondary excitement in overcoming the difficulties of rhythm and rhyme, no doubt, but this is not the emotional heat excited by the subject of the "poet's" treatment. True poetry, the best of it, is but the ashes of a burnt-out passion. The flame was in the eye and in the cheek, the coals may be still burning in the heart, but when we come to the words it leaves behind it, a little warmth, a cinder or two just glimmering under the dead gray ashes,—that is all we can look for. When it comes to the manufactured article, one is surprised to find how well the metrical artisans have learned to imitate the real thing. They catch all the phrases of the true poet. They imitate his metrical forms as a mimic copies the gait of the person he is representing.

—*Over the Teacups*, 84–5

I find the burden and restrictions of rhyme more and more troublesome as I grow older. There are times when it seems natural enough to employ that form of expression, but it is only occasionally; and the use of it as the vehicle of the commonplace is so prevalent that one is not much tempted to select it as the medium for his thoughts and emotions. The art of rhyming has almost become a part of a high-school education, and its practice is far from being an evidence of intellectual distinction. Mediocrity is as much forbidden to the poet in our days as it was in those of Horace,[27] and the immense majority of the verses written are stamped with hopeless mediocrity.

—Over the Teacups, 313

Wit and Humor

—Wonder why authors and actors are ashamed of being funny?—Why, there are obvious reasons, and deep philosophical ones. The clown knows very well that the women are not in love with him, but with Hamlet, the fellow in the black cloak and plumed hat. Passion never laughs. The wit knows that his place is at the tail of a procession.

—The Autocrat of the Breakfast-Table, 50

It is a very dangerous thing for a literary man to indulge his love for the ridiculous. People laugh *with* him just so long as he amuses them; but if he attempts to be serious, they must still have their laugh, and so they laugh *at* him. There is in addition, however, a deeper reason for this than would at first appear. Do you know that you feel a little superior to every man who makes you laugh, whether by faces or verses? Are you aware that you have a pleasant sense of patronizing him, when you condescend so far as to let him turn somersets, literal or literary, for your royal delight?

—The Autocrat of the Breakfast-Table, 90–1

Laughter and tears are meant to turn the wheels of the same machinery of sensibility; one is wind-power, and the other water-power; that is all.

—The Autocrat of the Breakfast-Table, 90

There is nothing harder to forgive than the sting of an epigram.

—Over the Teacups, 306

---

[27]Horace: Quintus Horatius Flaccus (65 B.C.–8 B.C.): Roman poet who famously wrote: "Mediocrity is not allowed to poets, either by the gods or man."

Critics

—I never saw an author in my life—saving, perhaps, one—that did not purr as audibly as a full-grown domestic cat (*Felis Catus*, Linn.) on having his fur smoothed in the right way by a skilful hand.

—The Autocrat of the Breakfast-Table, 49

We are literary cannibals, and our writers live on each other and each other's productions to a fearful extent. What the mulberry leaf is to the silk-worm, the author's book, treatise, essay, poem is to the critical larvæ that feed upon it.

—Over the Teacups, 23

I don't know what it is,—whether a spontaneous change, mental or bodily, or whether it is thorough experience of the thanklessness of critical honesty,—but it is a fact, that most writers, except sour and unsuccessful ones, get tired of finding fault at about the time when they are beginning to grow old. As a general thing, I would not give a great deal for the fair words of a critic, if he is himself an author, over fifty years of age. At thirty we are all trying to cut our names in big letters upon the walls of this tenement of life; twenty years later we have carved it, or shut up our jack-knives. Then we are ready to help others, and more anxious not to hinder any, because nobody's elbows are in our way.

—The Autocrat of the Breakfast-Table, 81–2

Epithets follow the isothermal lines pretty accurately. Grouping them in two families, one finds himself a clever, genial, witty, wise, brilliant, sparkling, thoughtful, distinguished, celebrated, illustrious scholar and perfect gentleman, and first writer of the age; or a dull, foolish, wicked, pert, shallow, ignorant, insolent, traitorous, black-hearted outcast, and a disgrace to civilization.

—The Autocrat of the Breakfast-Table, 114

What do I think determines the set of phrases a man gets? – Well, I should say a set of influences something like these:—1st. Relationships, political, religious, social, domestic. 2nd. Oysters, in the form of suppers given to gentlemen connected with criticism. . . . No, it isn't exactly bribery. One man has oysters and another epithets. It is an exchange of hospitalities; one gives a "spread" on linen, and the other on paper,—that is all.

—The Autocrat of the Breakfast-Table, 114–5

What a blessed thing it is, that Nature, when she invented, manufactured, and patented her authors, contrived to make critics out of the chips that were left!

—*The Professor at the Breakfast-Table*, 25

You may set it down as a truth which admits of few exceptions, that those who ask your *opinion* really want your *praise*, and will be contented with nothing less.

—*The Autocrat of the Breakfast-Table*, 294

I think, generally, that fear of open discussion implies feebleness of inward conviction, and great sensitiveness to the expression of individual opinion is a mark of weakness.

—*The Professor at the Breakfast-Table*, 109

It has long been a favorite rule with me, a rule which I have never lost sight of, however imperfectly I have carried it out: Try to know enough of a wide range of subjects to profit by the conversation of intelligent persons of different callings and various intellectual gifts and acquisitions. The cynic will paraphrase this into a shorter formula: Get a smattering in every sort of knowledge. I must therefore add a second piece of advice: Learn to hold as of small account the comments of the cynic. He is often amusing, sometimes really witty, occasionally, without meaning it, instructive; but his talk is to profitable conversation what the stone is to the pulp of the peach, what the cob is to the kernels of an ear of Indian corn.

—*Over the Teacups*, 148

Talent and Genius

The world is always ready to receive talent with open arms. Very often it does not know what to do with genius. Talent is a docile creature. It bows its head meekly while the world slips the collar over it. It backs into the shafts like a lamb. It draws its load cheerfully, and is patient of the bit and of the whip. But genius is always impatient of its harness; its wild blood makes it hard to train.

Talent seems, at first, in one sense, higher than genius,—namely, that it is more uniformly and absolutely submitted to the will, and therefore more distinctly human in its character. Genius, on the other hand, is much more like those instincts which govern the admirable movements of the lower creatures, and therefore seems to have something of the lower or animal character. A goose flies by a chart which the Royal Geographical Society could not mend. A poet, like the goose, sails without visible landmarks to unexplored regions of truth, which philosophy has yet to lay down on its atlas. The philosopher gets his track by observation; the poet trusts to his inner sense, and makes the straighter and swifter line.

And yet, to look at it in another light, is not even the lowest instinct more truly divine than any voluntary human act done by the suggestion of reason? . . .

Talent is a very common family-trait; genius belongs rather to individuals.

—*The Professor at the Breakfast-Table*, 240–1

Nothing is so common-place as to wish to be remarkable. Fame usually comes to those who are thinking about something else,—very rarely to those who say to themselves, "Go to, now, let us be a celebrated individual!" The struggle for fame, as such, commonly ends in notoriety;—that ladder is easy to climb, but it leads to the pillory which is crowded with fools who could not hold their tongues and rogues who could not hide their tricks.

If you have the consciousness of genius, do something to show it. The world is pretty quick, nowadays, to catch the flavor of true originality; . . . You may have genius. The contrary is of course probable, but it is not demonstrated. If you have, the world wants you more than you want it.

—*The Autocrat of the Breakfast-Table*, 290–1

The gift of genius is never to be reckoned upon beforehand, any more than a choice new variety of pear or peach in a seedling; it is always a surprise, but it is born with great advantages when the stock from which it springs has been long under cultivation.

—*Ralph Waldo Emerson*, 2

SOCIETY AND THE BODY POLITIC

The Body Politic

There are half a dozen men, or so, who carry in their brains the *ovarian eggs* of the next generation's or century's civilization. These eggs are not ready to be laid in the form of books as yet; some of them are hardly ready to be put into the form of talk. But as rudimentary ideas of inchoate tendencies, there they are; and these are what must form the future.

—*The Autocrat of the Breakfast-Table*, 195

This Republic is the chosen home of *minorities*, of the less power in the presence of the greater. It is a common error to speak of our distinction as consisting in the rule of the majority. Majorities, the greater material powers, have always ruled before. The history of most countries has been that of majorities. . . . In the old civilizations they root themselves like oaks in the soil; men must live in their shadow or cut them down. With us the majority is only the flower of the passing noon, and the minority is the bud which may open in the next morning's sun. We must be tolerant, for the thought which stammers on a single tongue today may organize itself in the growing consciousness of the time, and come back to us like the voice of the multitudinous waves of the ocean on the morrow.

—*Currents and Counter-Currents in Medical Science*, 206–7

Religion and government appear to me the two subjects which of all others should belong to the common talk of people who enjoy the blessings of freedom.

—*The Professor at the Breakfast-Table*, 107

We talk about our free institutions;—they are nothing but a coarse outside machinery to secure the freedom of individual thought. The President of the United States is only the engine-driver of our broad-gauge mail-train; and every honest, independent thinker has a seat in the first-class cars behind him.

—*The Professor at the Breakfast-Table*, 115–6

The very aim and end of our institutions is just this: that we may think what we like and say what we think.

—*The Professor at the Breakfast-Table*, 118

When the common people of New England stop talking politics and theology, it will be because they have got an Emperor to teach them the one, and a Pope to teach them the other!

—*The Professor at the Breakfast-Table*, 118

The old-world order of things is an arrangement of locks and canals, where everything depends on keeping the gates shut, and so holding the upper waters at their level; but the system under which the young republican American is born trusts the whole unimpeded tide of life to the great elemental influences, as the vast rivers of the continent settle their own level in obedience to the laws that govern the planet and the spheres that surround it.

—The Professor at the Breakfast-Table, 295

After all, every people must have its own forms of ostentation, pretence, and vulgarity. The ancient Romans had theirs, the English and the French have theirs as well,—why should not we Americans have ours? Educated and refined persons must recognize frequent internal conflicts between the "*Homo sum*" of Terence[28] and the "*Odi profanum vulgus*" of Horace.[29] The nobler sentiment should be that of every true American, and it is in that direction that our best civilization is constantly tending.

—Over the Teacups, 223

A crank is a man who does his own thinking. . . . There never was a religion founded but its Messiah was called a crank. There never was an idea started that woke up men out of their stupid indifference but its originator was spoken of as a crank. Do you want to know why that name is given to the men who do most for the world's progress? I will tell you. It is because cranks make all the wheels in all the machinery of the world go round.

—Over the Teacups, 161

Two things, at least, Napoleon accomplished: he opened the door for ability of all kinds, and he dealt the death-blow to the divine right of kings and all the abuses which clung to that superstition.

—One Hundred Days in Europe, 174

---

[28]Terence: Publius Terentius Afer (195 B.C. or 185 B.C.–150 B.C.): Roman playwright best known for his comedies. The full quotation, "*Homo sum, humani nil a me alienum puto*" ("I am a man, I consider nothing that is human alien to me," or "I am a human being, so nothing human is strange to me") can be taken as a good motto for physicians; for example, it was a favorite of the French neurologist Jean-Martin Charcot (1825–1893).
[29]Horace: See page 223, note 27. The full quotation, "*Odi profanum vulgus et arceo*" ("I hate the uninitiated crowd and keep them far" or "I hate the ignorant crowd and keep them at a distance") is a favorite of various elitists. (For an example of its use, see William Kristol, "Here the People Rule," *The New York Times*, 20 October 2008.)

Reason may be the lever, but sentiment gives you the fulcrum and the place to stand on if you want to move the world.

—*The Poet at the Breakfast-Table*, 135–6

We have learned that the law of life in a complex animal organism is local autonomy, with universal suffrage; the individual cell being the citizen of a federal republic; the various departments being distributed among the different viscera, its senate and legislature in the nervous centres, the chief of which is under the dome that crowns the living structure. Here was prefigured what we Americans consider the adult and completed development of civic order.

—*Medical Highways and Byways*, 508

The Civil War

We all know what the *war fever* is in our young men,—what a devouring passion it becomes in those whom it assails. Patriotism is the fire of it, no doubt, but this is fed with fuels of all sorts. The love of adventure, the contagion of example, the fear of losing the chance of participating in the great events of the time, the desire of personal distinction, all help to produce those singular transformations which we often witness, turning the most peaceful of our youth into the most ardent of our soldiers. But something of the same fever in a different form reaches a good many non-combatants, who have no thought of losing a drop of precious blood belonging to themselves or their families. Some of the symptoms we shall mention are almost universal; they are as plain in the people we meet everywhere as the marks of an influenza, when that is prevailing.

The first of these is a nervous restlessness of a very peculiar nature. Men cannot think, or write, or attend to their ordinary business.

—*Bread and the Newspaper*, 3

Whatever miseries this war brings upon us, it is making us wiser, and, we trust, better. Wiser, for we are learning our weakness, our narrowness, our selfishness, our ignorance, in lessons of sorrow and shame. Better, because all that is noble in men and women is demanded by the time, and our people are rising to the standard the time calls for. For this is the question the hour is putting to each of us: Are you ready, if need be, to sacrifice all that you have and hope for in this world, that the generations to follow you may inherit a whole country whose natural condition shall be peace, and not a broken province which must live under the perpetual threat, if not in the constant presence, of war and all that war brings with it? If we are all ready for this sacrifice, battles may be lost, but the campaign and its grand object must be won.

—*Bread and the Newspaper*, 14

The struggle in which we are engaged was inevitable; it might have come a little sooner, or a little later, but it must have come. The disease of the nation was organic, and not functional, and the rough chirurgery of war was its only remedy.

—*The Inevitable Trial*, 83

A simple diagram, within the reach of all, shows how idle it is to look for any other cause than slavery as having any material agency in dividing the country. Match the two broken pieces of the Union, and you will find the fissure that separates them zigzagging itself half across the continent like an isothermal line, shooting its splintery projections, and opening its reentering angles, not merely according to the limitations of particular States, but as a county or other limited section of ground belongs to freedom or to slavery.

—*The Inevitable Trial*, 87–8

Slavery gratifies at once the love of power, the love of money, and the love of ease; it finds a victim for anger who cannot smite back at his oppressor; and it offers to all, without measure, the seductive privileges which the Mormon gospel reserves for the true believers on earth, and the Bible of Mahomet[30] only dares promise to the saints in heaven.

—*The Inevitable Trial*, 88

Provincialism

I made a comparison at table some time since, which has often been quoted and received many compliments. It was that of the mind of a bigot to the pupil of the eye; the more light you pour on it, the more it contracts.

—*The Autocrat of the Breakfast-Table*, 144

---

[30]Bible of Mahomet (Mohammed): The Koran.

Provincialism has no *scale* of excellence in man or vegetable; it never knows a first-rate article of either kind when it has it, and is constantly taking second and third rate ones for Nature's best.

—*The Autocrat of the Breakfast-Table*, 233

It dwarfs the mind, I think,—said I,—to feed it on any localism. The full stature of manhood is shriveled.

—*The Professor at the Breakfast-Table*, 87

Boston

Boston State-House is the hub of the solar system. You couldn't pry that out of a Boston man if you had the tire of all creation straightened out for a crowbar.

—*The Autocrat of the Breakfast-Table*, 125

Boston has opened, and kept open, more turnpikes that lead straight to free thought and free speech and free deeds than any other city of live men or dead men,—I don't care how broad their streets are, nor how high their steeples!

—*The Professor at the Breakfast*-Table, 3–4

That's all I claim for Boston,—that it is the thinking centre of the continent, and therefore of the planet.

—*The Professor at the Breakfast-Table*, 83

—A man can see further, Sir, —he [a neighbor] said one day, —from the top of Boston State House, and see more that is worth seeing, than from all the pyramids and turrets and steeples in all the places of the world!

—*The Professor at the Breakfast-Table*, 217

I love this old place where I was born;—the heart of the world beats under the three hills of Boston, Sir!

—*The Professor at the Breakfast-Table*, 301

He comes of the *Brahmin caste of New England*. This is the harmless, inoffensive, untitled aristocracy referred to, and which many readers will at once acknowledge.

—*Elsie Venner*, 4

Material Progress and the Future

It seems as if the material world has been made over again since we were boys. It is but a short time since we were counting up the miracles we had lived to witness. The list is familiar enough: the railroad, the ocean steamer, photography, the spectroscope, the telegraph, telephone, phonograph, anæsthetics, electric illumination,—with such lesser wonders as the friction match, the sewing machine, and the bicycle. And now, we said, we must have come to the end of these unparalleled developments of the forces of nature. We must rest on our achievements. The nineteenth century is not likely to add to them; we must wait for the twentieth century. Many of us, perhaps most of us, felt in that way. We had seen our planet furnished by the art of man with a complete nervous system: a spinal cord beneath the ocean, secondary centres,—ganglions,—in all the chief places where men are gathered together, and ramifications extending throughout civilization. All at once, by the side of this talking and light-giving apparatus, we see another wire stretched over our heads, carrying force to a vast metallic muscular system,—a slender cord conveying the strength of a hundred men, of a score of horses, of a team of elephants. The lightning is tamed and harnessed, the thunderbolt has become a common carrier. No more surprises in this century! A voice whispers, *What next?*

—Over the Teacups, 31–2

Isn't it like splitting a toad out of a rock to think of this man of nineteen or twenty centuries hence coming out from his stony dwelling-place and speaking with us? What are the questions we should ask him? He has but a few minutes to stay. Make out your own list; I will set down a few that come up to me as I write.

—What is the prevalent religious creed of civilization?

—Has the planet met with any accident of importance?

—How general is the republican form of government?

—Do men fly yet?

—Has the universal language come into use?

—Is there a new fuel since the English coal-mines have given out?

—Is the euthanasia a recognized branch of medical science?

—Is the oldest inhabitant still living?

—Is the Daily Advertiser still published?

—And the Evening Transcript?[31]

—Is there much inquiry for the works of a writer of the nineteenth century (Old Style) by — the — name — of — of —

—The Poet at the Breakfast Table, 167

SELECTED NON-MEDICAL POEMS

Old Ironsides[32]

Ay, tear her tattered ensign down!
    Long has it waved on high,
And many an eye has danced to see
    That banner in the sky;
Beneath it rung the battle shout,
    And burst the cannon's roar;—
The meteor of the ocean air
    Shall sweep the clouds no more.

Her deck, once red with heroes' blood,
    Where knelt the vanquished foe,
When winds were hurrying o'er the flood,
    And waves were white below,
No more shall feel the victor's tread,
    Or know the conquered knee;—
The harpies of the shore shall pluck
    The eagle of the sea!

Oh better that her shattered hulk
    Should sink beneath the wave;
Her thunders shook the mighty deep,
    And there should be her grave;
Nail to the mast her holy flag,
    Set every threadbare sail,
And give her to the god of storms,
    The lightning and the gale!

---

[31] The *Daily Advertiser* ceased publication in 1929; the *Evening Transcript* ceased publication in 1941.
[32] Holmes wrote "Old Ironsides" after reading a notice in the *Boston Daily Advertiser* of September 14, 1830, that "the Secretary of the Navy has recommended to the Board of Navy Commissioners to dispose of the frigate Constitution." See page 6.

The Last Leaf [33]

I SAW him once before,
As he passed by the door,
   And again
The pavement stones resound,
As he totters o'er the ground
   With his cane.

They say that in his prime,
Ere the pruning-knife of Time
   Cut him down,
Not a better man was found
By the Crier on his round
   Through the town.

But now he walks the streets,
And he looks at all he meets
   Sad and wan,
And he shakes his feeble head,
That it seems as if he said,
   "They are gone."

The mossy marbles rest
On the lips that he has prest
   In their bloom,
And the names he loved to hear
Have been carved for many a year
   On the tomb.

My grandmamma has said—
Poor old lady, she is dead
   Long ago
That he had a Roman nose,
And his cheek was like a rose
   In the snow.

---

[33]Holmes revealed that "The Last Leaf" was inspired by "the appearance in one of a venerable relic of the Revolution, said to be one of the party who threw the tea overboard in Boston Harbor."

But now his nose is thin,
And it rests upon his chin
  Like a staff,
And a crook is in his back,
And a melancholy crack
  In his laugh.

I know it is a sin
For me to sit and grin
  At him here;
But the old three-cornered hat,
And the breeches, and all that,
  Are so queer!

And if I should live to be
The last leaf upon the tree
  In the spring,
Let them smile, as I do now,
At the old forsaken bough
  Where I cling.

The Chambered Nautilus[34]

THIS is the ship of pearl, which, poets feign,
  Sails the unshadowed main,—
  The venturous bark that flings
On the sweet summer wind its purpled wings
In gulfs enchanted, where the Siren sings,
  And coral reefs lie bare,
Where the cold sea-maids rise to sun their streaming hair.

---

[34]"The Chambered Nautilus," originally published in *The Atlantic Monthly* and then in book form in *The Autocrat of the Breakfast-Table*, is usually interpreted as a metaphor for the growth of the human soul and the soul's ultimate release from the body, as evinced by the closing verse. A nocturnal marine animal of the western Pacific and Indian Oceans, the chambered nautilus (*Nautilus pompilius*) makes progressively larger chambers for its exoskeleton, each time closing off the previous chamber which then adds to its buoyancy. The poem occurs toward the end of Holmes's fourth chapter, in which the Autocrat holds forth on the "direction we are moving," the lesson that "we outgrow all we love," and that each of us must make our own way in the "race of life." The animal's abandonment of all previous chambers suggests that we, too, should live forwards without looking back, building an edifice of achievement analogous to the animal's prized and somewhat hard-to-find spiral shell, its "ship of pearl." However, some critics see in this poem an ambivalence between the "Protestant work ethic" and the work of nurturing our inner lives.

Its webs of living gauze no more unfurl;
   Wrecked is the ship of pearl!
   And every chambered cell,
Where its dim dreaming life was wont to dwell,
As the frail tenant shaped his growing shell,
   Before thee lies revealed,—
Its irised ceiling rent, its sunless crypt unsealed!

Year after year beheld the silent toil
   That spread its lustrous coil;
   Still, as the spiral grew,
He left the past year's dwelling for the new,
Stole with soft step its shining archway through,
   Built up its idle door,
Stretched in his last-found home, and knew the old no more.

Thanks for the heavenly message brought by thee,
   Child of the wandering sea,
   Cast from her lap, forlorn!
From thy dead lips a clearer note is born
Than ever Triton[35] blew from wreathèd horn!
   While on mine ear it rings,
Through the deep caves of thought I heard a voice that sings:—

Build thee more stately mansions, O my soul,
   As the swift seasons roll!
Leave thy low-vaulted past!
Let each new temple, nobler than the last,
Shut thee from heaven with a dome more vast,
   Till thou at length art free,
Leaving thine outgrown shell by life's unresting sea!

---

[35]Triton: In Greek mythology, the messenger of the deep and the son of Poseidon (god of the sea) and Amphitrite (goddess of the sea).

The Deacon's Masterpiece,
or, the Wonderful "One-Hoss Shay"[36]

A LOGICAL STORY

HAVE you heard of the wonderful one-hoss shay,
That was built in such a logical way
It ran a hundred years to the day
And then, of a sudden, it—ah, but stay,
I'll tell you what happened without delay,
Scaring the parson into fits,
Frightening people out of their wits,—
Have you ever heard of that, I say?

Seventeen hundred and fifty-five,
Georgius Secundus was then alive,—
Snuffy old drone from the German hive.[37]
That was the year when Lisbon-town
Saw the earth open and gulp her down,
And Braddock's army was done so brown,
Left without a scalp to its crown.[38]
It was on the terrible Earthquake-day
That the Deacon finished the one-hoss shay.[39]

---

[36]"The Deacon's Masterpiece," often known by its subtitle the "One-Hoss Shay," is usually interpreted as a satire against Calvinism or other fixed dogmas.

[37]George II of Great Britain (1683–1760), who as Duke Georg August of Hanover was the last British monarch to have been born outside of Great Britain, was known especially for his difficult interpersonal relationships, especially with members of his own family (hence, "snuffy old drone").

[38]Holmes refers here to General Edward Braddock's 1755 defeat at the Battle of Monongahela, near what is now Pittsburgh, during the French and Indian War (also known as the Seven Year War of 1757–1764).

[39]Holmes constructs this poem around the irony that the Deacon completed his one-horse shay (a light, covered, two-wheeled carriage for two persons), built to last indefinitely, on the very day that a great natural disaster with far-reaching economic, political, cultural, and philosophical consequences shook the coasts of Europe and North Africa. The 1755 Lisbon earthquake, now estimated to have approached magnitude 9 on the Richter scale, destroyed about 85 percent of Lisbon's buildings and killed an estimated 30,000 to 40,000 of its population of about 200,000 people. Other cities and towns in Portugal, Spain, Morocco, and elsewhere were also affected. Much of the damage was caused by tsunamis (estimated to

Now in building the chaises, I tell you what,
There is always *somewhere* a weakest spot,—
In tub, tire, felloe, in spring or thill,
In panel, or crossbar, or floor, or sill,
In screw, bolt, thoroughbrace,—lurking still,
Find it somewhere you must and will,—
Above or below, or within or without,—
And that's the reason, beyond a doubt,
That a chaise *breaks down*, but doesn't *wear out*.

But the Deacon swore (as Deacons do),
With an "I dew vum," or an I tell *yeou*"
He would build one shay to beat the taown
'n' the keounty 'n' all the kentry raoun';
It should be so built that it *couldn'* break daown:
"Fur," said the Deacon, "'t's mighty plain
Thut the weakes' place mus' stan' the strain;
'n' the way t' fix it, uz I maintain,
    Is only jest
T' make that place uz strong uz the rest."

So the Deacon inquired of the village folk
Where he could find the strongest oak,
That couldn't be split nor bent nor broke,—

---

have been up to nearly 70 feet high) and fires. Of major concern was the earthquake's occurrence on the morning of November 1, the Catholic holiday of All Saint's Day. Many saw it as a manifestation of the wrath of God, perhaps in retribution for the 1754–1755 Portuguese massacres of thousands of natives and missionaries in South America, especially in Paraguay, which had been ordered by King Joseph I of Portugal. Philosophers and theologians debated the concept of divine justice (theodicy). The earthquake inspired the young Immanuel Kant (1724–1804) to elaborate on the philosophy of the sublime—the idea that certain phenomena surpass our ability to comprehend or even imagine. Kant also posited that the earthquake was due to natural, rather than supernatural, causes, and indeed many trace the birth of seismology and earthquake engineering to this event. Holmes thus invites the reader to ponder the irony of the carriage's apparent self-destruction on the centenary of the Great Lisbon Earthquake.

That was for spokes and floor and sills;
He sent for lancewood to make the thills;
The crossbars were ash, from the straightest trees,
The panels of white-wood, that cuts like cheese,
But lasts like iron for things like these;
The hubs of logs from the "Settler's ellum,"—
Last of its timber,—they couldn't sell 'em,
Never an axe had seen their chips,
And the wedges flew from between their lips,
Their blunt ends frizzled like celery-tips;
Step and prop-iron, bolt and screw,
Spring, tire, axle, and linchpin too,
Steel of the finest, bright and blue;
Thoroughbrace bison-skin, thick and wide;
Boot, top, dasher, from tough old hide
Found in the pit where the tanner died.
That was the way he "put her through."
"There!" said the Deacon, "naow she'll dew!"

Do! I tell you, I rather guess
She was a wonder, and nothing less!
Colts grew horses, beards turned gray,
Deacon and deaconess dropped away,
Children and grandchildren—where were they?
But there stood the stout old one-hoss shay
As fresh as on Lisbon-earthquake-day!

EIGHTEEN HUNDRED;—it came and found
The Deacon's masterpiece strong and sound.
Eighteen hundred increased by ten;—
"Hahnsum kerridge" they called it then.
Eighteen hundred and twenty came;—
Running as usual; much the same.
Thirty and forty at last arrive,
And then come fifty, and FIFTY-FIVE.

Little of all we value here
Wakes on the morn of its hundredth year
Without both feeling and looking queer.
In fact, there's nothing that keeps its youth,

So far as I know, but a tree and truth.
(There is a moral that runs at large;
Take it.—You're welcome.—No extra charge.)

FIRST OF NOVEMBER,—the Earthquake-day,—
There are traces of age in the one-hoss shay,
A general flavor of mild decay,
But nothing local, as one may say.
There couldn't be,—for the Deacon's art
Had made it so like in every part
That there wasn't a chance for one to start.
For the wheels were just as strong as the thills,
And the floor was just as strong as the sills,
And the panels just as strong as the floor,
And the whipple-tree neither less nor more,
And the back-crossbar as strong as the fore,
And spring and axle and hub *encore.*
And yet, *as a whole,* it is past a doubt
In another hour it will be *worn out!*

First of November, 'Fifty-five!
This morning the parson takes a drive.
Now, small boys, get out of the way!
Here comes the wonderful one-hoss shay,
Drawn by a rat-tailed, ewe-necked bay.
"Huddup!" said the parson.—Off went they.
The parson was working his Sunday's text,—
Had got to *fifthly,* and stopped perplexed
At what the—Moses—was coming next.
All at once the horse stood still,
Close by the meet'n'-house on the hill.
First a shiver, and then a thrill,
Then something decidedly like a spill,—
And the parson was sitting upon a rock,
At half past nine by the meet'n'-house clock,—
Just the hour of the Earthquake shock!
What do you think the parson found,
When he got up and stared around?
The poor old chaise in a heap or mound,
As if it had been to the mill and ground!

You see, of course, if you're not a dunce,
How it went to pieces all at once,—
All at once, and nothing first,—
Just as bubbles do when they burst.

End of the wonderful one-hoss shay.
Logic is logic. That's all I say.

Opening manuscript page of Holmes's 1879 introductory lecture to the incoming Harvard Medical School class. By permission of the Houghton Library, Harvard University.

"Introductory–
Sept. 26th, 1879"

EDITORIAL NOTE: *Holmes, at age seventy, delivered this previously unpublished lecture to the incoming first-year class at Harvard Medical School. We wish to extend our gratitude to the Houghton Library at Harvard University for permission to print this lecture in its entirety. Note that in several instances, marked with an asterisk, we have indented a new paragraph for the sake of readability.*

It was formerly the custom in this School, and is still in most of the Schools of this country, to open every course of Lectures with an Introductory Discourse. They were for the most part somewhat full-blown rhetorical performances, announced beforehand, often to the public and having a little the character of advertisements of the particular institution before whose faculty, students, friends and stray visitors they were delivered. Sometimes, commonly, indeed, they were delivered by one of the Professors chosen by his Colleagues for the purpose. Sometimes a distinguished or even an illustrious personage, not connected with the profession, or not conversant perhaps with any branch of science was prevailed upon to undertake the task. It was a serious matter for a statesman or a clergyman who did not know whether his lungs were above or below his diaphragm to address a body of experts and their pupils. But all His Excellency or His Reverence had to do was to make some salutary general remarks on education, to praise the Medical Profession, to speak of "the ills that flesh is heir to," to work in a few technical phrases from a medical book his doctor had lent him, to quote Scripture to the effect that we are "fearfully and wonderfully made,"[1] and sit down amidst the applause of the

---

[1] The complete verse (Psalm 139:14) reads: "I will praise thee; for I am fearfully and wonderfully made: marvelous are thy works; and that my soul knoweth right well."

audience. A correspondence would naturally follow in which the discourse was earnestly requested for publication, and yielded with seeming coy reluctance by the hardened old public speaker. So the discourse is published and redounds to the glory of the institution before which His Excellency or His Reverence has kindly consented to appear. I have a great collection of these Introductory Lectures sent me by the writers, and whenever I look them over I feel as if I were handling a pile of Barnum's Posters.[2]

We have given up the formal Introductory Lecture of late years. But there is no objection that I know of to any Professor's writing a modest private Introductory to his own course, in which he may take occasion to express himself a little more freely on some general topics than he would be like to when busy with the details of the subject on which he is entering. This is what I venture to do today at our first meeting.

I wish to impress on these young men before me the momentous character of the occupation to which they mean to consecrate their lives. I wish to fix their attention on the main purpose of all the manifold apparatus of instruction provided for them. The duties of the surgeon, the physician, the obstetrician involve responsibilities as great as a human being can well take upon himself. They demand a great amount of varied knowledge. I wish to insist on the paramount importance of the more immediately practical part of our teaching, and at the same time explain the wisdom of devoting the first year of training to studies which are in great measure subsidiary to their working knowledge. The object of this school is to teach the Art of Healing with so much of science as is needed for its intelligent practice. Other schools are devoted to science as such, but the business of this institution is to fix young men for the difficult and laborious practical duties of the Medical Profession in all its branches. Some of these young men may see fit to confine themselves to special provinces of medical practice, but many, the larger number probably, must be ready to deal with all the cases which come before them. Think what an extent of ground the practitioner's knowledge must cover!

Surgery requires that he should be familiarly acquainted with all the parts which can be reached mediately or immediately by mechanical appliances. Every bone, with a very few exceptions; every joint; every canal which can be explored; every vessel and nerve within reach; the position of every internal organ; all this and a great deal more he must have at his fin-

---

[2]Probably a reference to Phineas Taylor Barnum (1810–1891), the showman famous for his hoaxes and for his circus (later known as Ringling Bros. and Barnum & Bailey), who made no attempt to disguise his primary motive: making money.

gers' ends, as it were, or he is like to be at his wits' ends before he thinks of it. Is a man shot—he must know what organs lie in the track of the missile. Here is Mr. Rallock[3] with a bullet or two, it may be a slug somewhere in his body. What has it gone through and in what has it probably lodged? Is the precious life of that Apostle of the Lord endangered, or is he like to recover and resume his Christian task of blessing those that curse him? Here is a tumour which seems ready for the lancet. Shall it be opened? Yes, said a noted surgeon, Mr. Dease,[4] and plunging in his lancet, opened an aneurism, saw his patient die, and committed suicide. Here is a patient to be bled; the practitioner chooses the wrong place, goes too deep, opens an artery, the arm is lost, a jury awards ruinous damages, and it is thought necessary to circulate a subscription-paper throughout France to pay the sum which would bankrupt the luckless man who had forgotten his anatomy. Here is a sudden summons to a case of strangulated hernia; reduction proves impossible; have you a perfect remembrance of the parts to be divided and the position of the epigastric artery? Here is a dislocation of the femur,—do you remember what happened in that famous case in Maine, the legal consequences of which filled a volume?[5] Can you afford—not merely for your patient's sake, but for your own—to take any chance of consequences which may be utter ruin? Here is a child seemingly at its last

---

[3]Of all the proper nouns in the address, this one remains elusive; it is unclear to whom, if anyone, it refers.

[4]William Dease (1752–1798) was one of the founders of the Royal College of Surgeons of Ireland. It remains unclear whether he in fact committed suicide (by opening his own femoral artery) or died from an accidental injury or aneurysm. See the entry by Charles Creighton, *Dictionary of National Biography, from the Earliest Times to 1900*, ed. Sir Leslie Stephen and Sir Sidney Lee (London: Oxford University Press, 1888), 5: 712.

[5]In the lawsuit, *Lowell v. Faxon and Hawkes*, a Mr. Charles Lowell of Lubec, Maine, alleged that Dr. Micajah Collins Hawkes (1785–1863) and, to a much lesser extent, Dr. John Faxon (the referring physician), had acted improperly in the treatment of a dislocation of the femur sustained from falling from a horse. Dr. Hawkes reduced Lowell's dislocation and advised bed rest. The affected leg, however, remained longer than the other leg the rest of his life. Lowell engaged consultants in Boston (including Holmes's friend, Dr. John Collins Warren), who were, however, unable to correct the abnormality. The ensuing three trials attracted the attention of physicians throughout the United States. The third trial resulted in the case being dismissed, with the defendants being advised to pay their own costs. See Kenneth Allen De Ville, *Medical Malpractice in Nineteenth-Century America: Origins and Legacy* (New York: New York University Press, 1990), 9–24; John Collins Warren, *A Letter to the Honorable Isaac Parker, Chief Justice of the Supreme Court of the State of Massachusetts, Containing Remarks on the Dislocation of the Hip Joint, Occasioned by the Publication of a Trial which took place at Machias, in the State of Maine, June, 1824* (Cambridge: Hilliard and Metcalf, 1826). The "Lowell hip" continues to reside at the Warren Anatomical Museum at the Francis A. Countway Library of Medicine.

gasp with croup, despaired of by almost all around it—why should it not have a few whiffs of chloroform and so go to its dreamless sleep without a desperate fight for an hour perhaps of slow strangulation? A young surgeon stands by who is not afraid to risk his reputation in a dangerous, some of the experts think a desperate operation. He knows all about the arteries and veins that are liable to injury; his eye is keen, his hand is steady, his pulse is calm; he works with knowledge and therefore he moves to his purpose without fear, without hesitation, and so this child, for which the gates of death were standing ajar, is rescued. This is not an imaginary case; one of the younger instructors in this school was the chief actor—I was going to say, the hero of it.

I need not multiply examples to show the absolute necessity of extensive, exact, always ready knowledge on the part of the surgeon. But surgery is the branch of the healing art which is practiced in the daylight. Medicine is the branch which is practiced in the dark. The dial of the human chronometer is easily got at; the works can only be reached after the mainspring is broken and the wheels are still forever.

If then the surgeon requires all this knowledge which I have hinted at to deal with external disease how much training must the physician require, who has to infer the condition of internal parts from such marks as betray their injuries! Surgical diseases, speaking broadly, reveal themselves, as it were, in articulate confessions. The language of visceral disease is a kind of ventriloquy. We hardly know where the words come from. In questioning the state of a surgical patient we first examine the disease or injury and then ask the patient about his sensations. In examining a medical patient we ask him how he feels, or what is his chief source of suffering and thus overhaul his bodily conditions. Our method with the first, if we talked metaphysics, would be objective-subjective, and with the second subjective-objective. It is here that the physical signs, especially those furnished by auscultation and percussion, almost turn some medical diseases into surgical ones. I have made many an *ante-mortem autopsy*, which was as final in its result for me as if it had been made with the scalpel instead of the stethoscope. But the physician has frequent difficulties to meet which require the keenest exercise of the most carefully trained faculties and with all his knowledge will too often find the riddles of nature beyond his power to unravel. He must know the position of the internal organs as if they were encased in crystal. He must be able to tell by the secretions and excretions what mischief is going on in that laboratory of life which carries on its chemistry so secretly that often times it has poisoned the system before its dangerous or destructive work is suspected. He must have in his mind the normal working of all the chemical agencies, the proper modes of action of every mechanical adjustment of the complex machine, he must know above all how to estimate the vital force and its fluctuation, for on that he has [to] depend for all that he calls his cures of disease.

*He must know when he can interfere with disease to arrest it, and when he must let it have its way, only trying to steady and render easier its progress. He must be fertile in resources to combat symptoms; for symptoms are what the patient has to think of; the disease as a whole is not his special business. Just here it is that the most "scientific" physicians, as we call them are apt to be in fault. They are acute in diagnosis, they can give a good guess to the course and probable issue of a disease, but when it comes to meeting the lesser exigencies of the moment, they are perhaps not half as serviceable as the comparatively *un*scientific practitioner of the small island town—the shrewd-self-reliant "country doctor" who, having only himself to trust to keep his wits about him, and who has just enough of the nurse in him to think of all those little appliances which have so much to do with the comfort and sometimes with the recovery of a patient.

*Now all this can only be taught at the bedside. Clinical teaching is incomparably the most important part of a physician's training. All else, indeed, is quite secondary and subsidiary. Many excellent practitioners have owed all their professional education to the instructions of a wise physician, whose knowledge of chemistry, anatomy, physiology, and other secondary branches connected with the practice of medicine was of the slenderest amount. But it is obvious that if clinical teaching is the great means of making a good working physician—the educational means, that is—the right material for a doctor being given—it is obvious, I say, that a long period must be devoted to it. A course of lectures in anatomy, or chemistry or physiology can be begun and finished within a certain definite period. But clinical teaching involves the necessity of an indefinite time—in fact there is no proper end to it. The practitioner is teaching himself clinical medicine all his days, and if he had been carrying a student around with him every day for the whole three years of study he would not have transferred to him all or nearly all the results of his experience. I speak of course of that class [of] men who grow wiser with every additional two years of practice and not of mere mechanical routinists.

*The physician must not make mistakes where mistakes are avoidable. He must not take an abdominal tumor for pregnancy nor let the protests and indignant exclamations of injured innocence prevent his recognizing the consequences of an indiscreet moment until innocence is in the pangs of parturition. He must not take cerebral disease for typhoid fever, nor the first appearance of small pox for measles, nor nervous palpitations for cardiac disease, nor a catarrhal bark for the smothered cough of croup—nor make any of those not infrequent blunders which bring disaster to the patient and discredit to himself. In the matter of prognosis,—the foretelling the course and probable issue of disease—how much depends on his knowledge or ignorance! What misery, needless misery, can he occasion by an alarming shake of the head in a case which a wise man would feel sure was coming out right with a little patience! What happiness can he give to a despairing household by a bold promise of recovery, founded on sagacious experience, where ignorance would have left dismay and timidity have darkened the sick room with apprehensions!

In the matter of *treatment* of disease it by no means follows that those who are most skilful in diagnosis and prognosis will be most efficient and successful. It ought to be—no doubt it often is so, but we have seen men eminently well equipped in all that relates to the natural history of disease who were by no means the persons we should choose to prescribe for us and to attend us through any disease—especially a disease attended with many troublesome or distressing symptoms. There is a natural genius for therapeutics—the management of disease—as there is a natural gift for cooking. The great therapeutic agents are comparatively few. Old Dr. Holyoke, the centenarian, carried the late Dr. James Jackson[6] into his medicine room, surrounded with all its artillery of wide-mouthed jars and its infantry of narrow necked bottles and phials—formidable as an army with banners, and capable of as much mischief if not well generalled. "Look round," he said, "on this array of drugs and medicines. Four of them are worth all the rest: Opium, Calomel, Antimony, and Peruvian Bark." We should not select the same four out of our present pharmacopoeia, but we should select a very small number as of more value than all the others. But even in the use of these few remedies there is room for great sagacity and tact. No remedy is useful unless employed at the right moment is an ancient axiom. Now "the right moment" is just what one man decides, and another, perhaps a much better pathologist, overlooks. One has natural tact, swift apprehension, feminine delicacy of perception. I say *feminine* delicacy. I myself, all things considered, very much prefer a

---

[6]James Jackson (1777–1867), well-known therapeutic moderate under whom Holmes trained, himself trained under Edward Holyoke (1728–1829), first president of the Massachusetts Medical Society and a famed therapeutic moderate. See James Jackson Putnam, *A Memoir of Dr. James Jackson* (Boston: Houghton, Mifflin and Company, 1905).

male practitioner, but a woman's eye, a woman's instinct, a woman's divining power are special gifts which ought in some way to be made useful. If there were only a well-organized and well trained hermaphroditic physician, I am not sure I should not send for him—her—it—them—as likely to combine more excellences than any unisexual individual. Mainly, however, I think the ovarian sex finds its most congenial employment in the office of nurse; and I would give more for a good nurse to take care of me while I was alive than for the best pathologist that ever lived to cut me up after I was dead.

The practical conclusion from this is that the student's eye must be trained, that his tact and sagacity, whatever they are naturally, must be developed by patiently following an expert—a first-rate medical practitioner— from bedside to bedside. No matter how much genius a man may have for painting or sculpture, he must have teachers and models. No matter how well fitted by nature for a physician a man may be, he requires long and severe discipline to sharpen all his faculties. To give one more illustration of the difficulties of the physician's task let me refer to the whole imitative series of disorders to which Marshal[l] Hall gave the now somewhat obsolete name of *Mimoses*.[7] The anomalous nervous affections, of women more especially, simulate almost every malady. The treatment of such affections will probably be diametrically opposite to that of the diseases they so nearly resemble. If a man is not quick to detect the false show which tries to palm itself off as a real malady of much graver nature, he may be ever so great a pathologist, but any keen-eyed old woman who is learned in the tantrums of hysteria, will make a shrewder guess at what the matter is than the very erudite Doctor of Medicine. I cannot insist too strongly than on the vital importance of assiduous and long continued training at the bedside under a wise practitioner.

Let me add one more point to be remembered in summing up what is to be learned by the medical student. He should graduate not only knowing what remedies to administer, when to give them, how to give them, but also when to abstain from them. My own childhood was seriously embittered by the frequent administration of at least the threat and the fear of

---

[7]Marshall Hall described in 1818 a group of disorders affecting young women which he grouped under the term Mimosis (imitator). Symptoms often included diffuse abdominal pain. These patients were commonly diagnosed as having acute peritonitis and were bled. Hall expressed reservations about both the diagnosis and the treatment. See Diana E. Manuel, *Marshall Hall (1790–1857): Science and Medicine in Early Victorian Society* (Amsterdam: Rodopi, 1996), 66–77. For comment on Hall's influence on Holmes, see pages 8–9.

what the old doctor who had charge of my viscera always called "a puke." I doubt if it was ever needed—I know it occasioned me untold misery. A part of the student's business is to learn never to give a drug when it is not needed for cure or comfort; never to occasion any needless suffering or disgust by painful or loathsome prescriptions; but not the less to be ever vigilant for the first fruit of nature that she needs something more than hygienic treatment and to have in his memory every medicinal agent in which he knows he can place confidence. *In his memory*; patients do not like to see their physicians consult a printed conspectus. There are clinical teachers (or have been) who hardly ever used more than half a dozen formulæ and found themselves at a loss when an old dowager wanted a new pill in the place of her accustomed peristaltic persuader. There are others (or were) who were always prescribing new medicines and compounding new pills and mixtures—never keeping to anything long enough to know whether it was good for much or nothing. There are those who like the terrible old man I remember too well with his mingled aroma of rhubarb and ipecac, contrive to disgust their patients so that their stomachs are turned before their potion is swallowed. On the other hand I have heard that the success of Sir Henry Halford,[8] the sometime famous physician of British royalty, was in large measure due to his skill in prescription, especially in rendering his medicines acceptable to the fastidious palates of sick epicures.

I have spoken of the limited number of really powerful medicinal agents. I am certainly not one of those who are like to be accused of overconfidence in drugs. Indeed I once frightened a learned body almost out of its sense of propriety by a somewhat epigrammatic statement of a belief that they were very generally too much trusted in. Yet I would not despise the fractional benefit not rarely to be derived from the judicious administration of articles on the whole of quite secondary value. The Shaker who was assailed with the text from Paul's Epistle, "Bodily exercise profiteth little,"[9] replied with a knowing twinkle in his eye: "Yea, and that little we

---

[8]Of Sir Henry Halford (1766–1844), who attended such members of the British royal family as King George III, George IV, William IV, and Victoria, George Thomas Bettany would write: "For many years after Dr. Matthew Baillie's death he was indisputably at the head of London practice. . . . Halford was a good practical physician with quick perception and sound judgment, but he depreciated physical examination of patients, knew little of pathology, and disliked innovation. His courtly, formal manners and his aristocratic connection served him well." In *Dictionary of National Biography, from the Earliest Times to 1900*, ed. Sir Leslie Stephen and Sir Sidney Lee (London: Oxford University Press, 1890), 8: 923.
[9]The complete verse (1 Timothy 4:8) reads: "For bodily exercise profiteth little; but godliness is profitable unto all things, having promise of the life that now is, and of that which is to come."

mean to have." In the way of palliations—cordials, anodynes, and the like there is all the difference in the world between the rough handling of a physician who, perhaps really skilful and equal to the treatment of the gravest diseases, yet is obtuse in recognizing the susceptibilities of a delicate constitution and an invalid habit, and the nice care of a man of finer organization, not half so well equipped for his profession, it may be, as the other, who does notwithstanding fully enter into the whims of the sick man's palate and the susceptibilities of his stomach. I remember a case where a patient who required daily stimulants on account of great debility was taking brandy and soda-water. The next practitioner under whose hands this patient came, who would not have claimed anything like equal eminence in the profession, got great credit by ordering champagne and apollinaris water in place of the harsher stimulant.

There is no end, you see, to what is to be learned at the bedside. On the very last day of his pupilage, a student may see a case of disease for the first time which he may have to treat on his own responsibility during the first week of his practice.

The duties of the obstetrician require him to be both physician and surgeon. And the suddenness with which he is liable to be called upon for the exercise of all his knowledge, all his skill—the terrible urgency of the hour—it may be of the moment—in which his action or inaction, his choice of this or that course of treatment of the emergency may settle the question of the life or the death of the two human creatures entrusted to his care— all this invests his office with a peculiar gravity and anxiety. When the much loved Princess Charlotte and her new-born infant were lying dead, and the British nation was almost paralysed with grief, the unfortunate practitioner who had attended her, Sir Richard Croft, could not endure his position before the excited community and sought escape from it, like the surgeon I have spoken of in self-destruction.[11] The story has been told a thousand times how, when Marie Louise was in labour and a grave question arose, Dubois who was attending her appealed to Napoleon as to the possible

---

[11]Princess Charlotte Augusta of Wales (1796–1817), having had two previous miscarriages, was managed with great care during her third pregnancy according to the prevailing standards, which included caloric restriction and bloodletting. Her obstetrician, Sir Richard Croft (1762–1818), correctly diagnosed a transverse lie of the term infant but failed to resort to forceps delivery. The infant was stillborn and the princess died within six hours, presumably of an undetected hemorrhage. Croft committed suicide three months later. The case is known in medical history as "the triple obstetrical tragedy" and in general history for its effect on the British monarchy, as it resulted in Victoria's ascending to the throne. See, e.g., Hugh M. Shingleton, "A Famous Triple Death Tragedy," *ACOG Clinical Review* 10 (2005): 14–16.

risks of a certain course of action, and whether he was to take those risks. Treat her like the wife of a common citizen was the emperor's answer.[11] What more could he say,—for the woman about to become a mother appeals to every heart alike whether she wears the crown of an empress or only that crown of thorns which is worn by every woman who passes through the cruel martyrdom of maternity. The great danger is that human sympathy and the sense of all that is depending on his perfect self-command and mastery of all his resources should shake his nerves at the time when every faculty should be obedient to the will of the master.

I have spoken of the three leading branches of professional practice. They each, and still more all of them taken collectively must require a great amount of practical knowledge to do them justice. But there are many special branches each of which requires a large amount of exceptional knowledge and practical skill. The profession is returning in a remarkable manner to the old methods of the Egyptians, who divided the practice of medicine into many specialized branches, which were the exclusive province of certain individuals.[12] We have Dermatologists, Gynaecologists, Oculists, Aurists, Dentists, and may expect to hear before long of Laryngologists, Pneumonologists, Cardiologists, Urethrologists, Urinologists, Syphilologists and for aught I know Rectologists. We have besides, Orthopedists, Alienists,[13] Public-Hygienists, and the experts in Medical Jurisprudence. There is not one of these branches of which the properly accomplished physician can afford to be ignorant. There is not one of them on which he may not have to show himself competent to give advice—no specialty of them all as to which he has a right to profess entire ignorance, and in many of them he ought to have a certain degree of practical skill, if not equal to all their emergencies.

---

[11]Marie Louise (1791–1847), the second wife of Napoleon Bonaparte, gave birth to a son on March 20, 1811, after Napoleon famously instructed physicians to spare the mother's life if it was not possible to save both the mother and the child. Using forceps that he had invented in 1791, the surgeon and obstetrician Antoine Dubois (1756–1837) delivered an apparently dead fetus and then performed a successful resuscitation. The emperor immediately conferred upon Dubois a barony. The short-lived son, generally known as Napoléon II (1811–1832), spent most of his life in Austria. See June K. Burton, *Napoleon and the Woman Question: Discourses of the Other Sex in French Education, Medicine, and Medical Law, 1799–1815* (Lubbock: Texas Tech University Press, 2007), 15–24.

[12]Herodotus wrote of the Egyptians: "The art of medicine is thus divided among them: Each physician applies himself to one disease only, and not more. All places abound in physicians; some physicians are for the eyes, others for the teeth, others for the intestines, and others for internal disorders" (*Histories*, ii, 84). See Fielding H. Garrison, *An Introduction to the History of Medicine* (Philadelphia: W.B. Saunders Company, 1917), 48.

[13]Alienists: Psychiatrists.

In view of the vast amount of really practical knowledge which the student is expected to acquire in his three years,—three academic years of professional study, he may naturally ask some searching questions as to the time he should be expected to devote to those branches which are subsidiary only to his main object. What fraction of the knowledge which he obtains in his first year of study of Chemistry, of Anatomy, of Physiology is going to help him in the daily care of the patients he is to visit? Let us be honest about it. The greater part, by far the greater part of the knowledge acquired in the first year will have no direct, immediate bearing on his daily duties. He has a perfect right to ask his anatomical teacher of what possible use it is going to be to him to learn the five surfaces of the orbital process of the sphenoid bone. How will it help him, in any conceivable case like to come under his care, to remember all the little branches of Jacobson's nerve,[14] or the connections of the otic ganglion? Is he going to extirpate the sphenoid bone that he learns so much about it? Do the Professors of that branch think it sufficient reason for teaching the ramifications of a blood vessel or a nerve that they are laid down in some voluminous treatise of Anatomy, the author, or rather compiler of which thought it a matter of duty to put down everything that he had found in every other compilation lest some critic should prick his ears up and bray over his unpardonable omission?—In order once for all to convince the student that a teacher must leave out a great deal of what he could teach if he thought it worth while, I have been in the habit of showing to my classes the wonderful treatise of Fischer on the nerves of the lower extremities.[15] He will find in the plates of that miracle of industry more than five hundred branches of the sciatic and crural nerves distinguished and separately numbered. I doubt if any anatomist ever took the trouble to verify these extraordinary dissections, but to look at them is a lesson so useful that it more than excuses the laborious drudgery which was expended in their preparation and delineation. They show that the best anatomist must stop somewhere in his pursuit of minutiae. They show that the teacher must often stop short of the compiler. A medical student could not waste his time more effectually than over this treatise of Fischer. He had better read a novel, or row a boat or churn a bicycle and come back with some life in him to a book with some common sense [in] it, that has some idea of the kind

---

[14]Jacobson's nerve: Also known as the tympanic nerve, arising from the glossopharyngeal nerve and named after the Danish anatomist, Luwig Levin Jacobson (1783–1843).

[15]The Francis A. Countway Library of Medicine holds Holmes's copy of Johann Leonhard Fischer, *Descriptio Anatomica Nervorum Lumballium Sacralium et Extremitatum Inferiorum* (Leipzig: Apud S.L. Crusium, 1791). It seems to have been well-used.

and amount of knowledge he wants and makes it as plain for him as clear description and abundant and lucid illustration can make it.

These studies of the first year require a good deal of judgment in their administration. The student is not himself competent to decide what he ought to learn and what he ought to let alone. I have no right perhaps to speak of chemistry, but from my primitive knowledge of it as it exists today, I believe that the same caution which applies to my own branch is not superfluous with reference to this. Chemistry used to be a charming study in my younger days, perhaps it is so now. But the blooming faces that were so attractive in my academic days are not all they once were. Chemistry is fuller of new wrinkles than they are, but like them, is less alluring to youth than in its less mature period. A course of chemical lectures was one of the most agreeable of entertainments. To redden a vegetable blue; to precipitate a cloud of some carbonate or sulphate; to burn iron in oxygen; to inflate bubbles with hydrogen; on great occasions to solidify carbonic acid; to make a light with electricity or phosphorus which should blind everybody with its intensity; to mask a smell with sulphuretted hydrogen— which should cause all to hold their noses; such was a specimen of chemical teaching as I remember it. But since chemistry has waded beyond its depth among the compound radicals; since it has upset its nomenclature; since it deals so largely with unmanageable formulae, and impalpable abstractions it is no longer a matter of a retort, a crucible, a few test glasses, a few reagents, a balance and such other delightful toys, but a stern and difficult complication of problems, which to deal with as a master takes the devotion of a whole life.

Physiology, like chemistry, has become much more exact, much more complicated, and in some of its textbooks as it seems to me, much less interesting. I do not question the great increase in the matter of precision— though Hyrtl,[16] aggressive, good natured old cynic as he is, rather laughs at the pretensions of the modernized science in this regard. But when I see a text-book giving up a large portion of its pages to diagrams illustrating all the forms of contraction of a vessel, of a muscular fibre, under all sorts of conditions I cannot help thinking that M. Marey's pretty playthings are claiming more than their share of the students' attention.[17] When I see the young man who is going very soon to have to deal with the practical prob-

---

[16]Josef Hyrtl (1810–1894), Austrian anatomist.

[17]The pioneering physiologist Etienne Jules-Marey (1830–1904) was an early developer of the sphygmograph and of devices to measure motion. See François Dagognet, *Etienne-Jules Marey: A Passion for the Trace*, trans. Robert Galeta with Jeanine Herman (New York: Zone Books, 1992).

lems of dyspepsia and constipation and other grave matters of real and vital importance, puzzling his brains over parapeptone and dyspeptone, and metapeptone and hemipeptone; over antialbumose and hemialbumose and antialbumate and anti-albumid; perhaps writing a thesis proving that Kühne's anti-albumid is identical with Schützenberger's hemi-protein and Meissner's dyspeptone;[18] I seriously question with myself whether the apprentice as he would have been called, of an old time practitioner, a man of sense and experience, going round with him from house to house, seeing the average run of diseases, how his master called there, how he thought they would come out, and what he did for them, was not much better employed than the young man who has lost his bloom in puzzling over these fugacious polysyllabic compounds.

If then, as I assumed at the beginning this is a school for imparting practical skill in the healing art, with so much of the collateral sciences as contribute to its chief purposes, it may be naturally asked what is the object of the preliminary examination and the studies of the first year? The student does not expect to talk Latin, or French, or German to his patients. He does not expect to discourse on physics to them, or to require any great amount of knowledge of hydraulics or hydrostatics. Why then this examination in those who do not bring certificates from one of the higher Institutions that they have been through its regular course of instruction.

It is necessary that the student should know something of Physics to fit him for the study of Physiology. It is a great advantage to be acquainted with the language from which so many terms used in medical science are borrowed. But there is, I think a much better reason than these. What would be expected of a young man placed in the freshman class at Harvard—the examination having been dispensed with—without his having been "fitted for college," but taken raw as his own potatoes, green as his own cow-pasture, from his bucolic avocations? He could not stay there a week—no, nor a single day, for the first recitation would show him to be ridiculously incompetent. Just such hopeful subjects as this have been from time to time in the habit of resorting to medical schools, just as if no training whatsoever, no acquisitions beyond reading, writing, in a character one remove from pothooks, spelling, on a phonetic system of his own, and ciphering, within the limits of the multiplication-table were required for a scholar

---

[18]Wilhelm Kühne (1837–1900), German physiologist who coined the term "enzyme"; Paul Schützenberger (1829–1897), French chemist; Georg Meissner (1829–1905), German anatomist, histologist, and physiologist. For an account of such contemporary debate, written the same year as Holmes's lecture, see M. Foster, *A Text Book of Physiology*, third edition (London: Macmillan, 1879), 235–6. See also P. Schützenbeger, *On Fermentation* (New York: D. Appleton and Company, 1876).

who in the course of three years—in half that time in some institutions was to claim the title of Doctor, Teacher, that is Master of the great art and mystery of dealing in the issues of life and death. I have been long an Instructor and have therefore seen many strange things. I have seen students attending medical lectures whom I should have rather sent to a kinder-garden—except for the fear that they would tread on the little children. Do you wonder that we insist on a certain amount of previous training of the intelligence of the students whom we are to teach all that belongs to a serious and difficult calling?

And what shall I say about those branches pursued during the first year, a large part of which I have confessed has no immediate or essential bearing on the practice of medicine in any of its branches. I do not pretend that all the anatomy I teach will find a direct practical application. I have no claim to speak for my colleagues, but I do not question that the Professors of Physiology and of Chemistry will say the same thing of their several departments.

I have already explained what hardly needed explanation, the absolute necessity of a good deal of exact anatomical knowledge to enable the practitioner to deal confidently with most external and many internal diseases, as it is also with that natural process always liable to be complicated with conditions which require instant action founded on thorough acquaintance with all the normal and abnormal states belonging to the parts involved.

Not less needful is it that the practitioner should be acquainted with the normal state of all the functions, the proper character of all the products of secretion—all those conditions the changes of which mark the existence of disease and its nature in each given case. In other words he must have a certain amount of physiological knowledge—not simply for its own sake but because it is needed in his everyday work.

But he will not have gone far in physiology before finding out that some chemical knowledge is absolutely essential to a proper understanding of physiology. A physician suspects the existence of a certain disease of the kidneys. He wishes to know the condition of their secretion as furnishing evidence to guide him in his diagnosis, prognosis and treatment. Physiology teaches him the natural aspect and character of the fluid. Chemistry shows him how to test it—for the substance it calls albumen—for sugar, which sometimes is largely found in it. And so with regard to a great number of diseased conditions, physiology and chemistry go hand in hand shedding light upon their natural cause and treatment.

It is plain, then, that the student must know something, perhaps we are safe in saying a good deal of these three subsidiary branches, Anatomy, Physiology, Chemistry. Granting this, why teach those numerous details which form a part of every regular course of lectures—details which confessedly are not going to be of any real use to the practitioner?

The answer to this question is a very simple one. The most efficient and economical way of learning what must be learned of these three branches is to study them *systematically*. If only those facts were to be picked out of each of these branches which are like to find direct practical application, such fragmentary knowledge would be vastly less clear to the apprehension, very much less likely to be retained in the memory. Suppose, for instance, in teaching Anatomy I should leave out the description of such bones, muscles, vessels, nerves, as I thought were least likely to be of practical importance and allow considerable portions of the body to remain unexplained territory. The student would feel as one reading a volume feels when he finds leaves torn out and a chapter missing here and there. Many parts not in themselves of great importance to the practical man, help to fix the relations of facts that are important. But supposing they were without any even indirect practical significance, the mind of the intelligent student would demand the missing link in the chain of his knowledge. If when we came to the muscles of the back, a student should say "I think those muscles are of no great practical importance and I do not mean to trouble myself about them," I should not expect him to pass a good examination on the points that *are* most eminently practical. It is perfectly true that you will forget or at least seem to have forgotten many things that you have learned in the three branches of the first year. I say *seem to have forgotten*, because no man knows how much is stored away in his memory. He cannot summon each recollection at will from the dark mental recesses where it is laid away. But sooner or later, perhaps at the moment when it is needed, it suddenly emerges into consciousness. There are silent strings in the great harp of memory the chords to which may be struck half a dozen times perhaps in the course of a life, but when the right chord is struck they vibrate in response. We must not think our intellectual world is made up of the thoughts we can command at will. The unseen planet betrays itself by its action on the visible ones, and so the knowledge which we have lost sight of for the time is constantly acting on the thoughts which revolve in full view through our consciousness. As it is

"better to have loved and lost
Than never to have loved at all"

So it is better to have known and forgotten—if anything *can* be forgotten—than never to have known at all.

When the studies of this first year are finished you will find yourselves oppressed with the multiplicity of practical studies to which your attention

Holmes in 1887, outside his summer home at Beverly Farms. From the collection of the
Boston Medical Library in the Francis A. Countway Library of Medicine.

will be called. I have tried to impress upon you their extent and complexity. It will be of infinite comfort and help if you have faithfully employed
your time in these preparatory studies so that you can build on your
acquired knowledge as a solid foundation. If you neglect them you will
never repair the loss. The first year settles pretty conclusively what is like
to be the result of your professional education.

It were much to be wished that a longer time could be devoted to the
various practical branches. I believe you can learn anatomy enough, physiology enough, chemistry enough to begin the study of your special calling at the end of the first year. It is a very formidable task which lies before
you for those two years which follow. In fact I think the conviction is fast
growing that the time is not sufficient for its full demands, and it will not
be long, I believe, before this Institution, which has to act as the tug-boat
to drag other craft much bigger than itself out of their stagnant harbors,
will feel compelled by its own ever enlarging ideas of its duty to the medical community and to the public, to add a fourth year to its curriculum.[19]

---

[19]A fourth year was officially recommended for the first time by the faculty during the
1880–1881 academic year, but would not be implemented until the 1892–1893 academic
year.

Bibliography

CITED WORKS BY OLIVER WENDELL HOLMES[1]

Facts and Traditions Respecting the Existence of Indigenous Intermittent Fever in New England. In *Boylston Prize Dissertations for the Years 1836 and 1837* (Boston: Charles C. Little and James Brown, 1838).

On the Utility and Importance of Direct Exploration in Medical Practice. In *Boylston Prize Dissertations for the Years 1836 and 1837* (Boston: Charles C. Little and James Brown, 1838).

"Astrology and Alchemy [1842]," unpublished lecture before the Society for the Diffusion of Useful Knowledge. Houghton Library, Harvard University, MS Am 1234.7.

"Homœopathy and its Kindred Delusions [1842]," in *Medical Essays, 1842–1882* [The Works of Oliver Wendell Holmes, Standard Library Edition, Volume IX]. Boston: Houghton, Mifflin and Company, 1892, 1–102.

"The Contagiousness of Puerperal Fever [1843; reprinted with additions, 1855]," in *Medical Essays, 1842–1882* [The Works of Oliver Wendell Holmes, Standard Library Edition, Volume IX]. Boston: Houghton, Mifflin and Company, 1892, 103–72.

"The Position and Prospects of the Medical Student [1844]," in *Currents and Counter-Currents in Medical Science: With Other Addresses and Essays*. Boston: Ticknor and Fields, 1861, 279–322.

An Introductory Lecture, Delivered at the Massachusetts Medical College, November 3, 1847. Boston: William D. Ticknor and Company, 1847.

"Mechanism of Vital Actions [1857]," in *Currents and Counter-Currents in Medical Science: With Other Addresses and Essays*. Boston: Ticknor and Fields, 1861, 323–82.

"Some More Recent Views on Homœopathy [1857]," in *Currents and Counter-Currents in Medical Science: With Other Addresses and Essays*. Boston: Ticknor and Fields, 1861, 179–188.

"Valedictory Address delivered to the Medical Graduates of Harvard University, at the Annual Commencement, Wednesday, March 10, 1858 [1858]," in *Currents and Counter-Currents in Medical Science: With Other Addresses and Essays*. Boston: Ticknor and Fields, 1861, 383–406.

---

[1]The works by Holmes are listed by order of original publication. The most accessible printed version of each work (relying heavily upon The Works of Oliver Wendell Holmes, Standard Library Edition) is the one cited.

The Autocrat of the Breakfast-Table [1858]. The Works of Oliver Wendell Holmes, Standard Library Edition, Volume I. Boston: Houghton, Mifflin and Company, 1892.

The Professor at the Breakfast-Table [1859]. The Works of Oliver Wendell Holmes, Standard Library Edition, Volume II. Boston: Houghton, Mifflin and Company, 1892.

"Currents and Counter-Currents in Medical Science [1860]," in *Medical Essays, 1842–1882* [The Works of Oliver Wendell Holmes, Standard Library Edition, Volume IX]. Boston: Houghton, Mifflin and Company, 1892, 173–208.

"Preface [1861]," in *Currents and Counter-Currents in Medical Science: With Other Addresses and Essays*. Boston: Ticknor and Fields, 1861, iii–ix.

"Borderlines of Knowledge in Some Provinces of Medical Science [1861]," in *Medical Essays, 1842–1882* [The Works of Oliver Wendell Holmes, Standard Library Edition, Volume IX]. Boston: Houghton, Mifflin and Company, 1892, 209–72.

"Bread and the Newspaper [1861]," in *Pages from an Old Volume of Life* [The Works of Oliver Wendell Holmes, Standard Library Edition, Volume VIII]. Boston: Houghton, Mifflin and Company, 1892, 1–15.

Elsie Venner [1861]. The Works of Oliver Wendell Holmes, Standard Library Edition, Volume V. Boston: Houghton, Mifflin and Company, 1892.

"My Hunt after the Captain [1862]," in *Pages from an Old Volume of Life* [The Works of Oliver Wendell Holmes, Standard Library Edition, Volume VIII]. Boston: Houghton, Mifflin and Company, 1892, 16–77.

"The Inevitable Trial [1863]," in *Pages from an Old Volume of Life* [The Works of Oliver Wendell Holmes, Standard Library Edition, Volume VIII]. Boston: Houghton, Mifflin and Company, 1892, 78–120.

"Scholastic and Bedside Teaching [1867]," in *Medical Essays, 1842–1882* [The Works of Oliver Wendell Holmes, Standard Library Edition, Volume IX]. Boston: Houghton, Mifflin and Company, 1892, 273–311.

The Guardian Angel [1867]. The Works of Oliver Wendell Holmes, Standard Library Edition, Volume VI. Boston: Houghton, Mifflin and Company, 1892.

"Talk Concerning the Human Body and its Management [1869]," in *Pages from an Old Volume of Life* [The Works of Oliver Wendell Holmes, Standard Library Edition, Volume VIII]. Boston: Houghton, Mifflin and Company, 1892, 186–238.

"The Medical Profession in Massachusetts [1869]," in *Medical Essays, 1842–1882* [The Works of Oliver Wendell Holmes, Standard Library Edition, Volume IX]. Boston: Houghton, Mifflin and Company, 1892, 312–69.

"Mechanism in Thought and Morals [1870]," in *Pages from an Old Volume of Life* [The Works of Oliver Wendell Holmes, Standard Library Edition, Volume VIII]. Boston: Houghton, Mifflin and Company, 1892, 260–314.

"The Young Practitioner [1871]," in *Medical Essays, 1842–1882* [The Works of Oliver Wendell Holmes, Standard Library Edition, Volume IX]. Boston: Houghton, Mifflin and Company, 1892, 370–95.

The Poet at the Breakfast-Table [1872]. The Works of Oliver Wendell Holmes, Standard Library Edition, Volume III. Boston: Houghton, Mifflin and Company, 1892.

"Crime and Automatism [1875]," in *Pages from an Old Volume of Life* [The Works of Oliver Wendell Holmes, Standard Library Edition, Volume VIII]. Boston: Houghton, Mifflin and Company, 1892, 322–60.

"An Address Delivered at the Annual Meeting of the Boston Microscopical Society," *Boston Medical and Surgical Journal* 96 (1877): 601–12

"Medical Libraries [1878]," in *Medical Essays, 1842–1882* [The Works of Oliver Wendell Holmes, Standard Library Edition, Volume IX]. Boston: Houghton, Mifflin and Company, 1892, 396–419.

"Introductory—Sept. 26, 1879," unpublished lecture before the first-year class, Harvard Medical School. Houghton Library, Harvard University, Ms. 1234.7.

"Jonathan Edwards [1880]," in *Pages from an Old Volume of Life* [The Works of Oliver Wendell Holmes, Standard Library Edition, Volume VIII]. Boston: Houghton, Mifflin and Company, 1892, 361–401.

"Introductory Lecture—October 1881," unpublished lecture before the first-year class, Harvard Medical School. Houghton Library, Harvard University, Ms. 1234.7.

"The Pulpit and the Pew [1881]," in *Pages from an Old Volume of Life* [The Works of Oliver Wendell Holmes, Standard Library Edition, Volume VIII]. Boston: Houghton, Mifflin and Company, 1892, 402–33.

"Some of My Early Teachers [1882]," in *Medical Essays, 1842–1882* [The Works of Oliver Wendell Holmes, Standard Library Edition, Volume IX]. Boston: Houghton, Mifflin and Company, 1892, 420–45.

"Medical Highways and Byways," *Boston Medical and Surgical Journal* 106 (1882): 505–13.

"Address," in *Addresses and Exercises at the One Hundredth Anniversary of the Foundation of the Medical School of Harvard University*. Cambridge: John Wilson and Son, 1884, 3–35.

Ralph Waldo Emerson. John Lothrop Motley. Two Memoirs [1878, 1884]. The Works of Oliver Wendell Holmes, Standard Library Edition, Volume XI. Boston: Houghton, Mifflin and Company, 1892.

A Mortal Antipathy [1885]. The Works of Oliver Wendell Holmes, Standard Library Edition, Volume VII. Boston: Houghton, Mifflin and Company, 1892.

One Hundred Days in Europe [1887]. The Works of Oliver Wendell Holmes, Standard Library Edition, Volume X. Boston: Houghton, Mifflin and Company, 1892.

"Address before the Boston Medical Library Association," *Boston Medical and Surgical Journal* 120 (1889):129–31.

Over the Teacups [1890]. The Works of Oliver Wendell Holmes, Standard Library Edition, Volume IV. Boston: Houghton, Mifflin and Company, 1892.

"Preface to the New Edition [1891]," in *Medical Essays, 1842–1882* [The Works of Oliver Wendell Holmes, Standard Library Edition, Volume IX]. Boston: Houghton, Mifflin and Company, 1892, xii–xvii.

The Poetical Works of Oliver Wendell Holmes. The Works of Oliver Wendell Holmes, Standard Library Edition, Volumes XII and XIII. Boston: Houghton, Mifflin and Company, 1892.

"On Physicians," undated manuscript, Houghton Library, Harvard University, Ms. Am 1937, folder 68.

Cited Secondary Literature on
Oliver Wendell Holmes[2]

Ball, James. *Dr. Oliver Wendell Holmes and His Works, being a Brief Biography and Critical Review*. London: Elliot Stock, 1878.

Boewe, Charles. "Reflex Action in the Novels of Oliver Wendell Holmes." *American Literature* 26 (1954): 303–19.

Brown, E.E. *Life of Oliver Wendell Holmes*. Chicago: E.A. Weeks & Company, 1884.

Dowling, William C. *Oliver Wendell Holmes in Paris: Medicine, Theology, and The Autocrat of the Breakfast Table*. Durham, New Hampshire: University of New Hampshire Press, 2006.

Fischoff, Ephraim. *Oliver Wendell Holmes: Physician and Humanist*. Springfield, Illinois: The Pearson Museum Monograph Series, 1982.

Gibian, Peter. *Oliver Wendell Holmes and the Culture of Conversation*. Cambridge: Cambridge University Press, 2000.

Hoyt, Edwin P. *The Improper Bostonian: Dr. Oliver Wendell Holmes*. New York: William Morrow and Company, Inc., 1979.

Kennedy, William Sloan. *Oliver Wendell Holmes: Poet, Littérateur, Scientist*. Boston: S.E. Cassino and Co., 1883.

Morse, John T. *Life and Letters of Oliver Wendell Holmes*, Volumes I and II. Boston: Houghton, Mifflin and Company, 1896.

Oberdorf, Clarence P. *The Psychiatric Novels of Oliver Wendell Holmes*. New York: Columbia University Press, 1943.

Ticknor, Caroline (editor). *Dr. Holmes's Boston*. Boston: Houghton Mifflin and Company, 1915.

Tilton, Eleanor M. *Amiable Autocrat: A Biography of Dr. Oliver Wendell Holmes*. New York: Henry Schuman, 1947.

Warner, John Harley. *The Therapeutic Perspective: Medical Practice, Knowledge, and Identity in America, 1820–1885*. Cambridge: Harvard University Press, 1986.

Warner, John Harley. *Against the Spirit of System: The French Impulse in Nineteenth-Century American Medicine*. Princeton: Princeton University Press, 1998.

Weinstein, Michael A. *The Imaginative Prose of Oliver Wendell Holmes*. Columbia, Missouri: University of Missouri Press, 2006.

---

[2]Please note that this "bibliography" is meant as a guide to the essays and quotes included in this volume, rather than as a comprehensive or annotated Holmes bibliography itself. For those interested in more complete guides to the existing literature on Holmes, we would recommend starting with the bibliographic sections included in William Dowling's *Oliver Wendell Holmes in Paris*, and Michael Weinstein's *The Imaginative Prose of Oliver Wendell Holmes*, both cited herein.

Notes on Contributors

CHARLES S. BRYAN is director of the Institute of Internal Medicine and Family Practice, Providence Hospitals, Columbia, South Carolina. He is also Heyward Gibbes Distinguished Professor of Internal Medicine Emeritus at the University of South Carolina, where he served successively as director of the Division of Infectious Diseases, chair of the Department of Medicine, and director of the Center for Bioethics and Medical Humanities. His books include *A Most Satisfactory Man: The Story of Theodore Brevard Hayne, Last Martyr of Yellow Fever* (Waring Library Society, 1996), *Osler: Inspirations from a Great Physician* (Oxford University Press, 1997), and *The Quotable Osler* (with Mark E. Silverman and Jock Murray; American College of Physicians, 2003).

PETER GIBIAN is Associate Professor of English at McGill University, Montreal, Canada. He is the author of *Oliver Wendell Holmes and the Culture of Conversation* (Cambridge University Press, 2001). His ongoing book projects address cosmopolitanism in nineteenth-century American literature (*A Traveling Culture*); the mid-nineteenth century American "culture of conversation" (*Writing in Circles*); and the experience of nineteenth-century shopping arcades (*Shoppers in Glass Houses*).

JOHN S. HALLER, JR., is Emeritus Professor of History and Medical Humanities, Southern Illinois University at Carbondale. His books include *Outcasts from Evolution: Scientific Attitudes of Racial Inferiority, 1859–1900* (University of Illinois Press, 1971), *The Physician and Sexuality in Victorian America* (with Robin M. Haller; University of Illinois Press, 1974), *American Medicine in Transition, 1840–1910* (University of Illinois Press, 1981), *Medical Protestants: The Eclectics in American Medicine, 1825–1939* (Southern Illinois University Press, 1994), *Kindly Medicine: Physio-Medicalism in America, 1836–1911* (Kent State University Press, 1997), *A Profile in Alternative Medicine: The Eclectic Medical College of Cincinnati* (Kent State University Press, 1999), *The People's Doctors: Samuel Thomson and the American Botanical Movement, 1790–1860* (Southern Illinois University Press, 2000),

History of American Homeopathy: The Academic Years, 1920–1935 (Haworth Medical Press, 2005), *The History of American Homeopathy: From Rational Medicine to Holistic Health Care* (Rutgers University Press, 2009), and *Healing at the Intersection of Mind and Body: The Competing Worlds of Mesmer and Swedenborg* (forthcoming).

AMALIE M. KASS is lecturer in the History of Medicine in the Department of Global Health and Social Medicine at Harvard Medical School, Boston. She is the author of *Perfecting the World: The Life and Times of Dr. Thomas Hodgkin, 1798–1866* (with Edward H. Kass; Harcourt Brace Jovanovich, 1988) and *Midwifery and Medicine in Boston: Walter Channing, M.D., 1786–1876* (Northeastern University Press, 2002).

SCOTT H. PODOLSKY is director of the Center for the History of Medicine at the Countway Medical Library, assistant professor in the Department of Global Health and Social Medicine at Harvard Medical School, and a primary care physician at Massachusetts General Hospital, Boston. He is the author of *Generation of Diversity: Clonal Selection Theory and the Rise of Molecular Immunology* (with Alfred I. Tauber; Harvard University Press, 1997) and *Pneumonia Before Antibiotics: Therapeutic Evolution and Evaluation in Twentieth-century America* (Johns Hopkins University Press, 2006).

CHARLES E. ROSENBERG is Professor of the History of Science and Ernest Monrad Professor of the Social Sciences at Harvard University, Cambridge, Massachusetts. He previously served as Chair of the departments of History and the History and Sociology of Science at the University of Pennsylvania. His books include *The Cholera Years: The United States in 1832, 1849, and 1866* (The University of Chicago Press, 1962), *The Trial of the Assassin Guiteau: Psychiatry and Law in the Gilded Age* (University of Chicago Press, 1968), *No Other Gods: On Science and American Social Thought* (Johns Hopkins University Press, 1976), *The Therapeutic Revolution: Essays in the Social History of American Medicine* (with Morris Vogel; University of Pennsylvania Press, 1979), *The Care of Strangers: The Rise of America's Hospital System* (Basic Books, 1987), *Framing Disease: Studies in Cultural History* (with Janet Golden; Rutgers University Press, 1992), *Explaining Epidemics and Other Studies in the History of Medicine* (Cambridge University Press, 1992), *Right Living: An Anglo-American Tradition of Self-Help Medicine and Hygiene* (Johns Hopkins University Press, 2003), *History and Health Policy in the United States: Putting the Past Back In* (with Rosemary Stevens and Lawton R. Burns; Rutgers University Press, 2006), and *Our Present Complaint: American Medicine, Past and Present* (Johns Hopkins University Press, 2007).

MICHAEL A. WEINSTEIN is Professor of Political Science at Purdue University, West Lafayette, Indiana. His books include *Meaning and Appreciation: Time and Modern Political Life* (Purdue University Press, 1978), *Postmodern(ized) Simmel* (with Deena Weinstein; Routledge, 1993), *Data Trash: The Theory of Virtual Class* (with Arthur Kroker; Macmillan, 1994), *Culture/Flesh: Explorations of Postcivilized Modernity* (Rowman and Littlefield, 1995), and *The Imaginative Prose of Oliver Wendell Holmes* (University of Missouri Press, 2006).

Farewell Address of Dr. Oliver Wendell Holmes, Parkman Professor of Anatomy in the Medical School of Harvard University, Delivered Nov. 28, 1882: (Boston: Heliotype Printing, 1882) Courtesy Harvard Medical Library in the Francis A. Countway Library of Medicine.

Index